NEW WORLDS

The Renaissance was a time of great adventure—
for philosophers as well as for seafarers who
discovered new continents, for artists who
discovered new techniques, and for writers
who ventured into new realms of literature.
Giorgio de Santillana, the well-known historian
of thought, presents a selection from the basic
philosophical writings of this exciting period,
together with explanatory commentaries
illuminating an age of creative confusion when
thinkers dared to venture into territories not
previously considered the province of philosophy.

Here the reader will find the essential ideas of
Machiavelli, Montaigne, Michelangelo, Leonardo
da Vinci, and Copernicus on such subjects as the
strategy of politics, the fallibility of man, the
techniques of art, original theories of aesthetics,
man's place on earth. With these concepts, so
daring in their day that some of their originators
drew the censure of ecclesiastical and political
authorities, comes a feeling of high adventure
which illustrates the Renaissance's love of life and
its fearlessness in discovering new worlds of
intellectual—as well as geographical—nature.

GIORGIO DE SANTILLANA was Professor of
The History and Philosophy of Science at Massa-
chusetts Institute of Technology and also taught at
Harvard. His many works include *The Crime of
Galileo*, *The Development of Rationalism and
Empiricism* (with Edgar Zilsel), and *Hamlet's
Mill* (with Hertha Von Dechend).

The Meridian Philosophers

THE AGE OF ADVENTURE

The Renaissance Philosophers

SELECTED, WITH INTRODUCTION AND
INTERPRETIVE COMMENTARY

by

GIORGIO DE SANTILLANA

A MERIDIAN BOOK

NEW AMERICAN LIBRARY

NEW YORK AND SCARBOROUGH, ONTARIO

© 1956 by Giorgio de Santillana

ACKNOWLEDGMENTS AND COPYRIGHT NOTICES

The author wishes to thank the following publishers and
authorized representatives for their kind permission to
reprint from the books indicated below:

ELISABETH ABBOTT:
  Giordano Bruno, *Del' Infinito, Universo e Mondi* and
  Heroici Furori, translated by Arthur Livingston.

BOLLINGEN FOUNDATION, INC.:
  Paracelsus: Selected Writings, translated by Norbert Guterman, edited by Jolande Jacobi, Copyright 1951 by
  Bollingen Foundation, Inc., New York, N. Y. Wolfgang
  Pauli, "The Influence of Archetypal Ideas on the Scientific Theories of Kepler," translated by R. F. C. Hull
  and Priscilla Silz, in *The Interpretation of Nature and
  the Psyche* by C. G. Jung and Wolfgang Pauli. Copyright
  1955 by Bollingen Foundation, Inc., New York, N. Y.

JONATHAN CAPE, LTD:
  The Notebooks of Leonardo da Vinci, translated and
  edited by Edward MacCurdy.

ENCYCLOPAEDIA BRITANNICA:
  Copernicus, "Preface and Dedication to Pope Paul III,"
  in *On the Revolutions of the Heavenly Spheres,* translated
  by C. G. Wallis, Copyright 1939, by Encyclopaedia Britannica, Inc., from *Great Books of the Western World,*
  Volume 16.

HARCOURT, BRACE AND COMPANY, INC:
  The Notebooks of Leonardo da Vinci, translated and
  edited by Edward MacCurdy.

(*The following page constitutes an extension of this
copyright page.*)

METHUEN & CO., LTD:
    Jakob Boehme, *The Confessions*, compiled and edited
    by W. Scott Palmer.

ROUTLEDGE & KEGAN PAUL, LTD:
    Nicolaus Cusanus, *Of Learned Ignorance*, translated by
    Germain Heron. *Paracelsus: Selected Writings*, translated
    by Norbert Guterman, edited by Jolande Jacobi, Copy-
    right 1951 by Bollingen Foundation Inc., New York,
    N. Y. Wolfgang Pauli, "The Influence of Archetypal
    Ideas on the Scientific Theories of Kepler," translated
    by Priscilla Silz, in *The Interpretation of Nature and
    the Psyche* by C. G. Jung and Wolfgang Pauli, Copyright
    1955 by Bollingen Foundation, Inc., New York, N. Y.

VIKING PRESS, INC:
    Erasmus, "De Libero Arbitrio," translated by Mary
    Martin McLaughlin, from *The Portable Renaissance
    Reader*, Copyright 1953 by The Viking Press, Inc.

VISION PRESS, LTD:
    Michelangelo, "Sonnets III and IV," from *Sonnets*,
    translated by J. A. Symonds.

YALE UNIVERSITY PRESS
    Nicolaus Cusanus, *Of Learned Ignorance*, translated by
    Germain Heron.

The Age of Adventure previously appeared in a Mentor edition.

Library of Congress Catalog Card Number: 86-63905

 MERIDIAN TRADEMARK REG. U.S. PAT. OFF. AND FOREIGN COUNTRIES
REGISTERED TRADEMARK—MARCA REGISTRADA
HECHO EN WINNIPEG, CANADA

SIGNET, SIGNET CLASSIC, MENTOR, ONYX, PLUME, MERIDIAN and
NAL BOOKS are published *in the United States* by
NAL PENGUIN INC., 1633 Broadway, New York,
New York 10019 *in Canada* by The New American Library of
Canada Limited, 81 Mack Avenue, Scarborough, Ontario
M1L 1M8

1 2 3 4 5 6 7 8 9

Printed in Canada

To the memory of my friend
LAURO DE BOSIS
who died alone for freedom
over Rome
1901–1931

Contents

Introduction

ALL ERAS ARE OF TRANSITION, BUT SOME ARE MORE TRAN-
sitional than most. The Renaissance liked to consider itself
as a final return to proper intellectual conditions, a Restoration as it were. It was prompt to coin for what preceded
it the transitional term of "Middle Ages" (this term of
media aetas is used for the first time by Cusanus's secretary,
G. A. Bussi, about 1450). From our point of view, the
perspective is different. The thousand years of the Age of
Belief appear to us as a great fruition preceded by slow
and painful growth, whereas the Renaissance looks more
like an explosion. Between 1450 and 1550, America is
discovered, together with the Pacific and South Atlantic
oceans, the world is circumnavigated and its real size understood; the Copernican theory denies the common idea
of a well-enclosed universe with the Earth at the center;
the Reformation breaks out all over Western Europe; and
20 million volumes come out of the presses to replace
handwriting. All this together, and even separately, would
have taxed any capacity for adjustment.

Thus, far from being a re-establishment, the Renaissance becomes a quick rush along the whole front, urged
on by staggering innovations which could not be grasped
in their full import, a surge which in less than three centuries loses itself in the unending rapids of the scientific
era. This particular image of our time, born in its first form
in the mind of Hölderlin, is of course as subjective as any.
But so much ought to be fairly sure, that the Renaissance
as a specific period is a short-lived one of rapid transition,
without any recognizable points of stability except in the
arts.

Hence to characterize its coherent systems of thought is
not easy, nor would it be rewarding; the philosophical

effort is a helter-skelter advance, a reconnaissance expedition into unexplored territory. Intellectual coherence, as it is found, lies in the obstinate effort to transform old systems apace and enrich them with new elements without losing the essential ideas they carry from the past. At the end of the great adventure the landscape has changed utterly; new stars are shining in the sky.

Thus, what stands out for us in this period is not systematic philosophy; it is critical revision and creative thought embodied in powerful personalities who work out a momentary cosmos of their own. Evaluation of contemporary efforts at the truth is surely an essential part of philosophy too, and in such thinkers as Montaigne it goes together with the construction of a new idea of man.

What follows is, then, the story of how certain ideas of ours took shape and place, which seem now the unchallenged foundations of thought, but began at one time as high dreams, adventurous choices, sacrificial decisions based on remotely improbable guesses.

A modern trend among historians has undermined the conventional idea of Renaissance "uniqueness." It has brought up as many "Renaissances" in Northern Europe as there are centuries in the Middle Ages from Charlemagne onward. This is very sound insofar as it destroys the other conventional myth of medieval immobility, but it cannot do away with the hard fact that something immeasurably different happened in those two centuries starting with 1400 or just before. The Renaissance would stand, as Erwin Panofsky has remarked, all the more if a medieval like Robert Grosseteste had really had the telescope already—and had done nothing with it.

It was specifically born in Italy, just as Burckhardt maintained. It was affected by the particular conditions of Italian history at the time, and transmitted many of its specific features to the wider Renascence of Northern Europe. The table of values of Italian humanism was born in the Middle Ages of the burgher civilization of the free Communes: it carries with it the discovery of the initiative of man as the creator of his fortunes, the praise of worldly capacity and worldly success, and of the passions and feelings that go with them. Hence narrative realism and the introspective lyric, hence the discounting of scholastic thought, hence a free ethics, a lay conception of life.

Whence this word *humanism* which becomes all at once so important? We should be mindful of its origin. Today, it stands somewhat vaguely for something opposed to scientific and technical specialization; it has drifted away from its full meaning under the pressure of modern problems. So, too, has "liberal," a related term, which is at present loosely opposed to "conservative." Yet by definition the true liberal is always one kind of conservative. When the term arose in Spain, it was in contrast to "servil," the "servants of the king's arbitrary will."

Humanitas was born in Rome, out of the circle of the Scipios, around 150 B.C. It was the watchword of a new imperial civilization, the heir of Greece. It stood opposed to *barbaritas* or *feritas,* "the way of the wild ones," and it meant cultivated intelligence.

In the Christian era, the term took on a connotation of transiency and misery in the face of eternity: "Chétive créature humaine . . ." The Renaissance inherits thus an ampler meaning: *Humanitas* is again man's "high estate," but it implies also fallibility and frailty: hence venture, risk, responsibility, freedom, tolerance.

The great effort of medieval philosophy had come to its logical conclusion, as may be seen from the preceding volume, in Ockhamism. We have there a world of carefully defined and utterly separate ("absolute") entities, connected only by an abstract order, a discontinuous universe where even cause and effect become shadowy with respect to clear distinction and sharp separation of the objects of thought. It is a world of logical atomism, satisfactory to the pure analytical mind, but far removed indeed from the structural compactness of the Aristotelian vision whence it had issued. In this swirling dust of concepts, what is lost beyond repair is the poetic element that the Greeks had always retained to hold their cosmos together. Whatever poetic vision there was has been sublimated into supernatural truth and mystical intuition; it has left the world of nature, where Aquinas had tried to hold it fast.

We might, then, have as good a point as any for the start of Renaissance philosophy in the letter of Coluccio Salutati, the Florentine humanist and Chancellor, to an Ockhamist doctor in Padua, about 1390. "The truth," he says, "cannot be in all these distinctions, questions, and suppositions. Take away the sophistic dressing, give us back a knowledge of reality. . . . Turn above all things to poetry, whose seal is higher than that of logical knowledge, and alone is able to speak of God." Here "poetry" is meant in the ancient sense of *poiesis;* it corresponds to the fullness of activity and creation, to what was understood as *humanitas* itself.

"Do not believe, my friend," says Coluccio in another letter, "that to flee the crowd, to avoid the sight of beautiful things, to shut oneself up in a cloister, is the way to perfection. In fleeing from the world you may topple down from heaven to earth, whereas I, remaining among earthly things, shall be able to lift my heart securely up to heaven. In striving and working, in caring for your family, your friends, your city which comprises all, you cannot but follow the right way to please God."

This is not anti-philosophical, nor is it a sudden mutation. Salutati shares the mature medieval trend of thought, he is explicitly sympathetic to the Franciscan Ockhamists in the re-establishment of the priority of faith and will over intellectual subtlety; that is indeed why he declares that the proper object of study is not the secrets of Creation of which we can know so little, but the structure of language and law. "The aim of speculation," he remarks, "is truth, but we can reach only a semblance of it; the aim of the laws is the control of men's actions, it is hence the good, that which makes *us* good. . . . They have principles which are not in outer things, but in us, imposed by our minds, they hold together families, cities and nations, they come from the wisdom of God in us." This, goes on the good Chancellor, is what makes of Socrates the philosopher *par excellence,* and if he had died in the true faith, "he would certainly have been the greatest among our martyrs."

There is sound sense here, but also the seed of future grievous intellectual conflict. We can watch it coming to a head presently in the most renowned of Renaissance philosophical movements, namely, the Platonic Academy in Florence. Its chief representatives in history are Marsilio Ficino (1433-1499), the first editor and translator of Plato's text, and Giovanni Pico, Count of Mirandola (1463-1494), the author of the *Discourse on the Dignity of Man,* who died at thirty after a brief but prodigious career of learned activity.

The Florentine Platonists take it for granted that a science of nature on the Aristotelian level is acceptable, and this might well look discouraging in these great innovators. But let us consider that, until the advent of Galileo, it is not easy to move out of the classical orbit of ideas concerning knowledge. The "nature" of an object was understood as its tendency to fulfill its own purpose, and this was the answer to "why" it existed. So why not leave it to Aristotle, insofar as he ordered and described these purposes in the most logical system? For the Florentine Academy, Plato is not the master of intellectual method, he is the "divine philosopher" who gave wings to the soul and lifted it beyond nature to the transcendent realm. In fact, it is Neoplatonism which draws their interest. "The gold of Platonic doctrine," writes Ficino, was refined not only by Plotinus, but by Iamblichus and Porphyry, the masters of secret wisdom. What that means, inevitably, is getting involved in mysterious tradition and in all the fantastic echelons of spiritual entities and "intelligences" which move between us and the upper spheres. Hermes Trismegistus (i.e., "Thrice-Greatest"), the Jewish Kabbala, are brought in by Pico for still vaster concordances and speculations. Leibniz was to score effectively when he described this kind of thought as having reached out for transcendent and "hyperbolic" questions before dealing with fundamentals.

On the other hand, the new concern with infinity which appears here is far from pointless. Nicholas of Cusa had brought it into focus. In Pico and Ficino, it is romantically rather than logically developed, but it animates their thought. The very soul of man is characterized by the infinity of its possibilities. "The images of the divine entities whence it sprang," says Ficino, "it carries in itself as the reasons and models of the lower things that it re-creates as it were of its own. It is the center of all and possesses the

forces of all. It can turn to and penetrate this without
leaving that, for it is the true connection of things. Thus
it can be called rightly the center of nature, the middle
point of the universe, and the chain that links the world
together." The helpless yearning of nature toward a higher
reality cannot find assistance either in material things,
which are too bound, or in spiritual intelligences, too remote: it can work its way back only through the soul and
the action of man.

These are the kind of notions that Montaigne will make
merciless fun of, but then we shall see how Montaigne's
judgment remains curiously paralyzed by doubt; while
Ficino's weird prophesying does outline in a way the shape
of things to come:

"It is man's spirit which re-establishes the shaken universe, it is through its action that the physical world is
continually transmuted and led nearer toward those spiritual regions from which it once issued."

While Salutati had been trying, in the name of good
sense, to re-establish Socrates over Ockham, and to bring
philosophy down to the city, philosophy is sweepingly off
on a new tangent—as it will. And the conflict is out in the
open.

Philosophy and religion, after centuries of separation,
are becoming one again. Ficino's theory is currently described as mystical Neoplatonism; yet contemplative withdrawal looks more like the literary side of it, while its
intellectual ambition is strongly anchored to reality. It
strives, like Pico's, towards the conquest of "natural
magic," the capacity for command that comes to man's
soul from standing thus in the cockpit of the universe. The
creation of new habitable planets, as we unashamedly
discuss it today, would have been quite within the range
of credibility for this kind of imagination. It believes that
we can reach out for as yet unknown harmonies and
powers, for "nothing is incredible, and nothing is impossible. The possibilities that we deny are those that we do
not happen to know." To this bold affirmation of Ficino,
Pico brings a new and strikingly original content in his
Dignity of Man. Man's central position in the universe
would be, by itself, an old story many times rehearsed,

and so, too, is the mystic correspondence between the Microcosm of our nature and the universal Macrocosm. That correspondence involves the idea of two closed and achieved orders. It is an essentially ancient idea. The true distinction of man according to Pico is, much rather, that he has no fixed properties but has the power to share in the properties of all other beings, according to his own free choice. He is a universal and protean agent of transformation, hence it behooves him to orient his soul properly towards the good, so as not to use his powers wrongly. It is not so much his universality as his liberty which is stressed.

Men who can think thus are not seeing the world as a prison, or as a fleeting pageant. For the first time, the world is really open. And in it, man is very strong.

It is significant to see Ficino pick up in the storehouse of tradition, of all things, the story that Archimedes once built a model to imitate the motions of the planets, moved by an imagined "infusion of mercury" which ensured its perpetual motion:

【 Not every man can understand how and in what manner the skillful work of a clever artisan is constructed, but only he who possesses a like artistic genius. Certainly no one could understand how Archimedes constructed his brazen spheres and gave them motions like the heavenly motions unless he were endowed with a similar genius. He who can understand it because he has a like genius could doubtless, as soon as he has understood it, also construct another, provided he did not lack the proper material. Now, since man has observed the order of the heavens, when they move, whither they proceed and with what measures, and what they produce, who could deny that man possesses as it were almost the same genius as the Author of the heavens? And who could deny that man could somehow also make the heavens, could he only obtain the instruments and the heavenly material, since even now he makes them, though of a different material, but still with a very similar order? 】

ARCHIMEDES MIGHT HAVE TOLD FICINO THAT SUCH ME-chanical gadgets had nothing to do with true science which built abstract and rigorous mathematical models impossible to translate into mere clockworks; he would also have wondered whether the God thus indicated was at all consistent with the good man's own "Platonic theology"; but the very lack of strength and consistency in Ficino's thought makes him more interesting in that it allows him to be swayed by the trends of his time. A protégé of Lorenzo il Magnifico, a contemporary of Brunelleschi and Leonardo, Ficino forgets mystical escape and is taken along in the great engineering dream. The true Archimedes, reappearing through Copernicus and Galileo, will give that dream wings for a vaster flight.

Here, then, is the new orientation: intense civil life; creative poetry, "natural magic," the science which combines knowledge with a capacity to transform things. Man is no longer the contemplative soul, but is a transformer placed at the outside limit of absolute risk, a free force taking consciousness of itself. The new mythical symbols came up naturally, as it were, in Salutati's strong and quiet prose. They are Hercules at the crossroads, Prometheus and his ultimate decision. Man reflects himself in the heroic demi-gods. This is what Renaissance philosophy stands for; it is not to be found in the academic production of Nifo, Nizolius, Pendasius, and their like. Instead, it exists in this first period in the thinking of Leon Battista Alberti, the great architect, as he projects the ideal man, or gives a theory of the good family, as he describes its mores, its organization, its proper way of dwelling in town and country, of building, or running its estate. Or one finds it in the eloquence of Leonardo Bruni on history and civil subjects, in the profound creative speculations of Leonardo da Vinci, in the adventures of Pico della Mirandola among strange doctrines and strange languages. As it reaches out towards the unknown in a spirit of adventure, the Renaissance mind is also fascinated by the discovery of man's own past, and that is one of the most positive contents of humanism. Even for a man like Sir Walter Raleigh, who lived in the midst of the heroic Elizabethan expansion, the great conquest of the mind is history, which "hath carried our knowledge over the vast and devouring space of many thousands of years."

Is this properly philosophy? Let us consider what Lorenzo Valla has to say. Valla (1406-1457) is the sharpest humanistic mind and the most fearless critic of that early period, the avowed model of Erasmus. Like Erasmus, he had but qualified sympathy for the Church hierarchies; he wrote vigorously against their encroachments by showing the historical non-existence of the so-called Donation of Rome to the Pope by Constantine. He also wrote philosophical disquisitions on Pleasure (for) and on Free Will (against). But, in one revealing passage, he sets Quintilian above Cicero as a master of eloquence for this peculiar reason, that Quintilian did not regard philosophy as highly as Cicero did, but considered rhetoric as the more serious art, which allows one to control political assemblies and to sway the decisions of men.

Thus poetry, history, eloquence and what is in the ampler sense "philology" are simply the form in which a new philosophy of life is taking position against the old. Even Martin Luther, who could hardly be called a typical Renaissance character, belongs to this line of thought. As a Church philosopher, he still considered himself an Ockhamist of sorts, or "terminist," as the name was, "for it provides good means for calling a spade a spade," but in his Table Talk he rues the time spent "on philosophy and all that devil's muck, when I could have been busy with poetry and legend and so many good things."

This is indeed the happy phase of the Renaissance, the age of the unearthing of great texts, of the introduction of Greek, of brave hopes and memorable formulations of the dignity of man. It is also the age of the printing press and the discovery of America. It culminates in those decades between 1500 and 1520, which brought forth perhaps the greatest density of significant production that history can remember. "Immortal God!" writes Erasmus in 1517, "What a world I see dawning! Why can I not grow young again?" He was seeing "the near approach of a golden age" in which, he predicted, three great blessings would be restored to humanity, namely true Christian piety, learning of the best sort, and the lasting concord of Christendom.

A few years later he was a sorrowful disappointed old man. In a letter to Luther in 1526, he laments the irremediable confusion of everything "for which," he adds, "we have to thank only your uncontrollable nature." Many new factors, indeed, were at play. The turning point of the epoch may well be that year 1517, in which Erasmus and More are confronted with the new forces of Luther and Machiavelli. From then on the Renaissance enters the somber phase of theological dust and fury, of the wars of religion, of overreaching adventures of the mind, and of the awesomely unbounded revelations of the Copernican universe, from which its own world, so intense in its individualism, artistic imagination and local fantasy, cannot recover.

The worm has been in the apple from the beginning. We have remarked earlier that Italian humanism has its origin in the late medieval flourishing of the free cities. But by the time it has become fully conscious of its claims, the social structure that bears it has entered its decadence. The incredible tension of the world of Dante, paradoxically spanning the chasm between the universe and the pinpoint local event, between the mind of God and that of sharply etched individual characters, between cosmic meaning and city brawls, has brought forth at the limit a total order and an unrepeatable *tour de force*. The generation of Petrarch and Boccaccio is beyond that order, ripe for the new era, but its maturity is frail, like that of a flower already plucked. A great formal culture in its pride is born at a time in which the social underpinnings are giving way.

The great institutions are crumbling, the Empire has become a joke, the Papacy is by way of becoming a ceaselessly intriguing military principality in Latium, the Church is considered more than due for a thorough overhauling; wealth and worldliness have broken down the strict, austere and military-minded order of the early Communes. While Italy is exporting the literary, diplomatic and military techniques for the monarchies of the new era, we shall find Machiavelli ruefully meditating on the civil decay of his country and trying to figure out desperate countermeasures.

This, then, is how things stand at the very outset in the creative generations of Italian humanism: a civilization shooting forth wonderful sparklers, but out of balance and kilter, full of broken utopias and futile hopes, passionately rehearsing great motifs, but ready to settle down into the immobile splendor of a long decadence comforted with splendid dreams.

This is true, obviously, only so far as Italy goes. But what wonder if in this initial phase we find many of the inherited defects of late classical culture? In thought, we are not witnessing a "rebirth" of the early age of Greece, but a revival of learning, carried through in the first place by grammarians and rhetoricians rehearsing the accomplishment of a language not their own. The sense of daemonic presence, the vital immediacy and the no less vital incomprehension with which the medievals handled the fragments of antiquity of which they took notice, is replaced now by a kind of "show window" psychology with respect to the wonders of the past finally on display. There is a kind of nostalgia, an imitative and self-conscious quality, about much of the new production. The Latin language itself is transformed into a show object out of the reach of the vulgar. The Renaissance hits its creative stride only when it finds really new ground in the plastic arts. But a gap always remains between the originality in the arts and the derivative aspect of the purely intellectual and verbal achievements. The accent placed on personality is not always sufficient to fill that gap.

In an epoch, indeed, in which values are centered so strongly upon personal distinction and "fame," the counterfeit presentments of it, self-importance and self-advertising, give rise to the characteristic figures of the pedant, the doctor, the rhetorician, the facile expounder of philosophy as a literary genre. Much of that thought is running around in circles. This more than accounts for Valla's crack at Cicero, his master: "If Tully had claimed back rhetoric for civil life where it can be soundly employed, there would be left only the bloodless ghost of philosophy."

The truth is that, so long as there is nothing more effective to go by, words have to take all the place available; words, which may convey at times startling news or sharp criticism or wondrous intimations, but most of the time remain caught and sterilized inside the commonplaces of language. The weary gibes of Leonardo at the clamor of

the pedants pass **unnoticed**, for words can be brought to
heel only by some new contact with reality. By the time
of Galileo and Bacon, a new vision can replace the old
one. Simplicio the doctor still gravely explains that there
is nothing strange or interesting about what makes bodies
fall: "everyone knows that it is Gravity"; but Galileo is in
a position to reprove him gently:

[You are out, my dear Simplicio, you should say that
everyone knows that it is *called* Gravity: but I do not question you about the name, but about the essence of the thing,
of which essence you know not a tittle more than you
know the essence of the mover of the stars in gyration:
unless it be the name that has been put to this, and made
familiar and domestical, by the many experiences which
we see thereof every hour in the day: but not as if we
really understand any more what principle or vertue
that is, than when we say the stars are moved by 'intelligences.']

Our epoch has solved, even too effectively, the problem
of the independent intellectual personality. Scientific method provides a standard procedure whereby any individual,
without having to be endowed with a genius "similar to that
of Archimedes," can find a place in which his contribution dovetails with that of others to bring forth the imposing architecture of scientific or historical research. It
may end up in the purely instrumental conception of the
"mass attack" on important problems; it provides nonetheless a working place for talent in society. The Renaissance
had inherited from antiquity a set of rhetorical or Plutarch-
ian delusions whereby the intellectual was led to strike
classical poses and try for the unique opus apt to procure
for him "immortal fame." Too often he had nothing to
say; this did not prevent him from writing. To be conversant with the ancient and noble languages, to be able to
use them, was accounted a social distinction in itself.
Hence all the cumbersome erudition, the concordances,
the numberless quotations and "such like loitering gear,"
as Milton calls it.

The artist, unencumbered by status, had his work assessed by the whole community, but the scholar tended to fence in the intellectual patrimony; hence the universities fell behind, they no longer provided a place for creative intellects. As Copernicus remarked, the drones outnumbered the bees. In attendance, too, the regular philosophy courses show a significant shrinkage. Conventicles, academies, the favor of princes or the protection of the rich, these became the new media for cultural activity. But to please the new patrons, oratory is in order, or rather flattery, and, beyond that, anything apt to astonish and bemuse. Scientific curiosity flounders amid the strange and the sensational.

The Poetic Element

The tension between past and future imparts to the Renaissance, more than to any other period, a peculiar Janus-like quality. Like the two-headed god himself, it stands at the same time for the divide, the boundary and the gate. The only clarity that it can attain is thus poetic and artistic. As it looks backward, its aspect is that of humanism, passionately absorbed in the prototypes set by the past; as it gazes ahead, it projects a Faustian vision of undefined but unlimited power, the new anthropological myth of Man the Explorer, bent on an endless quest. We should leave it to Giordano Bruno to express it, since it is such thoughts that led him to the stake: "Another stump of the past, you say? A stump, if you wish, but destined to bloom with vigor; antique things, perhaps, too, but bound to come back; truth, long forgotten, but now recovered. It is a new light which dawns after a long darkness at the horizon of our knowledge, and rises apace until it will become the sun at noon." Here speaks indeed "the prophetic soul of the wide world dreaming of things to come." So intense is that dream that reality as a whole responds to it, becomes one with it, charged with mysterious power. The rigid dualism between matter and spirit yields to a pantheistic monism. The development of philosophical thought goes the way that unites and makes whole intuitively, and not the way which analytically separates. The Platonic-Aristotelian relation of the Gen-

eral to the Particular yields to the organic relation of the
Whole to its parts.

How far this may lead one from the beaten paths of
safe doctrine can be seen from these startlingly pantheistic
lines of Tommaso Campanella, a thinker who remained to
the end, or so he thought, a passionate Catholic and a
Dominican:

> Man was once child, was embryo, seed and blood,
> Bread, grass, and sundry things, in which it pleased
> Him to be what he was, nor did he crave
> To be what now he is;
> And what is now to him so frightening
> To become fire, and earth, and mouse, and snake
> Will be his pleasure then, and he'll be glad
> To be what he shall be, for in all things
> God's thought is shining through
> And all the past forgotten.

A further quotation will give us the compass of Campanella's thought:

[All living beings are inside that greatest of living beings
that is the world, like worms in an animal's belly, and so
are we; yet it is only man who knows what that great
animal is, its origin and course and life and death. Hence
man is there not only as a worm, but as a contemplator
and a representative of the cause and Architect of all
things. . . . And we see that man does not abide by the
nature of the elements, the Earth and the Sun, but aims
and yearns beyond them, and brings about effects higher
than any in nature. Thus, when man thinks, he thinks far
and away above the Sun, and yet further, and beyond
heaven; he thinks many worlds, aye an infinity of
them. . . .]

This was said by a Copernican, and by a champion of
Galileo. But the whole of the Renaissance is in it.

An age which found its fulfillment in form would hardly
have been the one to unravel the confusion, or shall we say
blending, between the empirical and the formal content of
thought, which had been going on for ages. It was rather
one to preserve and enhance it by stressing the traditional

relationship between Eloquence and Wisdom which made
for what we might call poetic logic.

There is in the Renaissance none of the later self-
conscious and somewhat guilty division between conceptual truth and imaginative or non-scientific truth. Poetic
lucidity, as T. S. Eliot remarked of Dante, does come first;
intellectual lucidity is supposed to be connatural with it;
in fact it follows up, carried by structures and form. A
famous example is the Michelangelo sonnet quoted on
page 155. An old definition of eloquence may bring us
nearer to the spirit of the thing. Eloquence, that is, the
capacity for expression, is said to overcome the weakness
of our nature, the difficulties inherent to knowledge, and
the fruitlessness of effort. It provides thus a solution by
itself, within the universe of discourse that is man's; it
sculptures, as it were, his capacities through expression,
and this is what Michelangelo ambiguously stresses.

The scientific image which startles us at times in Donne's
poems is really quite congruent with his thought. The instrument of knowledge—and were it the map or the telescope—is *also* an instrument of poetic thought. Conversely,
the anatomical tables of Vesalius, wherewith modern
medicine is supposed to begin, in 1544, are works of art
at least as much as instruments for science. The universe
still responds to the metaphysical imagination, for which
the discoveries of science are a stimulant and not a hindrance. It is only after the seventeenth century, when
mathematics takes over as the language proper to science,
that poetry *about* science becomes a second-rate genre. In
our own time, largely by merit of Auden and Empson,
poetic thought would again seem to have become able to
deal with science in its own terms. This may be tied up with
the fact that philosophy proper is left with little to say except logical analysis. But it is still too early to understand
what is actually taking place.

One might say that in the Renaissance, as in the ages of
myth, poetry was considered inseparable from whatever
science there was. It was expected to provide what Sir
Philip Sidney called the "Architectonicke." But that was
because it had been preceded by an "Analytic." If one was
an educated person in the sixteenth century, one was taught

from adolescence that the first step in disciplined thinking was to know what a thing is by reference to the ten Aristotelian categories or predicaments. The ones usually listed are: substance, quality, quantity, relation, manner of acting, manner of suffering, when and where. They were supposed to name "the very nature of things" (this was what everyone took for granted when one wanted to show "sound judgment"), and, as a schoolbook says as late as 1624, there is nothing "done either by Nature, or by Art, by Counsell or Chance" (note how these four are brought together) which may not be referred to these categories.

Thus, even the process of "finding" images, today utterly free, was subject to rigid logical rules. A well-invented figure did not only mean an ingenious figure, it meant a suitable figure, one which went to the heart of the true nature of the matter. It is not strange, then, that much of that poetry should be conceived as philosophical in a demonstrative way.

On the other side of the tapestry, we have the creative minds of science—Copernicus, Kepler, Galileo—starting their search from what is to them an obvious assumption, viz., that the world is "a perfect work of art," and that hence the clues to unravelling its complexities must be sought in beauty, simplicity and symmetry.

Great literature, as Whitehead remarked, has always been the laboratory of philosophical ideas. From the laboratory of Renaissance poetry, from the innumerable images meant to assist in evoking the true nature of something, there emerges the indication that the clock is being set back to some kind of Platonic realism, that is, the belief in the reality of ideas, as against hard-headed late medieval Nominalism; and indeed this is what we find also in the most characteristic strain of philosophical thought in the fifteenth century, the Platonism of the Florentine Academy. This "realist" attitude normally occurs where philosophy has struck some new and fertile ground; it is tantamount to a belief in what one is doing. Our age is, in philosophy, the "age of analysis"—it prides itself again in extreme Nominalism—yet our thought is inescapably tinged with Platonic realism for what concerns the time and space of General Relativity, or the entities in the

Freudian Unconscious, or the nature of the atomic nucleus, just as the nineteenth century had a "realist" attitude, from different sides, with respect to Matter, or the Hegelian Spirit, or Progress, or the electro-magnetic ether. In the Renaissance, this realism applied to aesthetic forms and substances.

When Donne wants to affirm his love as durable through time and wandering, he has recourse to the famous image of the compasses:

> Thy firmness draws my circle just
> And makes me end, where I begun.

It is not a conceit, not a rapprochement. It is a declaration in cosmic terms, value merging with fact. "What is eternal is circular, and what is circular is eternal," the Philosopher had said. The same theme reappears then on another level, as an anxious question, when he addresses the Jet Ring:

> What wouldst thou say? Shall both our properties
>   by thee be spoke,
> Nothing more endless, nothing sooner broke?

Donne is not following free association: he is really asking the black jet to "say" a meaningful abstraction, a particular to "speak" or express universals; and through them also his own human predicament. If the thing is true (and who could deny it, here is the Ring—the actualized reality of what in the compasses was still potential and free) it will have the signature of things on it, the Platonic "simple seal of truth," which speaks unerringly to the intellect. The ring does indeed convey things on more levels than the poet cares to expound. The circle of perfection which enclosed the universe, the meaning of circularity as expressing the order and eternity of the cosmos, were symbols deeply felt in their aesthetic and metaphysical import. The "breaking of the circle" effected by Copernicanism had meant, in Donne's time, a psychological trauma not to be overcome for generations. The divining mind of Pascal recoils before the coming reality: "the silence of infinite space frightens me."

It is a measure of man's resourcefulness that the Renaissance can show such vitality of thought while people feel that the fabric of the universe is shaking, and that this unleashed fireworks of fantastic novelties is a sign that "this tired world is nearing its end." This kind of "combat fatigue" or shock condition in the civilized consciousness is bound to last for a long time. The passionate Pythagorean—and revolutionary—faith of a Bruno, a Campanella, a Galileo or a Henry More may find joy in the intimations of infinite universal life, but most minds, like Donne, who witness with dread the breaking of "Nature's nest of boxes" will derive only despondency from it. As late as 1664, Henry Power, himself a robust optimist, mentions "the Universal Exclamation of the World's decay and approximation to its Period."

We, too, are living in such an age of anxiety, but the difference is worth noting. The critical or skeptical attitude in society we have learned to take in our stride. What we are concerned with is whether the physical powers we have actually unleashed may not destroy mankind. Renaissance opinion had not much to show in the way of new powers; it was concerned with the *hybris* itself, it felt that the overweening recklessness of man's mind was a sign and a symbol, more than a cause, of the declining powers of order in the cosmos. Those who lamented that "beauty's self, Proportion, is dead" implied that the thought of man was bringing subversion to the universe in the way disaffection among the subjects brings about the ruin of kingdoms. In a word, it was criticism, arrogance and the new insecurity which seemed to forebode a "flagitious exit."

The prodigious creative response of the Renaissance to the new open condition might well make us forget that we are looking only at what emerges, so to speak, and that nine-tenths of the intellectual effort is hidden from sight. That nine-tenths is critical activity. Let us examine this submerged portion. Medieval Nominalism had been the beginning of the critical offensive against Aquinas's way of using the intellect. The offensive develops now along what we might call the Erasmian line, leading up to Montaigne, Spinoza and Hume. Protestantism has a share in it too. The Reformation itself, that bombshell at the heart of the Renaissance, is far from forward-looking. It wants to be an unquestioning return to Christian fundamentals, a revival of mystical and anti-intellectual faith; yet in its attack on institutional thought, in its philological scrutiny of texts and documents, it puts into question more ideas than it revives.

Erasmus, the reformer who refused to be drawn into the Reformation (similar in that to his friend Sir Thomas More), takes his stand on rationalism. Within traditional religious thought, he is the man who changes the meaning of rationalism from its medieval to its modern connotation; that is, instead of using reason as a handmaiden in the service of faith, he chooses to follow it where it will lead him in the analysis of traditional theological structures as built up by the Fathers of the Church. It leads him to recognize their inconsistent and essentially composite character. His sharp philological scrutiny shows how the personal spiritual experience of Paul concerning our sinfulness has been built up by theologians into an untenable theory of the cosmos and of man's place in it. In his defense of free will against Luther, he first shows by textual criticism that the Gospels do not really uphold the Pauline denial of free will, and then proceeds to show how free will is the necessary presupposition both for the ethical and for the religious existence. How this can agree with the postulate of an omniscient deity, how it can agree, indeed, with dogma itself, he does not profess to understand. Here is for him the skeptical limit of reason; he hopes it is still possible, that is all.

This earned him the raging invectives of Luther: "Erasmus is an enemy of all religion, he is the true adversary of Christ, a perfect replica of Epicurus and Lucian. Whenever I pray, I pray for a curse on him." Most unfair towards a great scholar, judged his contemporaries: the typical violence of the religious dictator. Surely Erasmus's pious labors, his *Manual of the Christian Soldier,* which was a devotional vade mecum for a century, deserved more consideration. Yet we who know what followed are moved to wonder whether Luther, in the intemperance of his genius, had not seen right. Erasmus quietly notes that divine election and predestinarianism would make of the merciful God a fearful oppressor with respect to the reprobate. A God, he says, who gives orders in order to show that man can disobey them would not only be a tyrant but a perverse one. Jonathan Edwards was to give the full expression of predestinationism when he presented man as a loathsome spider suspended by the hand of God over the flames. This alone, Erasmus would have remarked, ought to show that such a theology is hardly compatible with the principles of humanism.

Whither the new attitude may lead the unflinching mind is not far to seek, if and when it decides to ignore the general Christian assumptions and to draw strictly "philosophical" conclusions in the technical mood. But it takes the cold audacity of Pietro Pomponazzi to put it in print long before Spinoza: "Those who maintain the mortality of the soul can be shown to save the essence and reason of virtue better than those who believe the soul immortal: for the hope of reward and the fear of punishment imply a certain servility which is incompatible with true and rational virtue." This expresses well the coldly rationalistic atmosphere of Italian universities like Padua and Bologna. Such conclusions are not for the general public, nor even for humanists. It is Erasmus the moderate, the enlightened Christian, who can speak for public opinion and become its leader.

What Erasmus does, armed with the prestige of his learning, is to undermine the whole of dogma in the name of the Gospel text. He wants to remain within ecumenic Catholicity, he is accepted as such, he is even offered a cardinalship, but his thought leads inexorably to that of his great Protestant countrymen and successors: Coornhert, Oldenbarneveldt, Grotius. It leads to a universal theism, almost to Unitarianism.

The Erasmian critique of the medieval philosophy of man is vigorously taken up from another side, after 1540, by the Italian Protestant refugees. Of these men who wander through Europe as "displaced persons," some find hospitality in Geneva under Calvin, others are too free-thinking for that. Bernardino Occhino and the Sozzini brothers, the Siennese founders of Socinianism, end up in Poland under the king's protection. Some are caught and burned: Michael Servetus, the great Catalan, by the Calvinist Inquisition, Francesco Pucci, the Florentine, by the Roman Holy Office.

These men of heroic temper were not overreaching prophets such as Bruno was to be. They were mostly lawyers and humanists in the line of Coluccio Salutati and Lorenzo Valla, who wanted to make Christianity acceptable to humanistic reason. What came under criticism was the central dogmatic complex built around original sin, inherited corruption, and divine atonement. Originally a powerful metaphysical complex valid in its own symbolic language, it had been converted into a rational or rather a rationalized structure by Augustine, Anselm and their successors. But if there is to be reason at all, the Socinians now insisted, let it be used according to its own rules. Could it be called fair on the part of the deity to deprive man once and forever of what he was created for, because of a single mistake, since such a mistake was inevitable, and inevitably needed for man to learn? Is it just to load the innocent progeny with a hereditary corruption which makes of them degenerates and cripples? To hamstring man and then scourge him because he cannot walk? What kind of mistake could it be anyway that made the whole order of Providence collapse? And who ever heard, in civilized law, of accepting the sacrifice of the innocent as an atonement for the guilty? If imperfect man knows how to forgive and forget, could not God in His perfection at least try? This literal-minded polemic ends up in the very position held by the Arminians and by Grotius: namely, "natural religion" as the only justifiable one, based on the fatherhood of God and the perfectibility of man. It is also powerfully upheld by the great French jurist Jean Bodin. There is a certain naïveté, no doubt, in this type of argument; it is the same vigorous naïveté that shines forth in Renaissance art, and bestows a contemporary worldly setting and assurance on the portraying of religious mysteries; it is also the fearless naïveté of men who have come to grips with fundamentals. So long as these questions have not been tackled, one way or another, philosophy cannot turn to its proper business; and, indeed, many problems have been laid to rest then and there that will never turn up again in serious thought. "Let these traducers of nature be silent, and not try to show her as depraved, since she has never taught us to like evil." These words of Lord Herbert of Cherbury might apply to the whole of Renaissance illuminism.

On the profit and loss side, we thus have religion rationally straightened out and made acceptable to the lay philosophic mind. But is it still religion? In its solid good sense and elephantine simplicity, "natural" or "rational" religion seems to announce modern economic production devices like "positive thinking." The profound metaphysical paradox at the core of Christianity, which made of it a stumbling block to the wise, has been removed; but with it has gone the spiritual experience and the life of the soul. At the end of that road there is only the inconclusive deism of Newtonian science.

Be that as it may, it sets a problem for future generations, a problem which each generation attempts to solve in its own way. In this period of the Renaissance, in which bloody religious struggles are leading up to the climax and holocaust of the Thirty Years' War, from which Europe was never morally to recover, a period in which theologians are as busy as a barrel of monkeys sharpening knives in Councils and Synods, in anathema and counter-anathema, there is a wonderfully positive content, and a content of evangelical hope, in that fight for justice and tolerance, in that affirmation of peaceful and cosmic religiosity, which goes from Erasmus all the way to Voltaire. Such men as Socinus, Coornhert, Grotius, Oldenbarnevelt, Bodin, Castellio, Sebastian Franck, are prophets, and some of them martyrs no less than Pucci, Servetus, or Bruno. They stand for philosophical rationalism and for a new definition of man. "Saint Socrates, pray for us," Erasmus had said, and Coluccio Salutati before him.

By the end of the century, that idea had become understandable to simple men of affairs. In 1596, this is what the Burgomaster of Amsterdam, Pieter van Hooft, wrote curtly to the Calvinist authorities on behalf of a poor craftsman who was interpreting the Bible in his own curious way: "I hear that he is being excommunicated. Now let the Church be content with that, and cease persecuting him and his family any further. These people live in the fear of the Lord, they worship him as far as their insight reaches, and that ought to be enough. A man's life should not be dependent on learned subtleties." It was well said, but there were still too few such forces, including even the Venetian Senate with its power, to stop "the horrible nurses itching to boil their children." As Montaigne says, "there is no enmity so excellent as the Christian." By 1648, at the signing of the Treaty of Westphalia, which provided an official if lame ending to the wars of religion, there was barely one half of the previous population left alive in Germany. Weariness was to deliver more than reason ever could.

The Philosophical Foundation

After getting rid of so much superstructure (and not only on paper, for such feats as the discovery of America are in themselves a spectacular piece of critique), what did the Renaissance have to rely on in the way of foundations? Inevitably, it was ancient thought as it had been discovered through humanism. Plato in his genuine content; the late scrapbooks of *Opinions* of dimly-known Greek masters; Cicero and Seneca as teachers not only of ethical life, but also of comparative philosophy: these were now the sources.

Through them, the men of the Renaissance realized that thinkers of no small consequence had held Pleasure to be the guiding principle, that others, manifestly great scientific minds, had been able to assert that all of nature is "in reality nothing but atoms and the void." They also rediscovered the spirit of ancient mathematics and physics and generally were able to discern intuitively what modern historical research has endorsed, namely, that the admirable order and tidiness of the Aristotelian system had been obtained at the price of a retreat with respect to the true possibilities of Greek thought.

Advanced knowledge is always in a tactically exposed position. Much of its force is tied up in risky expeditions caught deep in dangerous territory. In Aristotle's own time, there had been the daring mathematical cosmology of the Pythagoreans, the physics of the Ionians, the atomism of Democritus, the astronomy and the metamathematics of Eudoxus, the transcendent speculations of the Platonists. With astringent good sense and a remarkable lack of philosophical imagination, Aristotle wrote off or melted down all those ventures ("liquidate" is the modern word for it) and concentrated on setting up a well-organized encyclopedic arrangement, in which everything should find its place in a consistent order. This was done at the price of keeping physics on a primitive and already discounted level, of eschewing mathematics and its possibilities, of concocting an absurd mechanics. The strong points of the scheme had been chosen for what Aristotle considered the more serious needs: giving man and his activities the proper place, and describing adequately the experiences of the mind. Beyond that, it became strictly a paper universe, handled by means of verbal analysis, in essence very similar to the lawyer's world. Like the lawyer, the scholastic used the technique he had learned to dispose of problems in the sense required by society, rather than trying to deal with them on their own terms, or, even more embarrassingly, being faced with the discovery of new ones. The disposal technique was called disputation; it went by way of brief and counterbrief, and it was found most suitable by a spiritual authority mainly concerned with protecting man from his own *libido sciendi,* or lust after knowledge. But some unruly minds, who wanted to go deeper into the matter, were not long in realizing that Aristotle had been the first to use that disposal technique himself, to obliterate the ideas of his great predecessors. Bacon likens him to those Turkish sultans who reached the throne over the corpses of their brothers.

Still, to find out what was wrong with the system was easier said than done: even more difficult, to devise a better one. When Faustus has bought all of the devil's knowledge with his soul, what can the devil produce out of his files to serve him, but a more comprehensive edition of Aristotle's

Natural History? A small episode might show the temper of the times. François I of France, a lover of the arts but surely not a scholarly character, heard that a philosopher in Padua had been able to "refute" Aristotle. He promptly granted him 10,000 livres in token of appreciation, which was several times the value of today's Nobel prize. The philosopher, alas, turned out not to be a very potent refutator; nor could Peter Ramus really replace Aristotle either, while his whole celebrity in education was based on such a claim.

After all, Aristotle was the master of the language of direct experience and common sense, and it was a high kind of common sense; most of Renaissance thinking goes on inside that frame even when it tries to rebel against it; Bacon himself remains inadvertently within its orbit. But people are willing to try anything, even magic, to get out of it, once they have become aware of its sterility. Descartes will state the case crisply: "We could not better prove the falsity of those principles than by saying that man has made no progress in knowledge by their means during many ages."

By going back to classic sources, the Renaissance uncovered leads that had been buried by scholasticism, and which opened the way to modern thought. Inevitably, they were conflicting leads; but they gave at last the feeling of a thought at grips with life and reality: and this is what Faust, that most representative of characters, is desperately searching for:

> That I the weary task forgo
> Of saying things I do not know,
> That I may detect the inmost force
> Which binds the world, and guides its course
> Explore its latent powers and seeds,
> And deal not in empty words but deeds.

This is Man the Transformer. What does he have to proceed on? Antiquity has left him two main approaches to cosmological thought. One in which the world is conceived of as "designed" by the deity (or freely forming itself on the divine idea), another in which it is seen as "begotten" or emanated. Plato and Aristotle are examples of the first kind. Whether God be imagined mythically as the Demi-urge or metaphysically as the Good or the Unmoved Mover, there is always an idea, a *design* which carries itself out. Nature is explained by Aristotle on the analogy of a master builder or an artist with an intention as well as a design in his mind.

There is, then, the other approach, which is represented mainly by the Stoics and stems from the intuitive thought of Heraclitus the Obscure: reality as a *flux* of perpetually changing forms, a transmutation of all things into each other by virtue of an inherent Logos or universal law. The living flame, preserving and affirming its form as it feeds on and transforms all things, is the original image. With it goes the idea of a spirit or "breath" bringing life to that flame and vital heat to the universe. The metaphysics pre-supposed here is what Aristotle rather contemptuously refers to as "imagining all things to take their origin from 'Night' and 'Not-Being' "—in other words, irreducible mythology. There is no question that this sex-dominated conception is intellectually intractable. It does not lend it-self to tidy logical developments. In Oriental thought, whence it comes, it does in fact presuppose a first begetting out of Chaos, or from "the spirit floating on the face of the waters." In Genesis, it is the mysterious command which is underlined, the creative act: "Let there be light." In the version given by the Greek Stoics, who insisted on being rational philosophers and unyielding naturalists, the command takes the form of a *Law* intrinsic to the universe, which makes it into a closed system tightly articulated by the force of Necessity. We have thus not so much a mystical as a dynamic pantheism. All is matter in the Stoic world, animated matter as it were. Forces themselves are a form of matter, permeating other matter: they are varieties of one original force, as is shown by the unity of the world and the connection and agreement of its parts. This force, too, is corporeal, it is imagined as the fiery breath, "pneuma," which animates all things: and it is also rational, for it is God, the Logos of the universe and its soul. It is the mind of the world, providence, necessity, fate, nature, universal law, whichever is the aspect we choose. It ordains the flux of all things through all forms according to a rigid determinism, from which man himself is not exempt. Astrology, a very un-Greek novelty, becomes all at once here a deus ex machina. It provides the orderly system of cosmic influences and the timing device that makes of the universe a smoothly functioning organism. Posidonius of Rhodes is said to have devised this solution after watching the influence of the moon upon the tides; this gives some good reason for Galileo and Descartes, later, stubbornly to deny any such influence, which should have appeared even to them undeniable.

Stoic philosophy was, then, some "reasonable" form of scientific materialism, while atomism appeared as the more dogmatic and unreasonable; but both had to be condemned and excluded by Christian philosophy, which tried to obliterate even their memory. It so happened, however, that a good dose of Stoicism had entered the thought of the Neoplatonists. Plotinus does indeed preserve the high intellectual design and the transcendence of Plato; but insofar as his system requires a process, an "emanation" from the Ineffable One down to the level (hypostasis) of Intellect, and further down to that of Soul, which becomes the sensible world, the Stoic ideas of Posidonius were called in to help, and with them the ladder of multitudinous forces and "intelligences" moving between here and above. All this came then into the Renaissance orbit under an orthodox label, but it was highly exciting contraband stuff; we have seen how the Florentine Platonists were attracted to it like moths to a flame.

It was a yeasty mixture that could be drawn out of Neoplatonism by adventurous minds. There were Pythagorean intimations in it, geometrical mysteries, magic-monistic emanationism, all in one. Out of some of those leads, and with the help of Archimedes, will come later modern science. The more immediately tempting way, however, led towards "natural magic." There is no question that it looked really scientific. It also led to experiment. If there is a universal idea of determinism and "natural law" (in our sense, not the medieval) before Galileo, it is in the form of an organic living interaction between all parts of the universe by influx, correspondence and analogy. Francis Bacon, the "modern," was to write in a vein of common sense:

[It is certain that all bodies whatsoever, though they have no sense, yet they have perception: for when one body is applied to another, there is a kind of election to embrace that which is agreeable, and to exclude or expel that which is ingrate; and whether the body be alterant or altered, evermore a perception precedeth operation; for else all bodies would be alike one to another. And sometimes this perception, in some kind of bodies, is far more subtile than sense; so that sense is but a dull thing in comparison of it: we see a weatherglass will find the least difference of the weather in heat or cold, when we find it not. And this perception is sometimes at a distance, as well as upon the touch; as when the loadstone draweth iron; or flame naphtha of Babylon, a great distance off. It is therefore a subject of very noble enquiry, to enquire of the more subtile perceptions. . . .]

Even the doubting heart of Montaigne was stirred by similar views as it was not by the attempts at a physical "machinery." (See p. 167.) Kepler believed passionately in animistic forces, including astrology, and it was out of that belief that he could attain to the idea of a gravitational force in astronomy—as Galileo and Descartes could and would not.

Pomponazzi, Machiavelli's contemporary and no less tough-minded, tried to do away with the spiritual fancies and to revive a materialist physics on a qualitative basis. We have seen on p. 28 that he did not shun the consequences of his thought. He was, of course, simply reviving an old Stoic strain. He found sympathy among the hardheaded logicians of Padua, who were trying on their side to revive the naturalist aspect of Aristotle—the "scientific-minded" group of scoffers at pious comfort, those whom Petrarch had called "a horde of black ants wasting the fields of wisdom." But it remained a road with no exit.

Against such and like forces, the Church had long since devised a strategy. In the Age of Belief, when it took charge of the whole of thought, it organized a competent distribution: Aristotle, properly trimmed, was put in charge of "natural reason," i.e. philosophy, as befitted "the master of those who know." Owing to the Neoplatonic tradition, nature remained shot through with the influxes of the planets and mystical correspondence; but they were under control. Above was the transcendent realm where Neoplatonic speculation was in order; it was the reign of theology and mystical contemplation. But there still was a range of reality that could not be denied; witness these measured words of Albertus Magnus himself:

[I discovered an instructive account [of magic] in Avicenna's *Liber sextus naturalium,* which says that a certain power to alter things indwells in the human soul and subordinates the other things to her, particularly when she is swept into a great excess of love or hate or the like. When therefore the soul of man falls into a great excess of any passion, it can be proved by experiment that it [the excess] binds things [magically] and alters them in the way it wants, and for a long time I did not believe it, but after I had read the nigromantic books and others of the kind on signs and magic, I found that the emotionality of the human soul is the chief cause of all these things. . . .]

This range of magic, even if carefully referred here to the powers of man alone, could not but tie up with the Nether Powers on which the Church herself as a vested guardian of magic practiced unceasing exorcism. Hence it was strongly discountenanced as a whole. But it was clearly accepted on all sides as a reality, it had been organized by late Antiquity into a wondrous-looking Esoteric Doctrine, and the adventurous minds of the Renaissance could not but be irresistibly attracted. A cloud of dust was bound to arise.

The Overreachers

Somewhere within that cloud of dust, and amid vast swirls of futile speculation which screened it from the conservative minds, something decisive was taking place.

Whitehead remarked once that, since the time when a babe was born in a manger, nothing came into the world so quietly as modern science. The beginnings of that science are unmistakably in the Renaissance, coupled, strangely enough, with those of another incompatible yet almost equally world-shaking force, dialectical idealism. We have tried to mark this coexistence by giving a chapter of this volume to that strange triad, Paracelsus, Kepler and Boehme.

The advent of science is surely the decisive factor, which will ultimately determine all other developments. An outstanding political historian, Herbert Butterfield, has stated flatly that it outshines everything else since the rise of Christianity, and reduces the Renaissance itself and the Reformation to the rank of mere episodes, mere internal displacements within the system of medieval Christendom. We cannot but subscribe. For the first and only time in history, philosophy (in the aspect of "natural philosophy," as it was then called) is going to shatter the world of man and remold it on a different pattern.

Hence it ought to be very much to the point to see how, and in what surroundings, the concept of Truth itself gradually changes its connotations.

There is hardly a speculative mind in the Renaissance which does not respond to the idea of Truth as a *"mysterium fascinosum."* Even the hard-boiled skeptics are only rebelling against it in an ineffectual way. Cusanus's Pythagorean wisdom, Pico's occult concordances, Cardan's doctrine of "subtility," Paracelsus's "light of nature," Kepler's "cosmographic mysteries," are just high points in the pantheistic, panpsychistic jungle which luxuriates over the whole epoch. As thinkers find revealed in God the deepest elements of man's soul, they find also revealed the immanent presence of God in all things. Even the sedate Sir Thomas Browne will distrust rational theology and like to "lose himself in the contemplation of mystery." Most of this rests on the shadowy Secret Doctrine or Great Tradition.

It is characteristic of a secret doctrine not to exercise criticism over its own tenets nor to accept it from outside.

It is, by definition, aristocratic, since it is for the few. Unprepossessed analysis is to its believers what cold daylight would be to a photographer operating in a dark room. The Pythagoreans had made of acceptance an explicit rule. Thinking in these regions does not go by decision, but rather by accretion and perpetual reinterpretation, with new and "deeper" meanings being made explicit by each successive age, for the assumption is of a "perennial philosophy." The doctrine's weakness is that it will accept undiscriminatingly a medley and omnium-gatherum of transmission at all levels, going from a flotsam of primitive superstitions coming from the days of Sumer and Babylon to the most profound and sophisticated insights into the psychology of the unconscious. Into it go headlong and pell-mell the unwarranted intuition, the far-fetched analogy, the quest for non-existent secrets, the wild hopeful snatching at a hidden meaning, the preposterous but at times felicitous misunderstanding, the plain mystification. Why not? "All is possible," as Ficino had said. Nothing will be discarded, because the original contention is that nature, and man's nature in particular, contains each and all levels, from the dreadful theriomorph shapes of the powers of the deep (whose aspects and planetary connections show the Babylonian origin) to the hierarchies of divine intelligences described by the Christian mystics. After all, magic was not a theoretical science. Anything that worked, or had been reported to work, was as good as true. Whatever theory there was had to be exegesis; its logic went by analogy and correspondence, it was poetic and not abstract. Poetry received from it its ideas, it goes on bearing its imprint to this day. That some very profound insights could be gained thereby, is hardly to be denied. Leibniz himself for a period went into Rosicrucian thought; nor did Goethe work out the character of Faust as a pure skeptic out of the "Faustbooks." Strong elements of that occult tradition were incorporated without change in his natural philosophy and in that of his Romantic contemporaries.

The turbid but powerful stream of representations which comes from the first ages of mankind went twice in our

recorded history through the transforming influence of intellectual interpretation. The first is that which centers on
late antiquity, and which embodied itself for transmission
in many forms, chief among them Neo-Pythagorean writings, the Jewish Kabbala and the purported opus of
"Hermes Trice-Greatest" (hence the name of "Hermetic"
philosophy). The second is the Renaissance. It combined
there with the widespread Stoic idea of natural law, tried
to scale the heights of true science—and failed. The need
for a comprehensive knowledge which should include our
qualitative and our metaphysical experience of the world
is bitterly felt even today, but Alfred Whitehead himself
could not bring it to success. When such mathematical
minds as Galileo and Kepler, buttressed by the authority
of Platonism, insisted upon the quantitative approach as the
only secure one to acknowledge, they were met by traditionalists with an obstinate rejoinder which, in truth, could
be derived from Plato himself: magnitude and measure-
ment concerns the "more or less" of things, but has nothing to do with the essence. A man is a man whether straight
or crooked, tall or short, and so it is with all other beings
worth understanding. There was a point here, albeit fum-
blingly made. Kepler's contrary contention that the "essence" of physical reality lay in the mathematical formula
has not held very long either. The search for essences has
shifted slowly to the field of historical idealism, which is
another way of admitting frustration.

Philosophically, all this leaves us today in a quandary,
or rather in a void filled with the arguing of logicians. The
greatest among them, Wittgenstein, said years ago:
"Whereof one cannot speak, thereof one should be silent";
but his advice apparently was not heeded.

The lesson of the past would seem to be that quality and
form are unable to carry the weight of consistent thought.
Once one tries to go beyond the mere classifying or de-
scriptive attitude of the Aristotelian, one either achieves
the doubtful coherence of artistic criticism and Gestalt
thought, or one "goes primitive" the natural way, being
caught first in appearance and wishful thinking, then in
make-believe, especially if the field is open to the pressure

of ancient fears and desires for health, wealth and power. "A sound magician is a demi-god."

We should not forget, either, the social ferment in the Renaissance, the rise of new elements from the submerged classes. The sects which had resisted the Church in the Middle Ages, the predecessors of Free Masonry, had found recruitment among the craftsmen practicing dangerous trades, who had been left to cope with nature with whatever was available in the way of ancient tribal magics and techniques as well as with a demonology of mixed ancestry. They had been once in Northern countries the gnomes, the Little People, and the magicians of medieval legends, remnants of conquered populations, wise in the ways of nature and metals, reputed to have a *modus vivendi* with treasure-guarding dragons and evil spirits, indentured to their lords like Daedalus and Wayland Smith. They had had to cope alone and uninsured with the tragic dangers of mining and smithing and smelting and building and dyeing, alone they had faced disaster in underground shafts, on perilous vaults and hazardous scaffoldings. Their sons were solid burghers now, their names were Villard de Honnecourt, Biringuccio, Brunelleschi, Georg Agricola; good Christians all, but not altogether free of ancient resentments. The reserved and impenetrable disdain of Leonardo towards the Catholic Church, the snarling irony of Machiavelli, are not utterly exceptional behaviors.

The masters of the arts are properly contemptuous of the needy, seedy, fly-by-night professionals of current magic, but they cannot have much sympathy either for the gowned intellectuals unable to conceive that knowledge could have anything to do with the work of hands. Until Galileo will come to consult them with the respect that is due, they are left to their own devices, they have their own independent approach to the humanistic civilization. One thing they have sometimes in common with humanists, and that is, as we said, estrangement from official religion. It may take a conformist cover, or it may look openly for the more ancient and universal foundations of belief, or it may discard the whole thing impatiently; but it is as if, now that the people have been thoroughly Christianized through centuries of conversation, the leading minds were assessing the results and looking beyond.

Where, then, are knowledge and truth? Thought hovers between free artistic creativeness and covered esoteric intimations. Great creators like Paolo Uccello, Piero della Francesca and Leonardo reach for the mathematical truths underlying their own craft. Archimedes is to them a fabulous figure whose achievements are more guessed at than understood. Speculative minds like Cardan, Paracelsus, or Boehme turn, conversely, to the mysteries of the Art as a foundation for theoretical knowledge. Thought loses itself again and again in the indefinite region of magic. For magic, like poetry, resists precise definition; and in particular its connection with religion is perplexing. There would not appear to be any belief without some magic at its foundation, and on the other hand magic has always avidly incorporated any religious foundations available. They appear at times like incompatible Siamese twins. And so, in another way, are magic and philosophy. Only the pure logician is immune—but at the price of sterility. The idea of imposing our will on nature is able to coexist only with difficulty with the other idea of receiving through our nature the intimations of a higher mind, of going beyond our personal desires into detached knowledge and contemplation. The two come into powerful dialectical conflict in the Renaissance (much more so than in antiquity), and bring about the intellectual maelstrom of which the Prologue of Goethe's *Faust* is the best expression. This is where Northern Europe steps dominantly, if late, upon the scene.

The coexistence between those elements is more difficult than in antiquity, because of the Christian faith, which has monopolized magic under the form of miracles and damned all the rest of it into hell; it is also more fertile, in that after the long medieval constraint there is a more passionate philosophical hope of discovering the lost dimensions of an ampler and deeper truth, and it goes hand in hand with the dim feeling of having been "cut off" from a legitimate inheritance. It is no less alarming, for it does not go without a heightened attraction towards the perilous and the illicit, and it brings about violent reactions of fear on the part of society. Astrology and gold-making, like witch-burning, were considerably on the increase in the sixteenth and seventeenth century. The witch trials of Salem and the trial of Cagliostro lead into our own times.

Thus we are facing again that peculiar unclear nature of Renaissance thought, born of conflicting emotions and of a too rich intellectual mixture: on one side a restoration, a painstaking effort at imitating antique models, on the other a prophetic vision, an arrogant plunging ahead, a passion for adventurous quest into an expanding world, a heedless expenditure of curiosity, energy and inventiveness so well expressed by Ulrich von Hutten's "It is a joy to live."

Leibniz has rightly characterized this kind of thinking from the start as "hyperbolic." The particular "overreaching" genius and torment of the later Renaissance, the one that "breaks the circle" and goes beyond consecrated union, form and bound, is more profoundly expressed by Marlowe the seer than by Descartes the actual innovator, too proud of his clarity to be even aware of his intentions. Marlowe's Doctor Faustus is the hero who "taking to him the wings of an eagle, thought to flie over the whole world, and to know the secrets of heaven and earth"; we are able to see from our vantage point that the flight will lead him farther than he imagines. For the adventure turns out to be not the cheap magic from the books of nigromancy, but the power of the mind itself getting "off bounds," carried by what it has created. It is the inertial trajectory of materialist man (or the matter invented by him) through limitless silent space, until he attains indeed the achievements that magicians had dreamed of, but henceforward alone in a world he never made.

We are doing some interpretation here, assuredly. But the poetic imagination of Marlowe, discerning the future only through the Enchanted Glass, would seem to have discerned farther than the fragile hopes of a Locke or a Newton. There is in the work of this confirmed atheist an understanding of sin which excludes belief in salvation through generous intentions or romantic *Streben*, a realization of evil of inflexible intensity.

The playful allusions of Rabelais to the dangers of heed-

less knowledge, the grave warnings of Copernicus in his
Preface are here worked out to their full import. Contemporaries may have seen and accepted the "remedy
of the end" in Faustus' last despairing hour, but Marlowe's
own metaphysical sympathy and imagination clearly go
beyond it. The tale of the scientific adventurer who gained
control over nature while losing control of himself is not
terminated by his own contingent downfall ("O would I
had never seen Wittenberg, never read a book . . ."), for
the philosophical choice goes on forever in the adventurer's macrocosmic second self, Mephistophilis, who is able
to identify with the suffering Faustus, yet brings into the
action the bitter conscience that endures, the guilty but
unconquered ironic intellect. Mephistophilis is the mind
that can "stand up" and pay the price—and is not "standing up" what science, *episteme,* meant for the Greeks?
"Why *this* is hell, nor am I out of it. . . ." "All places
shall be hell that is not heaven."

The reading of Marlowe's idea is even clearer on a
wholly secular, non-metaphysical level. There the philosophical program is staked out in the proud words of Tam-
burlaine:

> Our soules, whose faculties can comprehend
> The wondrous Architecture of the world,
> And measure every wandring planets course,
> Still climing after knowledge infinite,
> And alwaies moving as the restless Spheares,
> Wils us to weare our selves and never rest,
> Until we reach the ripest fruit of all,
> That perfect blisse and sole felicitie,
> The sweet fruition of an earthly crowne.

As Harry Levin remarks rightly, such lines remind us
that Galileo was Marlowe's own contemporary, and that
Giordano Bruno was in England during his lifetime. They
remind us, too, of Ficino's sweet nonsense about Archimedes. Marlowe cuts out the nonsense and puts the accent
on the "earthly crown." It is a philosophy of conquest
and achievement, in which it becomes only incidental pas-
time to "make whole cities caper in the aire" ("take out"
is the modern word for it). There is a logical sequence
(in poetic logic, alas) from this to the desperate projection

of the conqueror's will into the impossible, at the very moment in which he is entering the shadow of death:

> Come let us march upon the powers of Heaven
> And plant black banners in the firmament
> To signify the slaughter of the gods.

This is said in the grand manner, but it is said for once explicitly, and the image has more philosophical content and perception than what is merely implied in Descartes's cool and preposterous statement half a century later: "I have come so far that I am confident I shall be able to account for the place of every star." The only excuse for such a statement is indeed that it is utterly unaware of its own implications.

Bruno's cosmic religion is surely closer to the spirit of contemplative science. But Bruno's noble vision and his incandescent monism end up in a dream; it is in philosophical inconsequence, out of sheer greatness of soul, that he faces the stake. It is Marlowe, not Bruno, not Descartes, who has been able to indicate what modern "natural magic" was really going to be about.

Thus the Renaissance, like the creative epoch it is, ends upon a note of grand confusion, with man launched into an insecure but magically fascinating condition. The adventures of a Leonardo, a Columbus, a Cortez, a Luther, a Copernicus, or a Giordano Bruno had been taking it beyond the limits of the imaginable. They were irretrievable ventures—the breaking of the beautifully enclosed enchanted circle of the Cosmos, the bursting of the bounds of the familiar world with the era of discoveries, the splitting asunder of ecumenical Christianity in the great storm of the Reformation. Not least, of course, the end of the closed and well-protected garden of learning through the advent of the printing press. A heroic age, it brings with it a breaking of taboos, the advance into an open world from which there is no return.

At the same time, the paradoxical intuitions of its transcendent thinkers lead the Renaissance into a hidden realm more divined than understood, seen only *per speculum et in aenigmate*. But, as Blake said, the way to the palace of wisdom leads through excess. As it clarifies and simplifies itself, pantheism will unfold into Spinozian rationalism. In the founding days of our Republic, there appear those same ancient strands woven through the fabric: a Stoic and Ciceronian South ("Nature's God") and a Calvinistic North held together by a common temper of cool Erasmian reason.

But the stable order of reason is no sooner announced than other forces from the same Age of Adventure come forward in their turn: for it is the very definition of man which has changed from that of a creature established once and forever in its degree, into that of a protean, restless wanderer engaged upon an unending adventure. Time itself has come to the fore, no longer the eternal circling of the heavens, but an onrushing stream which carries away all attempts at metaphysical consolidation. Yet, as those rapids are of our own making, so did we too devise the art for steering our way through them. The "art of separation" that the alchemists dreamed of has become Galileo's "resolutive method": the awful art whereby the true is decisively separated from the false, and knowledge from ignorance, such knowledge as transmutes itself irresistibly into terrible power. Thus the magic of that age, for good or bad, is still with us, and so, too, is Prospero's vision:

> The cloud-capp'd towers, the gorgeous palaces
> The solemn temples, the great globe itself
> Yea, all which it inherits, shall dissolve
> And like this insubstantial pageant faded
> Leave not a rack behind.

CHAPTER I

Nicholas of Cusa

NICHOLAS KREBS (IN ENGLISH IT WOULD HAVE BEEN "Crabbe"), the son of a boatman, was born in 1401 at Cues (Lat., Cusa) on the Moselle, opposite Bernkastel where they make such good wine. He was educated at the Brothers of the Common Life in Deventer, the famous school whence had come Thomas à Kempis a generation earlier, where Erasmus was to study two generations later. At sixteen he went to the University of Padua and entered the circle of Italian lawyers and humanists, which made of him an international mind. At twenty-five he became secretary to the papal legate to Germany and entered the Church. He soon became a leading figure in that difficult crisis centering around the Council of Basel (1433) in which the Church organization struggled with the conciliar or "democratic" tendencies in its midst, to emerge as a strongly centralized power. Having started out on the side of the Council, Nicholas became out of experience the strongest advocate of papal authority. In 1437, he was sent by Pope Eugene to Constantinople to attempt a reconciliation with the Eastern Church, and in fact did establish with them the agenda for a meeting in Florence which took place in the following year. It was for this meeting that Greek scholars came to Italy—and stayed. He was thus the key figure in the restoration of Greek culture to Western Europe.

A born conciliator, Nicholas came back with high dreams of reconciling Christianity with Mohammedanism itself. It was on his long sea voyage homeward that he had the "sudden insight," as he says, of his philosophical doctrine as it is set forth in the *Learned Ignorance*. From then on, the lawyer had become a philosopher; but he had become also a ruling figure in the Church, charged with the German problems first as papal legate, then as bishop of Brixen in the Tyrol and finally as cardinal (1445). He had thus scant time for meditation. When his friend Aeneas Sylvius Piccolomini ascended the pontifical throne under the name of Pius II, he moved to Rome as his deputy and remained from then on, virtually in charge of executive decisions. The two men died a few weeks from each other, in 1464; Nicholas's tomb is to be seen in the church of San Pietro in Vincoli in Rome, opposite to Michelangelo's Moses.

Cusa's philosophy is profound, quite obscure in parts, and has often led commentators astray. There is in him a prefiguration of that other international German genius, Gottfried Wilhelm Leibniz. Like him, too, he never had time to put his thoughts into organic shape, and his mature production is a scattering of brief artless works which were often dictated in the evening, as he says, after forty-mile rides on horseback. One wonders what Aeneas Sylvius, the elegant and worldly man of letters who reigned over the golden age of Humanism, must have thought of his friend's involved speculations. He may have decided that Nicholas was too good an administrator and diplomat to be wasted on such subtilities, but that apparently it enhanced his authority to philosophize thus paradoxically, in the obscure manner of those who dwelt north of the Alps.

There is no doubt that with Nicholas (or Cusanus as he is often called) German philosophy has entered the scene full-fledged, with some of its powerful characteristics well in evidence. The cardinal was deeply impressed with the "mystic night" and the humble searching meditation of his countryman Meister Eckhart, and he strove to combine it with Pythagorean wisdom. But he remains a humanistic and Italianate German, as he freely admits. His thought is not of the cloister, nor even of the halls of learning: even in the setting of his little dialogues, he tends to move out into the open air. "The Truth," he says, "is simple, it speaks aloud in the market place." A workman in a street of Rome, the Layman (*Idiota*) teaches the Orator and the Philosopher a Socratic lesson in Learned Ignorance; the pitching of a curve in a ball game (apparently a subject of enduring interest) provides in *De Ludo Globi* a fresh "hunting ground" for wisdom.

The central fact about Cusanus, which has been too often overlooked because he made no achievements in science proper, is that he is a creative mathematical mind who has in him already the modern idea of mathematics as the "science of the infinite." This idea, in itself, undercuts radically the conventional and rather simple-minded notion, entertained by the scholastics, of mathematics as the science of magnitude, "that is, of the more and less." A discipline thus described could hardly have been relevant to true knowledge, since that was supposedly concerned with "being" itself as articulated into substances and essences. In each part of, say, man, the form of "man" was conceived to be wholly present, unaffected by more and less, and thus mathematics could be safely relegated to the limbo of abstraction. But if the philosopher is told a very different thing, namely, that mathematics is the science of the infinite (which is indeed what the great Greek mathematicians had discovered, and Aristotle had tried to cover up), why, then his metaphysical emotions are apt to respond. To a mind with medieval training, infinity participates in the divine essence, and should be understood to be somehow at the core of all being. Mathematics ceases to be a science of mere abstractions and becomes a possible avenue to true knowledge of reality.

Moderns, who take for granted a science of nature successfully based on mathematics, may find this approach singularly roundabout; but that is because nothing succeeds like success, and it is easy to be pragmatic about science as we have it now. As our present assurance requires no great effort of thought, neither does it lead one very far philosophically. So long as mathematics had not "delivered the goods," its value had to be explored metaphysically and ontologically, which is what Plato and Cusanus did, as well as Galileo and Descartes. Cusanus with his new idea does have the bear by the tail, but he cannot work out the idea as he should for lack of intellectual tools, to be developed only centuries later by Leibniz and Cantor. He is also, as such minds are apt to be, an intellectual mystic. He has received the heritage of medieval Neoplatonists and of Scotus Erigena: he has had the intuition (this was clearly his experience on board ship) of a symbolic language in which those ideas can be made coherent, and he is led on by his geometrical imagination, which is of a high order; but, for lack of adequate concepts, his thought is left to meditate on the way of "conjecture" and essential inadequacy.

This groping in coming to deal with the finite by way of the infinite, this perpetual approach through inadequacy and approximation, is what Cusanus calls the "Learned Ignorance," and he opposes it firmly to the Ignorant Learnedness of the Aristotelians and the Thomists, which allows any dolt to become a doctor. To him, they are cranking forever a heavy foolproof machinery of concepts abstracted from common sense, resting on the flat common denominator of "being"; a "being" which is merely a grammatical category. Whereas he wants to show at every point a reality of deep paradox, the "coincidence of opposites," which is beyond common sense but reveals God in all things, "all in all," and restores the sense of the mystery of being:

[The greatest danger against which most men have warned us is that which comes from communicating intellectual secrets to minds become subservient to the authority of an inveterate habit, for such is the power of a long-lasting observance that most men prefer death to giving up their way of life. . . . Today, it is the Aristotelian sect which prevails, and it holds the coincidence of opposites for heretical, which yet is the only way to ascend towards mystical theology. It would truly be a miracle if they repudiated Aristotle and started on the path to the summits.]

IT IS VERY TRUE THAT THE ARISTOTELIANS HAD DELIBerately repudiated or flattened out all considerations touching the infinite, as had been presented by the subtle speculations of the Eleatics. (It is noteworthy that Pierre Bayle, three centuries later, will lead the fight for modern rationalism starting with this very same point, in his famous article on *Zeno*.) Now, according to Cusanus, the "path to the summits" is by way of the infinite.

The initial idea is this: The circle of infinite radius is *also* a straight line, and it is of the nature of the infinite to present thus perpetually revealing paradoxes to our mind, if we are willing to face them. Anselm had already compared supreme truth to the straight line. Others had seen a symbol of the mystery of the Trinity in a triangle which should be made of right angles, if such could be conceived. Others chose for symbols the circle or the sphere. All of these, remarks Cusanus, become identical statements at infinity, for that is where all those figures become one. This includes the sphere, too, for since it can be generated by the rotation of the circle, it is "identical with it at infinity where all possibles are actualized."

Moreover, the element which generates all lines and is potentially identical to all of them is the point. Hence—seen as it were from the perspective of the Infinite, where all potentials become actual—the point becomes identical to the straight line, the minimum and the maximum are seen to coincide. This is what is meant by that universal principle of the Coincidence of Opposites, which has become since the permanent lure of romantic philosophy. Cusanus, however, holds on quite soberly to his geometry. He knows that the infinity of points of the straight line can be mapped on the points of a finite segment, however small; this shows to him how infinity is present ("contracted") into each finite thing, in fact is the foundation, the reason, and the measure of its being. Caught between minimal and maximal infinities, but reaching neither, the finite thing is participant of being, but in a way which is only indeterminate. Knowledge is really a creative process of approximation and estimation. Now this sounds much like Plato, and the cardinal in fact insists on the agreement with time-honored doctrine, but it is not really the same, because the very process of knowing is conceived differently.

Consider the idea of the infinite being mapped on a finite segment; this goes down to the yet-to-be invented infinitesimal. The line and the angle are conceived as being already such beneath all magnitude, in the nascent state, so to speak. This explains why the point is strangely considered here not only the generator, but the "completion and totality" of the line: the intellect perceives through it the unity, even as the sparkle of the diamond shows the same whether the stone be large or small. Whereas ancient thought had insisted on substances and forms as what the mind apprehends directly, we have here the intellectual process itself grasping the action of the minimal thing, its *law*, which becomes its real substance; and reaching out from there, provoked as it were by perception, to work its way through the extended and the composite, conquering as it goes the indeterminacy of the object which has provoked it. Thus the conquest of the sensible consists in weaving far out beyond it a net of abstract relations which gradually enclose it and tend to a limit. What started out as Platonism has taken a turn towards our own conception of science.

The analogic deduction from geometry to metaphysics may sound somewhat arbitrary, the more so when it aims at providing a complete rationale for Christian dogma. But we should consider that Descartes, Leibniz and Malebranche adhere with no less literalness to their own guiding mathematical ideas. After all, there are only two ways of abstracting a metaphysics: out of common language, or out of the mathematical. The first way leads from Socrates to such moderns as Hegel; the second goes from Parmenides to Descartes, Leibniz and beyond them to modern pan-mathematism. Relying as it does on the rigor and clarity of the mathematical concept, it is able to proceed boldly into remote speculative realms, and provides the philosophical background on which science can develop. If Cusanus had been able to avail himself of the modern concepts of the transfinite, of transformation group theory and n-dimensional spaces, he would have produced an incomparably richer symbolism to meet his needs. As it was, his thought had to remain often inarticulate and obscure. But it can go on to extreme and creative unconventionality.

The universe, remarks Cusanus, must be itself a "relative maximum" and a mere comprehensive symbol of the true one. If every single thing is a particular manifestation of Infinite Being, the universe must be seen not merely as the sum of things but as the progressive "explication" of the initial "complication" at every point—a contrast and oxymoron which portrays the relation of God and the world. And this is what is really implicit in the idea of the infinite sphere as the most complete symbol. Hence, concludes Cusanus devastatingly · (fortifying himself with a somewhat similar statement attributed to Hermes Trismegistus himself), the universe can only be such a "sphere," *whose circumference is nowhere and whose center is everywhere.* It will have a peculiar kind of "general relativity" of its own, since there is no absolute space or frame of reference, and motion and rest depend from the point of observation: the condition being that the cosmos must be symmetrical to all of its parts, i.e., at each point it must appear as if this were the center. Thence also there can be no motionless "hub" as the Earth was supposed to be, but motion is everywhere; the only real "rest" would be infinite velocity, since maximum and minimum coincide. The resemblance here with present-day cosmological speculation based on the expanding universe, although shadowy, is by no means fortuitous. The closed sphere of the Aristotelian world has been exploded, consequences out of sight are coming up.

Scientifically, of course, the thing is still helpless. Nicholas wants to have the Earth move, but is at a loss for a mechanism; the result is that it moves very little, in fact, imperceptibly: there is no pre-Copernican idea there. On the other hand, the involved philosophical obscurity hides the seeds of important ideas to which it is impossible to do justice in this brief sketch. Even as it stands, that thought remained impressive enough. Its paradoxes of the Infinite and its lofty Pythagorean adumbrations were to inspire an epoch which had had enough of the verbalism of scholastics; they made a heady brew. We know that such men as Pico della Mirandola, Leonardo, Bruno, Kepler, Campanella, pondered the chapters on the infinity of the universe and the plurality of worlds. Such ideas coming from a premier cardinal of the Church (even if, perhaps rather because if, qualified in strange medieval ways), caused many ecclesiastics to think like the worldly archbishop in Shaw's *Saint Joan*: "There is a new spirit rising in men: we are at the dawning of a wider epoch. If I were a simple monk, and had not to rule men, I would seek my peace with the philosophers and Pythagoras rather than with the saints and their miracles."

The following "paradigmatic figure" or "figure P," to which Nicholas refers often, is to be found in *De Conjecturis*:

[Imagine a cone of Light which protrudes into the darkness, and a cone of darkness which protrudes into the light; you should bring back to this figure every object of inquiry, so that this sensible image may lead you by the hand, so to speak, into the secrets that are being conjectured about. Then, for instance, consider the Universe as a whole through this figure.

Note that God who is Unity is as it were the base of Light; the base of darkness is Nothingness. Now it is between God and Nothingness that we have to think that all creatures take their place. The upper world as you see it is not without darkness, but because of its essential simplicity they seem to be absorbed by light. In the lower world darkness reigns, yet light is not absent. But as the figure indicates, it is so to speak hidden in the darkness and does not show.]

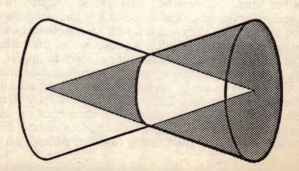

The following is from Cusanus's fundamental treatise, "Of Learned Ignorance" (*De docta ignorantia*).*

I. HOW KNOWLEDGE IS IGNORANCE

Every enquiry consists in a relation of comparison that is easy or difficult to draw; for this reason the infinite as infinite is unknown, since it is away and above all comparison. Now, while proportion expresses an agreement in some one thing, it expresses at the same time a distinction, so that it cannot be understood without number. Number, in consequence, includes all things that are capable of comparison. It is not then in quantity only that number produces proportion; it produces it in all things that are capable of agreement and difference in any way at all, whether substantially or accidentally. That is why Pythagoras was so insistent on maintaining that in virtue of numbers all things were understood.

It so far surpasses human reason, however, to know the precision of the combinations in material things and how exactly the known has to be adapted to the unknown that Socrates thought he knew nothing save his own ignorance, whilst Solomon, the Wise, affirmed that in all things there are difficulties which beggar explanation in words; and we have it from another, who was divinely inspired, that wisdom and the locality of the understanding lie hidden from the eyes of all the living. If this is so—and even the most profound Aristotle in his First Philosophy affirms it to be true of the things most evident to us in nature—then in presence of such difficulty we may be compared to owls trying to look at the sun; but since the natural desire in us for knowledge is not without a purpose, its immediate object is our own ignorance. If we can fully realize this desire, we will acquire learned ignorance. . . .

II. PRELIMINARY EXPLANATION OF ALL THAT FOLLOWS

As I am about to deal with ignorance as the greatest learning, I consider it necessary to determine the precise meaning of the maximum or greatest. We speak of a thing

*Nicolaus de Cusa, *Of Learned Ignorance*, trans. from the Latin by Germain Heron. London: Routledge & Kegan Paul; New Haven: Yale University Press, 1954.

being the greatest or maximum when nothing greater than
it can exist. But to one being alone does plenitude belong,
with the result that unity, which is also being, and the
maximum are identical; for if such a unity is itself in every
way and entirely without restriction then it is clear that
there is nothing to be placed in opposition to it, since it is
the absolute maximum. Consequently, the absolute maximum is one and it is all; all things are in it because it is
the maximum. Moreover, it is in all things for this reason
that the minimum at once coincides with it, since there is
nothing that can be placed in opposition to it. Because it
is absolute, it is in actuality all possible being, limiting all
things and receiving no limitation from any. In the First
Book I will endeavour to study this maximum, who without any doubt is believed to be the God of all nations. It
is a study that is above reason and cannot be conducted
on the lines of human comprehension; and for my guide I
will take him alone who dwells in light inaccessible.

In the second place, just as we have the absolute maximum, which is the absolute entity by which all things are
what they are, so we have from it the universal unity of
being which is called the maximum effect of the absolute.
In consequence, its existence as the universe is finite, and
its unity, which could not be absolute, is the relative unity
of a plurality. . . .

An understanding of this matter will be attained rather
by our rising above the literal sense of the words, than by
insisting upon their natural properties, for these natural
properties cannot be effectively adapted to such intellectual
mysteries. For the reader we must even use drawings as
illustrations, but he must rise above these in leaving aside
what is sensible in them in order to arrive unimpeded at
what is purely intelligible. In pursuing this method I have
eagerly tried, by the avoidance of all difficulties of expressions, to make it as clear as possible to the average mind
that the foundation for learned ignorance is the fact that
absolute truth is beyond our grasp.

III. ABSOLUTE TRUTH IS BEYOND OUR GRASP

From the self-evident fact that there is no gradation
from infinite to finite, it is clear that the simple maximum

is not to be found where we meet degrees of more and less; for such degrees are finite, whereas the simple maximum is necessarily infinite. It is manifest, therefore, that when anything other than the simple maximum itself is given, it will always be possible to find something greater. Equality, we find, is a matter of degree: with things that are alike one is more equal to this than to that, in-so-far as they belong, or do not belong, to the same genus or species, or in-so-far as they are, or are not, related in time, place or influence. For that reason it is evident that two or more things cannot be so alike and equal that an infinite number of similar objects cannot still be found. No matter, then, how equal the measure and the thing measured are, they will remain for ever different.

A finite intellect, therefore, cannot by means of comparison reach the absolute truth of things. Being by nature indivisible, truth excludes "more" or "less," so that nothing but truth itself can be the exact measure of truth: for instance, that which is not a circle cannot be the measure of a circle, for the nature of a circle is one and indivisible. In consequence, our intellect, which is not the truth, never grasps the truth with such precision that it could not be comprehended with infinitely greater precision. The relationship of our intellect to the truth is like that of a polygon to a circle; the resemblance to the circle grows with the multiplication of the angles of the polygon; but apart from its being reduced to identity with the circle, no multiplication, even if it were infinite, of its angles will make the polygon equal the circle.

It is clear, therefore, that all we know of the truth is that the absolute truth, such as it is, is beyond our reach. The truth, which can be neither more nor less than it is, is the most absolute necessity, while, in contrast with it, our intellect is possibility. Therefore, the quiddity of things, which is ontological truth, is unattainable in its entirety; and though it has been the objective of all philosophers, by none has it been found as it really is. The more profoundly we learn this lesson of ignorance, the closer we draw to truth itself.

There can be nothing greater in existence than the simple, absolute maximum; and since it is greater than our powers of comprehension—for it is infinite truth—our knowledge of it can never mean that we comprehend it. It is above all that we can conceive, for its nature excludes degrees of "more" and "less." All the things, in fact, that we apprehend by our senses, reason or intellect are so different from one another that there is no precise equality between them. The maximum equality, therefore, in which there is no diversity or difference from any other, is completely beyond our understanding; and for that reason the absolute maximum is in act most perfect, since it is in act all that it can be. Being all that it can be, it is, for one and the same reason, as great as it can be and as small as it can be. By definition the minimum is that which cannot be less than it is; and since that is also true of the maximum, it is evident that the minimum is identified with the maximum.

*　　*　　*　　*　　*　　*　　*　　*　　*

Our proof has been that, because unity is eternal, and equality eternal, the connection is likewise eternal. But it is impossible for several eternals to exist; if several were to exist, then, because unity precedes all plurality, there would exist something which would be prior by nature to eternity, which is absurd. Besides if there were several eternal beings, one would possess something which another lacked and so none of them would be perfect; in other words, there would exist an eternal which was not eternal at all, since it is imperfect. This absurdity manifests the impossibility of several eternals. We are left with the conclusion that unity, equality and connection, which are equally eternal, are one. That is the unity which is at once a trinity that Pythagoras—the first of philosophers and the honour of Italy and Greece—held up for adoration. . . .

All our greatest philosophers and theologians unanimously assert that the visible universe is a faithful reflection of the invisible, and that from creatures we can rise to a knowledge of the Creator, "in a mirror and in a dark manner," as it were. The fundamental reason for the use of symbolism in the study of spiritual things, which in themselves are beyond our reach, has already been given. Though we neither perceive it nor understand it, we know for a fact that all things stand in some sort of relation to one another; that, in virtue of this inter-relation, all the individuals constitute one universe and that in the one Absolute the multiplicity of beings is unity itself. Every image is an approximate reproduction of the exemplar; yet, apart from the Absolute image or the Exemplar itself in unity of nature, no image will so faithfully or precisely reproduce the exemplar as to rule out the possibility of an infinity of more faithful and precise images, as we have already made clear.

When we use an image and try to reach analogically what is as yet unknown, there must be no doubt at all about the image; for it is only by way of postulates and things certain that we can arrive at the unknown. But in all things sensible material possibility abounds which explains their being in a continual state of flux. Our knowledge of things is not acquired by completely disregarding their material conditions, without which no image of them could be formed; nor is it wholly subject to their possible variations; but the more we abstract from sensible conditions, the more certain and solid our knowledge is.

*   *   *   *   *   *   *   *   *

The power to share an essence with the most perfect equality is solely possessed by the Maximum or the Infinite Essence itself. Just as there is but one most perfect unity, so there can be only one equality of unity; and because this is the most perfect equality, it is the essence of all things.

Likewise, there is but one infinite line and it is the essence of all finite lines; and since the finite necessarily comes from the infinite line, by that very fact it can no more be its own essence than it can be at once finite and infinite. Consequently, just as it is impossible to have two precisely equal finite lines (since exact equality, which is the greatest equality, is Infinity itself), so it is also impossible to find two lines sharing equally the essence which is the one essence of all.

Moreover, as we have already said, in a line of two feet the infinite line is neither more nor less than two feet, in a line of three feet, neither more nor less than three feet, and so on; it is entire in each finite line since it is one and indivisible. Yet it is not as finite and participated that it is entire in each; for if it were it could not be entire in a line of three feet while it was entire in one of two feet, because a two-feet line is not a three-feet line. It is, therefore, whole and entire in each, because it is none of them, and the distinction of one line from others is due to the fact that they are finite.

The infinite line, then, is entire in each line and each is in it. If we consider these two statements together—and we must—we clearly see how the Maximum is in each thing and in no one thing in particular. Since it is by the same essence that it is in each thing and each thing in it, and since it is itself this very essence, then it is no other than the Maximum, which is then the Maximum in se: The Maximum which is the rule and measure of all things is really one and the same as the Absolute Maximum in se: the Maximum is the Maximum. The Maximum alone of all beings exists in se, and all things are in it as in their own essence, because the Maximum is their essence.

These considerations, and in particular the simile of the infinite line, can be a great aid to the intellect as it moves forward in sacred ignorance towards the Absolute Maximum which is above all understanding. For since beings have only a participation in being, we now clearly see how we arrive at God by eliminating that participation from all beings; once that is suppressed there remains only entity in its infinite simplicity, which is the essence of all beings. It is only by the most learned ignorance that the mind grasps such an entity, for nothing seems to be left once I mentally remove all that has participated being. For that very reason Denis the Great [the Areopagite] says that an understanding of God is not so much an approach towards something as towards nothing; and sacred ignorance teaches one that what seems nothing to the intellect is the incomprehensible Maximum.

XXII. IN THE PROVIDENCE OF GOD CONTRADICTORIES ARE RECONCILED

That we may be the more conscious of the deep insight we now have from our previous reflections, let us now turn to the study of God's Providence. It is clear, from what has been said, that God encompasses all things, even contradictories. . . .

. . . It will be useful, then, to add a few words on negative theology.

Sacred ignorance has taught us that God is ineffable, because He is infinitely greater than anything that words can express. So true is this that it is by the process of elimination and the use of negative propositions that we come nearer the truth about Him. For that reason the most noble Denis would not have Him called Truth or Intellect or Light or any name that man can utter; and in this he was followed by Rabbi Salomon and all the wise. According to this negative theology, therefore, He is neither Father nor Son nor Holy Ghost; one word alone may be used of Him: Infinite. Infinity, as such, does not engender, is not engendered and does not proceed,—which called from Hilary of Poitiers, whilst distinguishing the Persons, these subtle words: "In aeterno infinitas, species in imagine, usus in munere." His meaning is that all we see in eternity is infinity; and, while it is true that infinity is eternity, yet infinity is a negative and for that reason it cannot be conceived as a principle of generation. Eternity, on the other hand, clearly can be so conceived, for eternity is an affirmation of infinite unity or of the infinite present, and is, therefore, a principle that does not proceed from any other. "Species in imagine" express the principle that proceeds from a principle and "usus in munere" signifies procession from both.

*   *   *   *   *   *   *   *   *

. . . As far as negative theology is concerned, then, we must conclude that God cannot be known in this life or in the life to come. God alone knows Himself; He is as incomprehensible to creatures as infinite light is to darkness.

From this it is clear how in theology negative propositions are true and affirmative ones inadequate; and that of the negative ones those are truer which eliminate greater imperfections from the infinitely Perfect. It is truer, for example, to deny that God is a stone than to deny that He is life or intelligence. . . . In affirmative propositions the contrary holds good: It is truer to assert that God is intelligence and life than to assert that He is earth, stone or anything material.

All these points, which must now be abundantly clear, leave us with the conclusion that, in a way we cannot comprehend, absolute truth enlightens the darkness of our ignorance. That, then, is the learned ignorance for which we have been searching. . . .

BOOK II

I. FROM PROPOSITIONS ALREADY ESTABLISHED THE UNITY AND INFINITY OF THE UNIVERSE IS INFERRED

*   *   *   *   *   *   *   *   *

We have taken it as a fundamental principle that where degrees of difference are found it is impossible to arrive at a maximum which is actual and the greatest possible. From that we went on to see that absolute equality is predicable of God alone, with the result that, apart from Him, all beings necessarily differ from one another. No movement, therefore, can be the equal of another nor can one be the measure of another by reason of the necessary difference existing between the measure and the measured. . . .

In consequence, it is impossible to have a movement that would be simply the greatest, for it and rest would coincide. No movement, therefore, is absolute, for absolute movement is rest. It is God, and in Him all movements are contained.

*   *   *   *   *   *   *   *   *

The fact that the ignorance which is learning has shown the truth of the foregoing doctrine will perhaps be a surprise to those who had not heard of such teaching before. By it we now know that the universe is a trinity; that there is not a being in the universe which is not a unity composed of potency, act and the movement connecting them, and that none of these three is capable of absolute subsistence without the others, with the result that they are necessarily found in all things in the greatest diversity of degrees—in degrees so different that it is impossible to find in the universe two beings perfectly equal in all things. Consequently, once we have taken the different movements of the stars (orbium) into account, we see that it is impossible for the motor of the world to have the material earth, air, fire or anything else for a fixed, immovable centre. In movement there is no absolute minimum, like a fixed centre, since necessarily the minimum and the maximum are identical.

Therefore the centre and the circumference are identical. Now the world has no circumference. It would certainly have a circumference if it had a centre, in which case it would contain within itself its own beginning and end; and that would mean that there was some other thing which imposed a limit to the world—another being existing in space outside the world. All of these conclusions are false. Since, then, the world cannot be enclosed within a material circumference and centre, it is unintelligible without God as its centre and circumference. It is not infinite, yet it cannot be conceived as finite, since there are no limits within which it is enclosed.

The earth, which cannot be the centre, must in some way be in motion; in fact, its movement even must be such that it could be infinitely less. Just as the earth is not the centre of the world, so the circumference of the world is not the sphere of the fixed stars, despite the fact that by comparison the earth seems nearer the centre and heaven nearer the circumference. The earth, then, is not the centre of the eighth or any other sphere.

CHAPTER II

The Academic Scholar
or, The Intelligible Ass

CUSANUS IN HIS ORIGINALITY IS UNIQUE. YET WE HAVE seen how carefully he presents his thought as an exegesis of ancient truths. He is proud to maintain that it has all been said before, even by Pythagoras and Dionysius the Areopagite and Rabbi Salomon—all characters for whom later history has been unwilling to vouch. So, too, do the artists of his time think that they are imitating classical models while they are being most inimitably creative. In philosophy, at least, the attitude has a good reason. The corpus of organized knowledge from antiquity was as yet only half discovered, and it was natural for a thinker to assume that it surpassed anything he might work out unaided. He would be pleased no end to find in some unclear document of the past a confirmation of his own views.

Scholarship held, thus, more or less the place in public awareness that science holds in our own time. Erasmus or Scaliger enjoyed the same renown that today attaches to the name of Einstein or Freud. But so long as the pace had not been set for actual discovery, much of the "rebirth" could only be an elaborate rehearsing and embellishment of past themes, the proper field for the erudite antiquarian and the rhetorical humanist. The scholastic heritage of pedantry, too, still weighed heavily upon Europe, and the best minds had come to terms with it: even Leonardo wishes pathetically he could "allegate the authors" so as to win respect for his contentions. Here now is one kind of man who knows how to "allegate the authors." He will be very much around for two more centuries at least, witness Dr. Slop. This particular portrait is taken from Overbury's *Characters*. Sir Thomas Overbury is best known, of course, as the victim of one of the most sensational crimes in English history, as it was he who was poisoned in the Tower in 1613 by the young countess of Essex, determined "that he should return no more to this stage." If he talked against her to his friend Rochester as he knew how to write, we may understand her desperate decision.

A MERE SCHOLAR IS AN INTELLIGIBLE ASS, OR A SILLY fellow in black, that speaks sentences more familiarly than sense. The antiquity of his university is his creed, and the excellency of his college (though but for a match at football) an article of his faith. He speaks Latin better than his mother-tongue; and is a stranger in no part of the world but his own country. He does usually tell great stories of himself to small purpose, for they are commonly ridiculous, be they true or false. His ambition is, that he either is or shall be a graduate: but if ever he get a fellowship, he has then no fellow. In spite of all logic he dare swear and maintain it, that a cuckold and a townsman are *termini convertibiles,* though his mother's husband be an alderman. He was never begotten (as it seems) without much wrangling; for his whole life is spent in *pro* and *contra*. His tongue always goes before his wit, like a gentleman-usher, but somewhat faster. That he is a complete gallant in all points, *cap à pie,* witness his horsemanship and the wearing of his weapons. He is commonly longwinded, able to speak more with ease than any man can endure to hear with patience. . . . His phrase, the apparel of his mind, is made of divers shreds like a cushion, and when it goes plainest, it hath a rash outside and fustian linings. The current of his speech is closed with an *ergo;* and whatever be the question, the truth is on his side. 'Tis a wrong to his reputation to be ignorant of any thing; and yet he knows not that he knows nothing. He gives directions for husbandry from Virgil's *Georgics;* for cattle from his *Bucolics;* for warlike stratagems from his *Aeneid*, or Caesar's *Commentaries*. He orders all things by the book, is skilful in all trades, and thrives in none. He is led more by his ears than his understanding, taking the sound of words for their true sense: and does therefore confidently believe, that Erra Pater was the father of heretics; Rodulphus Agricola a substantial farmer; and will not stick to aver that Systema's *Logic* doth excel Keckerman's. His ill luck is not so much in being a fool, as in being put to such pains to express it to the world: for what in others is natural, in him (with much-a-do) is artificial. His poverty is his happiness, for it makes some men believe, that he is none of fortune's favourites. That learning which he hath, was in his nonage put in backward like a clyster, and 'tis now like ware mislaid in a pedlar's pack; 'a has it, but knows not where it is. In a word, he is the index of a man, and the title-page of a scholar; or a puritan in morality; much in profession, nothing in practice.]

CHAPTER III

Leonardo da Vinci

[AND IF YOU SAY THAT SIGHT IS APT TO IMPEDE THE steady and subtle thinking of the mind, with which it penetrates the divine sciences, . . . I reply that such eye, as lord of the senses, does its duty in giving a fall to those confused and lying, not sciences, but discourses, through which men are always disputing with noise and much moving of hands. . . . Where there is shouting there is no true science, for truth has only one term, which being declared, the disputation is ended for all time.]

IN THIS MANNER DOES LEONARDO DA VINCI (1452-1519) deal with professional philosophy. The intent and unforgiving eye has brought into focus the philosopher himself in a quick cartoon, and pinned him down in the ludicrous forensics which make of him a variety of the legal profession.

This is the way of the outsider, who has always distrusted the learning that is in books, although he acknowledges at times "the authority of men of great reverence." He is free to follow his bent, and to take up as it were by instinct from the great Ionian naturalists where they left off.

The passage we quoted would almost appear a deliberate answer to Plato's choice in the *Phaedo* against those "who turn their eye intently on things in the hope of grasping them through the senses." The idealist endeavor to find the truth in the realm of pure ideas above this world has expended itself into "vain clamor" over eighteen centuries; it is time to look at things again.

Philosophers in turn have repeatedly—and heatedly—denied Leonardo, the "man without letters," a place in

their midst, inasmuch as he did not "think steadily" enough
to their standard, and did not work out formal principles
into a system. Actually, the universal discourse of his
thought is far from lacking coherence. The universe that
Leonardo *saw* was a logically tight universe, fit for profound meditation; but he was not interested in trying for
what he felt could not be done, namely, translating that
universe into purely verbal tightness. He refused to think
in words only, as the scholastics did. He was searching for
a passage towards a new language. What that language
itself might be, Leonardo tried to establish through soundings that range over many depths, from the portrayal of
form to applied mathematics. When he writes: "the definition of the whatness of the elements is not in the power of
man, but many of their effects are known," a modern would
find no difficulty in agreeing with him; still, he is expressing
but an intuition, which cannot be worked out before the
advent of the experimental method. In his own time, the
great project of recognizing "whatnesses" or *quiddities*
could not be given up so lightly; for at least it could be
worked out to a conclusion with the means at hand. Two
centuries later, Spinoza still believed that this was what he
was doing.

What is knowing, then, if it is not by way of "whatness"
or of names representing substances? "You who speculate
on the nature of things, do not be sure you know the things
that nature in her order leads by herself to her own ends,
but be glad if so be that you know the issue of such things
as your mind designs." Translators, including McCurdy,
have misconstrued this whole passage by using "conceives"
for "designs." Yet Leonardo's meaning ought to be clear.
It is a strong epistemological position, a prelude to what
Vico will develop in his own way two centuries later: man
cannot know the truth about nature, but only about what
he "makes" himself, namely, history. Leonardo does not
mean it that way, however; his mind is not turned towards
our past. He is thinking of what man is able to create, both
artistically and technically. Nature can only be guessed at;
she gives at most "clues" to her own designs: but the unlimited world of man's creation is his very own.

There is little point in trying from this and from his engineering discoveries to make Leonardo into a "modern," whatever that may be taken to mean. The word would really have to change meaning with every generation. He was the most original natural philosopher of his own time. That time did not possess what *we* call science, but it possessed art in a sense that is lost to us.

Leonardo's guiding idea was not that the eye alone is able to see reality; but that the trained intent eye, the eye "knowing how to see," which controls the skilled hand, can come as close to the hidden structure of reality as it is possible for man to read—insofar as he has redesigned it himself. This is not mere observational knowledge as we would understand it, neither is it experimental knowledge, for even the word "experiment" does not go beyond the meaning of "experience" (and when Galileo will create the modern meaning he will have to call it "the ordeal of experience"). It is operational and creative knowledge, or, as Leonardo calls it, "exact fantasy." The artist is the "true philosopher" in that he re-creates a nature in more quintessential terms, as it were; he has extracted from nature more than "meets the eye"—or the mind either. "Mental things which have not gone in through the senses are vain and bring forth no truth except detrimental." What is detrimental are the universal statements which close our minds to reality. On the other hand, what the "senses" receive without creative participation can also be detrimental, and the artist knows it too well, for he is the magician who can arouse passions at his will. Leonardo tells with a shade of irony of the owner of one of his Madonnas who had to sell it again in haste, because "in spite of the reverence owed it, he had fallen desperately in love with the image."

The artist himself, like the philosopher, is above passion, for his mind is on the hidden substructure which reveals itself through his effort. Geometry, perspective, proportion and mechanics are the means whereby he is able, as artist and as engineer, to create or build afresh; they represent the law of operating inside nature, a law not wholly reducible to abstractions, but forever embodied in plastic reality and in operation.

This idea of mathematics is essentially different from that of the Greeks, which had led them to organize a world of abstract entities fit only for contemplation, and to geometrize the heavens into a system of eternal and uniform circles. Leonardo, who wrote "no one should read me who is not a mathematician," refuses to see the bare fabric of geometry in the heavens, where yet it has worked so brilliantly, and tries to think of the stars in terms of the behavior of living beings. Conversely, he dreams of expanding earthly mechanics to gigantic proportions. But it is always inside the "live force" of things that he seeks the subtle mysteries of balance, proportion and exact compensation. "Mechanics is the paradise of mathematical sciences, because it is there that one plucks the mathematical fruit." Is he thinking in terms of the ancient temptation of Eden? It is a total new *physics,* really, that he is aiming at. He cannot use the word, for it is still pre-empted by the old Aristotelian cosmology, and, like Galileo, he fixes his gaze on the science that Archimedes had built up into the model and example of the coming mathematical physics; but he straightway applies it to the balance and the action of the living body.

[Write [he reminds himself, for to him writing and drawing are all one], write the tongue of the woodpecker and the jaw of the crocodile. Write the flight of the fourth kind of chewing butterflies and of the flying ants, and the three chief positions of the wings of birds in descent. . . . Write of the regions of the air and the formation of clouds, and the cause of snow and hail, and of the new shapes that snow forms in the air, and of the trees in cold countries with the new shape of the leaves. . . . Write whether the percussion made by water upon its object is equal in power to the whole mass of water supposed suspended in the air, or no.]

HIS INDEFATIGABLE ENDEAVOR SURVEYS THE WHOLE TERrain of experience in search of the outline of a science as yet dimly seen but which he thinks can be eventually grasped only from the whole. It is a science which is expected, on the first level, to yield the laws of shock and fall, and also of dynamic equilibrium through the principle of virtual velocities (on this Leonardo had more penetrating insights than most of his successors) but should then proceed to levels not simply reducible to mechanics, nor dominated by the mechanical model.

Time itself, Leonardo remarks, is a continuous quantity, but yet "does not fall under the power of geometry." Time is the pulse of creation and destruction and of the unfolding and change of forms. For there reappears here, after twenty centuries of silence, the idea of organic evolution, and of the past and future of the globe as a life cycle. In a sequence of grandiose drawings, Leonardo lets his imagination dwell on the hurricane of final dissolution. We see again here why Leonardo would not go along with geometry in the heavens. The world model based on astronomical periodicity, which had shown time to the Greeks as the steady beat of uniform eternity, bringing forth forever uniform results, a model which goes on to inspire the Newtonian universe in the next century, begins here to yield to a richer and subtler conception of physical time, which will find understanding only in our own epoch.

By the same token, the concept of cause undergoes a sea-change: there is no longer the preconception of general causes dispensing down particular effects, but of varying causes transmitting themselves wholly and with precision into effects. Reality tends to become functions of variables. But of such variables there must be more than we can conceive: "Nature is full of infinite reasons which never were in experience." A mind which thinks thus will never feel impelled to concentrate on a single level of causes, as later mathematical physicists. It will go on exploring and sounding reality at all depths. Hence it will never reach the systematic clarity that we expect of the scientist. The most important part of Leonardo's thinking remained in the form of scattered notes interwoven with sketches, written mirrorwise from right to left to discourage prying curiosity.

An attempt of this order could not but end in stoically accepted failure and solitude. As Michelangelo said scornfully (and repented later): "He would have all sorts of big ideas, and he could not find a man to drive his bellows." But the tragedy of Leonardo is a fully accepted tragedy.

He is Faustus who never sold out to the Devil, and did
not have to face that last hour before midnight.

If we try, for what we can, to understand him on his
own terms, and from his own fragments, we have to follow
uncertain intuition more often than reason. But this much,
at least, stands out: the man who achieved such transcendent heights of Christian imagery as the *Last Supper* and the
Virgin of the Rocks is also the man in whom lives the style,
the grand old naturalism, and the wondering speculation
of the pre-Socratic Greeks. He feels at ease among them.
The first centuries of Greece, as Nietzsche remarked, have
provided all the molds for our thought. Leonardo instinctively, knowing but little about it, goes back to the ampler
mold, the one which contains vaster, still dormant but implicit possibilities. "There is no point in distinguishing between things natural and things divine," as Hippocrates
had written, "for all of them are natural and all of them are
divine too, whichever way we choose to look at them."

The soul, too, is for Leonardo what philosophical speculation has been "forever unable to define," but which can
be perceived in its actions as a force of nature: "Shock
does not travel far in the earth; much more does water
struck by water, as it moves in circles afar; even farther
goes sound in the air, and farther still the spirit in the
universe; but as it, too, is finite, it cannot extend throughout the infinite." This might well have sounded rawly primitive to minds schooled in Platonic or scholastic speculation, who assumed the spirit to be at home in the realm
of ideas and of eternal principles beyond the world, but
this is just the point: Leonardo sidesteps nineteen centuries
of philosophy (and Christian speculation) based on the
dualism of matter and spirit, and looks intently at reality
with fresh eyes. The detail of a plant or the serene gaze of
Isabella d'Este, the geometric design of a fossil or the intricate fabric of the hand, are to him structural elements
of the philosophic discourse, and he sees a more awesome
subject of meditation in that "miraculous point," the pupil
of the eye (see p. 83), in which the universe converges,
than does idealist philosophy in the truth which transcends
Being. "Mind passes in an instant from east to west; it is

even swifter than sight, and all great incorporeal things approach this latter in speed."

We may call this monistic naturalism, tinged with mythical vision. To develop it more explicitly would have led Leonardo into the depths of avowed heresy. He leaves it there, to work by implication. But we perceive his thoughts all moving on the level of vast potentialities, where observation, theoretical analysis and aesthetic creation can meet and merge. It is the level where everything is seen combining into a true Cosmos of forces such as those indicated by Heraclitus: "Immortals mortals, mortals immortals, living each other's death, dying each other's life."

There is a significant ambiguity in this thought, concerning the subject of infinity. We have seen it implied of space, in that it cannot be reached by the spirit "extending through the universe." Elsewhere we find: "Which is the thing that is not given in reality, and if it were given it would not be itself? It is infinity." This turns out to mean: infinite are the potentialities of nature, but perforce never wholly realized at one time, and this seems to apply even to geometrical space itself. Reality is a tension in the "now" between an infinity towards which it tends and the nothingness into which it lapses through time.

Such thoughts are wholly justified for a world which is conceived essentially as form and flux of form. The formal and the empirical element are inextricably interlocked in it; and so long as the aesthetic element of understanding persists, the hesitation about infinity has to persist too. It is to be found even, significantly enough, in Galileo. It vanishes when the analytical conception of science gets into stride with Descartes, by whom infinity is taken for granted. In present-day physics, where we have again something akin to intrinsic form emerging on the atomic level, we may watch, and not quite coincidentally, the correlative emergence of a closed expanding space.

Leonardo's universe is surely one of aesthetic rigor; it is also a universe of physical clarity and total immanence, where nothing is fixed but all is life, motion and exchange —a Pythagorean idea which will later again dominate Galileo's thought—where reign harsh necessity and an impassive justice, where hidden harmony and the coincidence of opposites contain in themselves good and evil in an ambivalent duality; a cosmos where all is beauty unaware of itself.

There is a strong logic in it, which expresses the supreme science of that First Mover Leonardo calls "a force divine or otherwise," which knew how to distribute to each power its meed of effect in the needed measure. The universe is a fully functioning affair, fully expressed, which knows no frustration. The basic law is: all forces are born from a break in equilibrium. "Lightness is born of weight and weight of lightness; they pay at the same instant for the benefit of their creation by waxing in life in the measure of motion, and they extinguish each other, too, at the same time, by destroying each other in the mutual expiation of death." This might be Anaximander speaking in 600 B.C., but it is Leonardo, and his thought moves on from there to investigate the rise and decline of its components.

Force is a true component, as "a great incorporeal thing." it is born in sudden violence, and dies victoriously "in gentle freedom," to transmute itself into forms; and indeed no greater violence than the first source of it all, the furnace of the sun, "from which all souls descend, because the heat that is in living animals comes from the soul, and there is no heat or light in the world except through the sun." We may see here again that seemingly illogical short turn of thought, which deals traditionally with force in terms of soul, only to imply that the soul itself has its origin in the sun's flow of energy, instead of preserving the distinction which makes of the sun the physical symbol of divine power. The Florentine Platonists had tried to establish the unity of the universe by conceiving of it as a continuous gradation from matter to spirit. Leonardo short-circuits it into one essential energy, and this prepares the way for Galileo's idea of light as the true nature of things.

Force becomes the elemental shapes and thus life. The rhythm of the pulse, of the wave, of the tides, the curl of running water around an obstacle, the spiraling filament again portrayed in the abstract spiral of causal processes, the whirl from conflicting currents, the flexuous curves of woman's hair or of the tender plant, the axial symmetry of the body or of the leaf—these, and not the simple uniformity of geometric circles, are the true components. What Leonardo would have needed to advance further into these regions are the sophisticated modern techniques of harmonic analysis, which have come to represent so great a part of present physical theory; but then they would have been true forms no longer.

Joy is a true component of this universe and not an epiphenomenon; we might call it, in Whiteheadian language, an "eternal object." It is the joy to be found in the young being and in the artist who contemplates it, of children, foals and kittens at play; then there appears force in full action; grandeur, ferocity, the carefully explored comparative physiognomy of furious men, charging horses, wolves and lions in attack; and there is the hardening and helpless freezing of decay. But as force gains perception, there is suffering—also a true component. "Where is most power of feeling, there is the most suffering. Great martyrdom."

What is man in all this? Leonardo's anthropology outlines itself gradually from his conception of nature. Man is for him, in true Renaissance manner, a microcosm within that macrocosm. So are all great units, like the earth and the stars. But man is at the "cockpit," he is an active transformer with all the possibilities within reach. So much Pico would have acknowledged. Leonardo looks now searchingly at man's actual behavior inside nature. Man, just because of his range, acts as a variable of fearsome instability. He may turn out to have been nature's greatest mistake. In nature good and evil are ambiguously present everywhere. The unconscious cruelty of animals is a just part of nature's design for richness and multiplicity (see p. 84), but man alone *knows* what suffering is, hence in inflicting it he becomes a monster. In a world of order and reason, man alone is disorganized and senseless. He calls it following his own purposes, but in the light of Leonardo's cosmic religiosity they stand as perpetual blasphemy. Man's role in nature has become that of the subverter, the ransacker and the destroyer.

The use of the intellect, Nature's gift, for egotistic purposes is a perpetual snare and a delusion. It is Nature's trap for hastening dissolution. This is almost the single

theme on which Leonardo plays numberless variations in
his fables, of which we give a couple of the shortest as an
example.

The fact that man does exert restraints of a sort towards
his own kind, that he has created laws and civilizations
which have bespoken most of his philosophical endeavor,
seems to touch the artist not at all. The foundation of
society is still violence, as his friend Machiavelli may have
reminded him. "Savage is he who saves himself."

Yet there is this other side: man alone is the author of
himself. He has steered the shaping forces which make the
wild beast into his own buildup, and he has become their
plaything. How is the philosopher-prophet to save him?
By orienting his capacity for change in the direction of his
true nature, which is that of the user of reason. So much
had been indicated by Plato and Aristotle. But how different Leonardo's way of understanding it. There are still "infinite causes in nature" that man can turn his energy to
constrain, if he is given scope in the guiltless unbounded
realms of artistic and technological creation. The prodigious engineering inventiveness of Leonardo stems from
this; it should not be seen merely as a response to the
demands made on him. Most of his machines were of no
use to his time. Some of them would require modern engines, and even engines with the modern ratio of weight to
power, in order to be made to work at all. Others are
machines to make machines, machines to solve problems
which had not yet come up by far. "The great swan which
will bring glory to its maker," the submarine designs that
Leonardo prefers not to divulge, are a Daedalean flight
into a new dimension, into the realm proper to man, as the
medieval myth suggested which made Alexander the Great
attempt the air and the depths of the sea after he found
there was no more land to conquer. In such achievements,
thinks Leonardo, man may find at last his true role as
transformer of nature, and rediscover innocence. His greatest artistic effort is aimed at expressing the crucial symbol
of man's mistake. The *Last Supper*, at which he worked so
long, and whose construction is as deeply thought out as
that of the *Divine Comedy*, carries a whole world of meaning. We watch the shock wave of the fatal announcement

traveling through the disciples, in a first movement of fright and flight; it is reflected on the stiffened outer figures of Simon and Bartholomew; it comes back towards the Master in a surge of dedication. But there is now a hesitant ripple in it, and the icy seizure of betrayal aware of itself. We feel it will further move away in a sense of awful destiny, go on moving through time. The twelve men know that they are henceforth alone. What is contained there is perhaps the cryptogram of a not wholly Christian idea: Man, the revealed image of the cosmos, again and again failed by mankind.

The following passages are from *The Notebooks of Leonardo da Vinci.**

[1. MAN AND EXPERIENCE
The painter contends with—and rivals nature.

* * * * * * * *

Wrongly do men cry out against experience and with bitter reproaches accuse her of deceitfulness. Let experience alone, and rather turn your complaints against your own ignorance, which causes you to be so carried away by your vain and insensate desires as to expect from experience things which are not within her power!

* * * * * * * *

The lover is drawn by the thing loved, as the sense is by that which it perceives, and it unites with it, and they become one and the same thing. The work is the first thing born of the union; if the thing that is loved be base, the lover becomes base. When the thing taken into union is in harmony with that which receives it, there follow rejoicing and pleasure and satisfaction. When the lover is united to that which is loved it finds rest there: when the burden is laid down there it finds rest.

* * * * * * * *

Behold now the hope and desire to go back to our own country, and to return to our former state, how like it is to the moth with the light! And the man who with perpetual longing ever looks forward with joy to each new spring and

* Edward MacCurdy (ed. and trans.). London: Jonathan Cape; New York: Reynal & Hitchcock, 1938.

each new summer, and to the new months and the new
years, deeming that the things he longs for are too slow in
coming, does not perceive that he is longing for his own
destruction. But this longing is the quintessence and spirit
of the elements, which, finding itself imprisoned within the
life of the human body, desires continually to return to its
source. And I would have you know that this very same
longing is that quintessence inherent in nature, and that
man is a type of the world.

*   *   *   *   *   *   *   *

O thou that sleepest, what is sleep? Sleep is an image of
death. Oh, why not let your work be such that after death
you become an image of immortality; as in life you become
when sleeping like unto the hapless dead.

*   *   *   *   *   *   *   *

While I thought that I was learning how to live, I have
been learning how to die.

2. THE SCIENCE OF NATURE

There is no certainty where one can neither apply any of
the mathematical sciences nor any of those which are based
upon the mathematical sciences.

*   *   *   *   *   *   *   *

There is no result in nature without a cause; understand
the cause and you will have no need of the experience.

*   *   *   *   *   *   *   *

Necessity is the mistress and guide of nature. Necessity
is the theme and artificer of nature, the bridle and the
eternal law.

*   *   *   *   *   *   *   *

How admirable thy justice, O thou first mover! Thou
hast not willed that any power should lack the processes or
qualities necessary for its results.

*   *   *   *   *   *   *   *

Instrumental or mechanical science is the noblest and
above all others the most useful, seeing that by means of
it all animated bodies which have movement perform all
their actions; and the origin of these movements is at the
centre of their gravity, which is placed in the middle with

unequal weight at the sides of it, and it has scarcity or abundance of muscles and also the action of a lever and counter lever.

*   *   *   *   *   *   *   *

Falsehood is so utterly vile that though it should praise the great works of God it offends against His divinity; truth is of such excellence that if it praise the meanest things they become ennobled.

Of Spirits

The definition of a spirit is a power united to a body, because of itself it can neither offer resistance nor take any kind of local movement; and if you say that it does in itself offer resistance, this cannot be so within the elements, because if the spirit is a quantity without a body, this quantity is what is called a vacuum, and the vacuum does not exist in nature, and granting that one were formed, it would be instantly filled up by the falling in of that element within which such a vacuum had been created. So by the definition of weight, which says that gravity is a fortuitous power created by one element being drawn or impelled towards another, it follows that any element, though without weight when in the same element, acquires weight in the element above it, which is lighter than itself; so one sees that one part of the water has neither gravity nor levity in the rest of the water, but if you draw it up into the air then it will acquire weight, and if you draw the air under the water then on finding itself above this air it acquires weight, which weight it cannot support of itself, and consequently its descent is inevitable, and therefore it falls into the air, at the very spot which had been left a vacuum by this water. The same thing would happen to a spirit if it were among the elements, for it would continually create a vacuum in whatever element it chanced to find itself; and for this reason it would be necessarily in perpetual flight towards the sky until it had passed out of these elements.

Whether the Spirit Has A Body Among the Elements

We have proved how the spirit cannot of itself exist among the elements without a body, not yet move of itself by voluntary movement except to rise upwards. We now proceed to say that such a spirit in taking a body of air must of necessity spread itself through this air; for if it remained united, it would be separated from it and would fall, and so create a vacuum, as is said above; and therefore it is necessary, if it is to be able to remain suspended in the air, that it should spread itself over a certain quantity of air; and if it becomes mingled with the air two difficulties ensue, namely, that it rarefies that quantity of air within which it is mingled, and consequently this air, becoming rarefied, flies upwards of its own accord, and will not remain among the air that is heavier than itself; and moreover, that as this aethereal essence is spread out, the parts of it become separated, and its nature becomes modified, and it thereby loses something of its former power. To these there is also added a third difficulty, and that is that this body of air assumed by the spirit is exposed to the penetrating force of the winds, which are incessantly severing and tearing in pieces the connected portions of the air, spinning them round and whirling them amid the other air; and therefore the spirit which was spread through this air would be dismembered or rent in pieces and broken. . . .

Plurality of Worlds

If you look at the stars without their rays,—as may be done by looking at them through a small hole made with the extreme point of a fine needle and placed so as almost to touch the eye,—you will perceive these stars to be so small that nothing appears less; and in truth the great distance gives them a natural diminution, although there are many there which are a great many times larger than the star which is our earth together with the water. Think, then, what this star of ours would seem like at so great a distance, and then consider how many stars might be set longitudinally and latitudinally amid these stars which are scattered throughout this dark expanse.

Microcosm and Macrocosm

Man has been called by the ancients a lesser world, and indeed the term is rightly applied, seeing that if man is

compounded of earth, water, air and fire, this body of the
earth is the same; and as man has within himself bones as
a stay and framework for the flesh, so the world has the
rocks which are the supports of the earth; as man has within
him a pool of blood wherein the lungs as he breathes expand
and contract, so the body of the earth has its ocean, which
also rises and falls every six hours with the breathing of the
world; as the veins spread out their branches throughout
the human body, in just the same manner the ocean fills
the body of the earth with an infinite number of veins of
water. In this body of the earth there is lacking, however,
the sinews, and these are absent because sinews are created
for the purpose of movement, and as the world is perpetually stable within itself no movement ever takes place
there, and in the absence of any movement the sinews are
not necessary; but in all other things man and the world
show a great resemblance.

The Physics of Scripture

Here a doubt arises, and that is as to whether the Flood
which came in the time of Noah was universal or not, and
this would seem not to have been the case for the reasons
which will now be given. We have it in the Bible that the
said Flood was caused by forty days and forty nights of
continuous and universal rain, and that this rain rose ten
cubits above the highest mountain in the world. But, consequently, if it had been the case that the rain was universal,
it would have formed in itself a covering around our globe
which is spherical in shape; and a sphere has every part of
its circumference equally distant from its centre, and therefore, on the sphere of water finding itself in the aforesaid
condition, it becomes impossible for the water on its surface to move, since water does not move of its own accord
unless to descend. How then did the waters of so great a
Flood depart if it is proved that they had no power of
motion? If it departed, how did it move, unless it went upwards? At this point natural causes fail us, and therefore
in order to resolve such a doubt we must needs either call
in a miracle to our aid or else say that all this water was
evaporated by the heat of the sun.

If you should say that the shells which are visible at the present time within the borders of Italy, far away from the sea and at great heights, are due to the Flood having deposited them there, I reply that, granting this Flood to have risen seven cubits above the highest mountain, as he has written who measured it, these shells which always inhabit near the shores of the sea ought to be found lying on the mountain sides, and not at so short a distance above their bases, and all at the same level, layer upon layer.

Should you say that the nature of these shells is to keep near the edge of the sea, and that as the sea rose in height the shells left their highest level:—to this I reply that the cockle is a creature incapable of more rapid movement than the snail out of water, or is even somewhat slower, since it does not swim, but makes a furrow in the sand, and supporting itself by means of the sides of this furrow it will travel between three and four ells in a day; and therefore with such a motion as this it could not have travelled from the Adriatic Sea as far as Monferrato in Lombardy, a distance of two hundred and fifty miles in forty days,—as he has said who kept a record of that time.

If you should say that the shells were empty and dead when carried by the waves, I reply that where the dead ones went the living were not far distant, and in these mountains are found all living ones, for they are known by the shells being in pairs and by their being in a row without any dead, and a little higher up is the place where all the dead with their shells separated have been cast up by the waves near where the rivers plunged in mighty chasm into the sea.

On A Fossil Fish

O how many times hast thou been amid the waves of the mighty, swelling ocean, towering like a mountain, and sinking ships with the flailing of thy tail amid thunderous noise! How many kingdoms and nations have flourished and passed and been forgotten since thy black-finned back ploughed through the waves with proud and stately bearing! Now thy form, a rock among rocks, is bearing the mountain above thee.

Force or Energy

Force I define as an incorporeal agency, an invisible power, which by means of unforeseen external pressure is caused by the movement stored up and diffused within bodies which are withheld and turned aside from their natural uses; imparting to these an active life of marvellous power, it constrains all created things to change of form and position, and hastens furiously to its desired death, changing as it goes according to circumstances. When it is slow its strength is increased, and speed enfeebles it. It is born in violence and dies in liberty; and the greater it is the more quickly it is consumed. It drives away in fury whatever opposes its destruction. It desires to conquer and slay the cause of opposition, and in conquering destroys itself. It waxes more powerful where it finds the greater obstacle. Everything when under constraint itself constrains other things. Without force nothing moves. The body in which it is born neither grows in weight nor in form. None of the movements that it makes are lasting. It increases by effort and disappears when at rest. The body within which it is confined is deprived of liberty. Often also by its movement it generates new force.

The Pupil of the Eye

Seeing that the images of the objects are all spread throughout all the air which surrounds them, and are all in every point of the same, it must be that the images of our hemisphere enter and pass together with those of all the heavenly bodies through the natural point [the pupil], in which they merge and become united by mutually penetrating and intersecting each other, whereby the image of the moon in the east and the image of the sun in the west at this natural point become united and blended together with our hemisphere.

O marvellous Necessity, thou with supreme reason constrainest all effects to be the direct result of their causes, and by a supreme and irrevocable law every natural action obeys thee by the shortest possible process!

Who would believe that so small a space could contain the images of all the universe? O mighty process! What talent can avail to penetrate a nature such as thine? What tongue will it be that can unfold so great a wonder? Verily, none! This it is that guides the human discourse to the considering of divine things.

Here the figures, here the colours, here all the images of every part of the universe are contracted to a point.

O what point is so marvellous!

O wonderful, O stupendous Necessity, thou by thy law constrainest all effects to issue from their causes in the briefest possible way! These are the miracles, . . . forms already lost, mingled together in so small a space, it can recreate and reconstitute. . . .

Fitness of Organisms

Though nature has given sensibility to pain to such living organisms as have the power of movement,—in order thereby to preserve the members which in this movement are liable to diminish and be destroyed,—the living organisms which have no power of movement do not have to encounter opposing objects, and plants consequently do not need to have a sensibility to pain, and so it comes about that if you break them they do not feel anguish in their members as do the animals.

The Balance of Life

Nature being capricious, and taking pleasure in creating and producing a succession of new lives and forms because she knows that they serve to increase her terrestrial substance, is more ready and swift so to create than time is to destroy; and therefore she has ordained that many of the animals shall serve as food one for the other. And as her desire is still unsatisfied, she frequently sends forth certain noisome and pestillential vapours upon the rapidly increasing herds of animals, and especially upon men, who increase very rapidly because other animals do not feed upon them, and if these causes were removed the results would cease. So therefore this earth seeks to lose its life, desiring only constant reproduction, and as, for the reason which you have assigned and expounded, the effects are generally in harmony with their causes, so animals are a type of the life of the world.

The Flight of Birds

The bird in its flight without the help of the wind drops half the wing downwards, and thrusts the other half towards the tip backwards; and the part which is moved down prevents the descent of the bird, and that which goes backwards drives the bird forward. . . .

Of whether birds when continually descending without beating their wings will proceed a greater distance in one sustained curve, or by frequently making some reflex movement; and whether when they wish to pass in flight from one spot to another they will go more quickly by making impetuous, headlong movements, and then rising up with reflex movement and again making a fresh descent, and so continuing.—To speak of this subject you must needs in the first book explain the nature of the resistance of the air, in the second the anatomy of the bird and of its wings, in the third the method of working of the wings in their various movements, in the fourth the power of the wings and of the tail, at such time as the wings are not being moved and the wind is favourable to serve as a guide in different movements.

Dissect the bat, study it carefully, and on this model construct the machine.

*   *   *   *   *   *   *   *

The great bird will take its first flight upon the back of the great swan, filling the whole world with amazement and filling all records with its fame; and it will bring eternal glory to the nest where it was born.

How He Who Despises Painting Has No Love for the Philosophy in Nature

If you despise painting, which is the sole imitator of all the visible works of nature, it is certain that you will be

despising a subtle invention which with philosophical and
ingenious speculation takes as its theme all the various
kinds of forms, airs, and scenes, plants, animals, grasses
and flowers, which are surrounded by light and shade. And
this truly is a science and the true-born daughter of nature,
since painting is the offspring of nature. But in order to
speak more correctly we may call it the grandchild of nature; for all visible things derive their existence from nature,
and from these same things is born painting. So therefore
we may justly speak of it as the grandchild of nature and
as related to God Himself.

The Fables of the Crab and of the Flame

The crab having posted himself beneath a narrow cleft in
the stream to catch the fish, came a flood with sudden
ruinous rolling of rock whereby said crab was crushed to
death.

A flame had lived for a month in a glass furnace, when
espying a candle nearby she contrived to leap over and
settle on it; and having with wondrous gluttony devoured
it, she wished for dear life she could go back to the furnace,
but in vain, whence perforce amid tears and repentance
she was turned in the end into noisome smoke, leaving her
sisters in long-lived harmony and splendid beauty.

The Cavern (a fragment)

. . . Drawn by invincible desire and much wanting to
see the great multitude of various and strange forms designed by the cunning of Nature, I followed a twisting way
among dark rocks, and came at last to the entrance of a
great cave. In front of it I halted bewildered in ignorance;
arching my back, my weary left hand resting on my knee, I
shadowed my narrowed eyes with the right hand, and bent
to and fro trying to see if I could discern anything therein;
which was in vain because of the great darkness. And as I
tarried there, I was assailed by both fear and desire. Fear of
the dark and dangerous abyss, desire of seeing what miraculous things it might contain . . .

A cautionary thought
concerning the "Last Supper" perhaps

When I portrayed the Lord God as a child, you cast me in prison; if now I portray him as a man, you'll do me worse.

Of Man (in the manner of a prophecy)

Creatures shall be seen upon the earth who will always be fighting one with another, with very great losses and frequent deaths on either side. These shall set no bounds to their malice; by their fierce limbs a great number of the trees in the immense forests of the world shall be laid level with the ground; and when they have crammed themselves with food it shall gratify their desire to deal out death, affliction, labours, terrors and banishment to every living thing. And by reason of their boundless pride they shall wish to rise towards heaven, but the excessive weight of their limbs shall hold them down. There shall be nothing remaining on the earth or under the earth or in the waters that shall not be pursued and molested or destroyed, and that which is in one country taken away to another; and their own bodies shall be made the tomb and the means of transit of all the living bodies which they have slain. O Earth! what delays thee to open and hurl them headlong into the deep fissures of thy huge abysses and caverns, and no longer to display in the sight of heaven so savage and ruthless a monster?

CHAPTER IV

Sir Thomas More

ABOUT 1510, THOMAS MORE, A LAWYER OF THE TEMPLE, looked with concern at the English landscape as it was being transformed by the new Tudor aristocracy, and thought, as he was to write later, that "sheep were eating men." This was the beginning of the new capitalistic era, and he did not like it. In 1516, Henry VIII asked him to become his counselor. By way of memorandum, he gave the king a fanciful tract of his own, entitled *Utopia,* or a visit to the Island of Nowhere. It was a sharp satire of the England of his days, and the king, who was a clever man, did not take it amiss.

Thus More was drawn reluctantly into a high career. A great lawyer and administrator, he became successively Chancellor of the Exchequer and, after Wolsey's downfall, Lord Chancellor of the Realm. Three years later, rather than endorse the king's projected marriage with Anne Boleyn, and the religious break that followed, he retired from office. The man who had drawn the highest legal fees in England went back to live in comparative poverty, and reappeared in Westminster Hall only when he was summoned to tender the Oath of Supremacy, whereby the king became the final religious authority in England. He respectfully but steadfastly refused, and was beheaded as a traitor. His head was set up on a pole on London Bridge. The Catholic Church has canonized him since, and he is now Saint Thomas More, Martyr of the Faith.

Delicately poised between two eras, Sir Thomas More is in a way the *beau idéal* of Conservatism. Like Socrates, he had to pay for it with his life, and, like Socrates too, he was no abstract speculator, but acted on a circle of friends through an exemplary existence. To the solitary and wandering Erasmus, More's house on the Embankment was a frequent haven of refuge, and he describes it as full of music and the laughter of children, but also of piety and prayers. In a time used to grave demeanor, it seemed wonderful to him to see this man laden with the greatest affairs of state romping with his grandchildren and their pet animals, and being ever "merry, jocund and pleasant among them." And, he remarked, "such is the excellence of his disposition that whatever happeneth that could not be helped, he is as cheerful and as well pleased as though the best thing possible had been done."

Holbein has left us an admirable likeness of More's sensitive keen face with its restless eyes, "grey and speckled, which kind of eyes do commonly betoken a very good and sharp wit." We may catch a hint in it of what Nicholas Harpsfield says further, that it was "resembling and tending to the fashion of one that would laugh." Sir Thomas did not belie that temper even in his last days. When the King's Lieutenant who had charge of him in the Tower used the customary apologies for the poor fare, he replied: "I assure you, Mr. Lieutenant, I do not dislike my cheer, but whensoever I do, then thrust me out of your doors." And when he was taken to the scaffold, on seeing it weak and rickety, he said with mock concern: "I pray you, Mr. Lieutenant, see me safe up; and for my coming down, let me shift for myself."

The serenity and composure of Sir Thomas More's personage are the result of a strong ancient discipline; underneath them, his soul had experienced to the full the great conflicts of his time, and gone through many an "agonizing reappraisal." He had taught tolerance and then had to lead repression, only to be cast out in his turn; he who belonged wholly in the ancient frame of medieval Christendom had brought into England the New Learning that was to undermine it; his flight into the rational Utopia of the future is inspired by the story of Vespucci's travels, for his Ancient Mariner, Master Raphael Hythloday, is imagined to have followed that route to discover the Ideal Community.

In his youth, More had retired for four years to monastic life, hoping to follow a religious vocation. Even after he went back to the world, he always wore a hairshirt of penance under his clothes; and he preserved to the last the stately medieval faith. His son-in-law Roper tells us in his biography how his daughter Margaret met him when she was admitted to see him for the last time in the Tower: "At whose coming, after the seven psalms and litany said —which whensoever she came to him, ere he fell in talk of any worldly matters, he used accustomably to say with her —among other communication he said to her: 'I believe, Meg, that they that have put me here ween they have done me a high displeasure. But I assure you on my faith, my own dear daughter, if it had not been for my wife and you my children, whom I account the chief part of my charge, I would not have failed, long ere this, to have closed myself in as strait a room and straiter too.' "

Yet this is the same man in whose house Erasmus wrote the *Praise of Folly,* and who could jest with him over the evil ways of monks and the absurdities of schoolmen; who wrote of the happy republic where religion rested on no authority but that of reason, and who was the most powerful advocate in England of the New Learning.

Men like Erasmus, Colet and More were first and foremost apostles of Culture, the reformers of the educational system, and the founders of the modern English school system, of which St. Paul's was the first example. More compared the school to "the wooden horse in which were concealed armed Greeks for the destruction of barbarous Troy"; but the Troy that these new Greek scholars were bent on wrecking was the stronghold of medieval learning. Cramped it was, no doubt, and crowded with useless logic; but it was also the stronghold of medieval thought. The freedom that More and Erasmus invoked, of going back to Plato and to the Fathers, was a dangerous one for orthodoxy, and it bore the seeds of the Reformation. Both of them were, indeed, reformers. They believed in a Christianity shorn of its cumbersome intellectual machinery, and brought down to its moral essentials. But both of them refused to become heretics or even schismatics. Erasmus's early sympathy with Luther turned to open hostility towards this new and aggressive kind of fundamentalism. As for More, his position was clear: the king had showered his favors upon him, but he would not for all that go against the ancient constitutions of Christendom, which prescribed that spiritual and temporal authority must not be vested in the same person.

On surrendering the Great Seal to Sir Thomas Cromwell, the masterful Machiavellian bureaucrat who was to usher in the new State, he said: "Mr. Cromwell, if you will follow my poor advice, you shall, in counsel giving unto His Grace, ever tell him what he ought to do, but never tell him what he is able to do, so shall you show yourself a true faithful servant and a right worthy Councillor." This was Conservative wisdom, in full accord with More's past as a parliamentarian who had fearlessly resisted the encroachments of the king's prerogative. His poor advice was not taken; Europe was entering upon the era of absolute monarchies, with the metaphysics attendant thereunto, of which in the next volume. As for More, he went home to face penury, refusing a gift of £5000 that was offered him by the Convocation of Catholic bishops for his labors on their behalf. "But," he told his family characteristically, "it shall not be best for us to fall to the lowest fare first. We will begin with Lincoln's Inn diet—then will we, if need be, the next year after go one step down to New Inn fare, wherewith many an honest man is well contented. If that exceed our ability, too, then will we the next year after descend to Oxford fare, where many grave, ancient and learned Fathers be conversant continually, which if our ability stretch not to maintain neither, then may we yet with bags and wallets go a-begging together, and hoping that for pity some good folks will give their charity at every man's door to sing *salve Regina*, and so still keep company merrily together."

The word *Utopia* has had a long career since. Utopianism has become an essential component of our civilization. It cannot be denied that More's ideal state looks drearily Spartan; so was Plato's Republic, which was its avowed model. But then, the idea was not to escape in fancy to some happy land of Cockaigne; it was to project a pattern of a truly rational society, through which most of the horrors of the actual one were shown to be unjustified. If, from poverty and persecution, from a land infested by robberies where destitute and desperate men are strung up "by the twenties" for petty thievery, we are to move forward to a decent standard of living and a six-hour working day, More perceived no way to do it except by cutting down on usury, luxury and conspicuous waste. This is a logic which imposed itself on all reformers, and as late as Proudhon, so long as it was not understood that the Industrial Revolution could bring numberless "mechanical slaves" to our aid. Within the unescapable limits of his time, More's Utopia is a very pure expression of the spirit of the Renaissance, which would bring reason into every corner of life and of the universe.

In youth, More had taught Augustine's City of God, and dreamt of bringing it to earth. The price for making historical reality rational is, unfortunately, unless we bring to it Hegelian logic, to freeze it into an unvarying order. In his youth, too, More had written a *Life of Picus, Count of Mirandola,* and it shows enough how he shared the dream of a total concordance and consistency of visible and invisible reality, mystical and open love, rational and revealed truths, in a kind of "block universe" of the mind. For him as for Erasmus, the Christian revelation denied nothing, it only crowned the edifice. This is not what Augustine had meant, surely, nor why ancient thought had undergone such previous pruning in the Middle Ages. But it might be said that men of More's type were so completely molded by Christian thought that they could not see the use for such restraints.

The religious tolerance expressed in *Utopia* is the swan song of the old ecumenic catholicity, matured in humanistic idealism. Had More foreseen the Lutheran revolt and the Anabaptist upheavals that were to follow almost immediately, he would never have dared write as he did. The later years of his life are riven by the new awareness. As Lord Chancellor, he had to persecute harshly the new Protestants and their thought: "For evil books have sprongen up so thick, full of pestilent errors and pernicious heresies, that they have infected and killed, I fear me, more silly simple souls than the famine of the dear years destroyed bodies." Yet, even in the midst of improvised action, he showed a prophetic insight which, if it had been shared by later statesmen, might have prevented the horrors of the Thirty Years' War: "Son Roper, I pray God that some of us, as high as we seem to sit upon the mountains treading heretics under our feet like ants, live not the day that we gladly would wish to be at league and composition with them to let them have their churches quietly to themselves, so that they would be contented to let us have ours quietly to ourselves."

In making the case for religious tolerance, More speaks as a Christian, yet his plea is based on a universal theism of Platonic inspiration, somewhat similar to that of Cusanus and Pico della Mirandola.

The passages which follow are from *Utopia* (1516), written in Latin, based on the translation of Ralph Robinson (1551).

[They also which do not agree to Christ's religion fear no man from it, nor speak against any man that hath received it. Saving that one of our company in my presence was sharply punished. He as soon as he was baptised began against our wills, with more earnest affection than wisdom, to reason of Christ's religion; and began to wax so hot in his matter, that he did not only prefer our religion before all other, but also did utterly despise and condemn all others, calling them profane, and the followers of them wicked and devilish and the children of everlasting damnation. When he had thus long reasoned the matter, they laid hold on him, accused him and condemned him into exile, not as a despiser of religion, but as a seditious person and a raiser up of dissension among the people. For this is one of the ancientest laws among them; that no man shall be blamed for reasoning in the maintenance of his own religion. For King Utopus, even at the first beginning, hearing that the inhabitants of the land were, before his coming thither, at continual dissension and strife among themselves for their religions; perceiving also that this common dissension (whiles every several sect took several parts in fighting for their country) was the only occasion of his conquest over them all; as soon as he had gotten the victory, first of all he made a decree, that it should be lawful for every man to favour and follow what religion he would, and that he might do the best he could to bring other to his opinion, so that he did it peaceably, gently, quietly, and soberly, without haste and contentious rebuking and inveighing against other. If he could not by fair and gentle speech induce them unto his opinion yet he should use no kind of violence, and refrain from displeasant and seditious words. To him that would vehemently and fervently in this cause strive and contend was decreed banishment or bondage. This law did King Utopus make not only for the maintenance of peace, which he saw through continual contention and mortal hatred utterly extinguished; but also because he thought this decree should make for the furtherance of religion. Whereof he durst define and determine nothing unadvisedly, as doubting whether God desiring manifold and divers sorts of honour, would inspire sundry men with sundry kinds of religion. And this surely he thought a very unmeet and foolish thing, and a point of arrogant presumption, to compel all others by violence and threatenings to agree to the same that thou believest to be true. Furthermore though there be one religion which alone is true, and all other vain and superstitious, yet did he well foresee (so the matter were handled with reason and sober modesty) that the truth of its own power would at the last issue out and come to light. But if contention and debate in that behalf should continually be used, as the worst men be most obstinate and stubborn, and in their evil opinion most constant; he perceived that then the best and holiest religion would be trodden underfoot and destroyed by most vain superstitions, even as good wheat is by thorns and weeds overgrown and choked. Therefore all this matter he left undiscussed, and gave to every man free liberty and choice to believe what he would. Saving that he earnestly and straitly charged them, that no man should conceive so vile and base an opinion of the dignity of man's nature, as to think that the souls do die and perish with the body; or that the world runneth at all adventures governed by no divine providence. And therefore they believe that after this life vices be extremely punished and virtues bountifully rewarded. Him that is of a contrary opinion they count not in the number of men, as one that hath abased the high nature of his soul to the vileness of brute beast's bodies, much less in the number of their citizens, whose laws and ordinances, if it were not for fear, he would nothing at all esteem. For you may be sure that he will study either with craft privily to mock, or else violently to break the common laws of his country, in whom remaineth no further fear than of the laws, nor no further hope than the body. Wherefore he that is thus minded is deprived of all honours, excluded from all offices and rejected from all common administrations in the public weal. And thus he is of all sorts despised, as of an unprofitable and of a base and vile nature. Howbeit they put him to no punishment, because they be persuaded that it is in no man's power to believe what he list.]

AN IMPORTANT QUESTION IS, WHAT KIND OF ADVICE SHOULD be given to rulers? This discussion is obviously intended for the eyes of Henry VIII. With his customary gentle irony, More takes the side of the worldly-wise statesman, and allows himself to be sternly corrected by Master Raphael Hythloday, the ancient voyager who has discovered Utopia. It comes out a prophetic criticism, a century in advance, of Francis Bacon's well-rounded wisdom.

[To be plain with you (quoth I) truly I cannot allow that such communication shall be used, or such counsel given, as you be sure shall never be regarded nor received. For how can so strange informations be profitable, and how can they be beaten into their heads, whose minds be already prevented with clean contrary persuasions? This school philosophy is not unpleasant among friends in familiar communication, but in the councils of kings, where great matters be debated and reasoned with great authority, these things have no place.

That is it which I meant (quoth he) when I said philosophy had no place among kings.

Indeed (quoth I) this school philosophy hath not, which

thinketh all things meet for every place. But there is another philosophy more civil, which knoweth, as ye would say, her own stage, and thereafter ordering and behaving herself in the play that she hath in hand, playeth her part accordingly with comeliness, uttering nothing out of due order and fashion. And this is the philosophy that you must use . . . and so it is in the consultations of kings and princes. If evil opinions and naughty persuasions cannot be utterly and quite plucked out of their hearts, if you cannot, even as you would, remedy vices, which use and custom hath confirmed: yet for this cause you must not leave and forsake the commonwealth; you must not forsake the ship in a tempest, because you cannot rule and keep down the winds. No, nor you must labour to drive into their heads new and strange informations, which you know well shall be nothing regarded with them that be of clean contrary minds. But you must with a crafty wile and a subtle train study and endeavour yourself, as much as in you lieth, to handle the matter wittily and handsomely for the purpose, and that which you cannot turn to good, so to order it that it be not very bad. For it is not possible for all things to be well, unless all men were good. Which I think will not be yet these good many years.

By this means (quoth he) nothing else will be brought to pass, but while that I go about to remedy the madness of others, I should be even as mad as they. For if I would speak such things that be true I must needs speak such things; but as for to speak false things, whether that be a philosopher's part or no I cannot tell, truly it is not my part. Howbeit this communication of mine, though peradventure it may seem unpleasant to them, yet can I not see why it should seem strange, or foolishly newfangled. If so be that I should speak those things that Plato feigneth in his Republic, or that the Utopians do in theirs, these things though they were (as they be indeed) better, yet they might seem spoken out of place. Forasmuch as here amongst us, every man hath his possessions several to himself, and in Utopia all things be common. But what was in my communication contained, that might not and ought not in any place to be spoken? Saving that to them which

have thoroughly decreed and determined with themselves
to run headlong the contrary way it cannot be acceptable
and pleasant, because it calleth them back, and showeth
them the jeopardies. Verily if all things that evil and vicious manners have caused to seem inconvenient and
nought should be refused, as things unmeet and reproachful, then we must among Christian people wink at the most
part of all those things which Christ taught us, and so
strictly forbade them to be winked at, that those things
also which he whispered in the ears of his disciples he
commanded to be proclaimed in houses. And yet the most
part of them is more dissident from the manners of the
world nowadays, than my communication was. But preach-
ers, sly and wily men, following your counsel (as I suppose) because they saw men unwilling to frame their manners to Christ's rule, they have wrestled and perverted his
doctrine, and like a [ductile] rule of lead have applied it
to men's manners: that by some means at the leastways,
they might agree together. Whereby I cannot see what
good they have done: but that men may more sickerly be
evil. And I truly should prevail even as little in king's councils. For either I must say otherways than they say, and
then I were as good to say nothing, or else I must say the
same that they say, and (as Mitio saith in Terence) help
to further their madness. For that crafty wile and subtle
train of yours, I cannot perceive to what purpose it serveth,
wherewith you would have me to study and endeavour
myself, if all things cannot be made good, yet to handle
them wittily and handsomely for the purpose, that as far
forth as is possible they may not be very evil. For there is
no place to dissemble in, nor to wink in. Naughty counsels
must be openly allowed and very pestilent decrees must be
approved. He shall be counted worse than a spy, yea almost as evil as a traitor, that with a faint heart doth praise
evil and noisome decrees. Moreover a man can have no
occasion to do good chancing into the company of them
which will sooner pervert a good man, than be made good
themselves: through whose evil company he shall be
marred, or else if he remain good and innocent, yet the
wickedness and folly of others shall be imputed to him, and

laid in his neck. So that it is impossible with that crafty wile and subtle train to turn anything to better.]

AS REGARDS INTERNATIONAL POLITICS, ON THE OTHER hand, Master Hythloday the pro-Utopian is no "utopian" at all. He speaks as an experienced statesman, and reason in matters of power is for him, as it will be for Machiavelli, *Realpolitik*. This shift allows More opportunity for bitter irony directed at Christian princes and even at the Catholic hierarchy, in whose obedience he was to die without illusions.

[As touching leagues, which in other places between country and country be so oft concluded, broken and renewed, Utopians never make none with any nation. For to what purpose serve leagues? say they. As though nature had not set sufficient love between man and man. And who so regardeth not nature, think you that he will pass for words? They be brought into this opinion chiefly because that, in those parts of the world, leagues between princes be wont to be kept and observed very slenderly. For here in Europe, and especially in these parts where the faith and religion of Christ reigneth, the majesty of leagues is everywhere esteemed holy and inviolable, partly through the justice and goodness of princes, and partly at the reverence and motion of the head bishops. Which like as they make no promises themselves but they do very religiously perform the same, so they exhort all princes in any wise to abide by their promises, and them that refuse or deny so to do, by their pontifical power and authority they compel thereto. And surely they think well that it might seem a very reproachful thing, if in the leagues of them which by a peculiar name be called faithful, faith should have no place. But in that new found part of the world, which is scarcely so far from us beyond the line equinoctial as our life and manners be dissident from theirs, no trust nor confidence is in leagues. But the more and holier ceremonies the league is knit up with, the sooner it is broken by some cavillation found in the words, which many times of purpose be so craftily put in and placed, that the bands can never be so sure nor so strong, but they will find some hole open to creep out at, and to break both league and truth. The which crafty dealing, yea the which fraud and deceit, if they should know it to be practised among private men in their bargains and contracts, they would incontinent cry out at it with an open mouth and a sour countenance, as an offence most detestable and worthy to be punished with a shameful death: yea even very they that advance themselves authors of like counsel given to princes. Wherefore it may well be thought, either that all justice is but a base and a low virtue, and which abaseth itself far under the high dignity of kings; or at the leastwise that there be two justices, the one meet for the inferior sort of the people, going afoot and creeping low by the ground, and bound down on every side with many bands because it shall not run at rovers; the other a princely virtue, which like as it is of much higher majesty than the other poor justice, so also it is of much more liberty, as to the which nothing is unlawful that it lusteth after.]

FINALLY—AND THIS MAKES OF HIM A TRUE MODERN Utopian—More faces unflinchingly the most dangerous and "radical" aspect of the whole issue. Far in advance of his age, he raises the problem of the economic foundations of society. His terse definition of the capitalist state which closes this section has been echoed by the masters of modern socialism.

[Wherefore when I consider with myself and weigh in my mind the wise and godly ordinances of the Utopians, among whom with very few laws all things be so well and wealthily ordered, that virtue is had in price and estimation, and yet; all things being there common, every man hath abundance of everything. Again on the other part, when I compare with them so many nations ever making new laws; where every man calleth that he hath gotten his own proper and private goods; where so many new laws daily made be not sufficient for every man to enjoy, defend, and know from another man's that which he calleth his own; which thing the infinite controversies in the law, daily rising, never to be ended, plainly declare to be true. These things (I say) when I consider with myself, I hold well with Plato, and do nothing marvel, that he would make no laws for them that refused those laws, whereby all men should have and enjoy equal portions of wealth and commodities. For the wise man did easily foresee this to be the one and only way to the wealth of a commonalty, if equality of all things should be brought in and established. Which I think is not possible to be observed, where every man's goods be proper and peculiar to himself. For where every man under certain titles and pretences draweth and pluckcheth to himself as much as he can, so that a few divide among themselves all the whole riches, be there never so much abundance and store, there to the residue is left lack and poverty. And for the most part it chanceth, that this latter sort is more worthy to enjoy that state of wealth, than the other be: because the rich men be covetous, crafty and unprofitable. On the other part the poor be lowly, simple, and by their daily labour more profitable to the commonwealth than to themselves. Thus I do fully persuade myself that no equal and just distribution of things can be made, nor that perfect wealth shall ever be among men, unless this property be exiled and banished. But so long as it shall continue, so long shall remain among the most and best part of men the heavy and inevitable burden of poverty and wretchedness. Which, as I grant that it may be somewhat eased, so I utterly deny that it can wholly be taken away. For if there were a statute made, that no man should possess above a certain measure of ground, and that no man should have in his stock above a prescript and appointed sum of money: if it were by certain laws decreed that neither the king should be of too great power, neither the people too haughty and wealthy, and that offices should not be obtained by inordinate suit, or by bribes and gifts: that they should neither be bought nor sold, nor that it should be needful for the officers, to be at any cost or charge in their offices, for so occasion is given to them by fraud and ravin to gather up their money again, and by reason of gifts and bribes the offices be given to rich men, which should rather have been executed of wise men: by such laws I say, like as sick bodies that be desperate and past cure be wont with continual good cherishing to be

kept and botched up for a time: so these evils also might
be lightened and mitigated. But that they may be perfectly
cured, and brought to a good and upright state, it is not to
be hoped for, whiles every man is master of his own to
himself. Yea, and while you go about to do your cure of
one part, you shall make bigger the sore of another part, so
the help of one causeth another's harm: forasmuch as
nothing can be given to any one, unless it be taken from
another. . . .

Now I have declared and described unto you as truly as
I could the form and order of that commonwealth, which
verily in my judgment is not only the best, but also that
which alone of good right may claim and take upon it the
name of a commonwealth or public weal. For in other
places they speak still of the commonwealth, but every
man procureth his own private gain. Here where nothing
is private, the common affairs be earnestly looked upon.
And truly on both parts they have good cause so to do as
they do. For in other countries who knoweth not that he
shall starve for hunger, unless he make some several provision for himself, though the commonwealth flourish
never so much in riches? And therefore he is compelled
even of very necessity to have regard to himself, rather
than to the people, that is to say, to others. Contrariwise
there, where all things be common to every man, it is not
to be doubted that any man shall lack anything necessary
for his private uses, so the common storehouses and
barns be sufficiently stored. For there nothing is distributed
after a niggardly sort, neither there is any poor man or
beggar. And though no man have anything, yet every man
is rich. For what can be more rich, than to live joyfully
and merrily, without all grief and pensiveness; not caring
for his own living, nor vexed or troubled with his wife's
importunate complaints, nor dreading poverty to his son,
nor sorrowing for his daughter's dowry? Yea they take no
care at all for the living and wealth of themselves and all
theirs, of their wives, their children, their nephews, their
children's children, and all the succession that ever shall
follow in their posterity. And yet besides this there is no
less provision for them that were once labourers and be

now weak and impotent, than for them that do now labour
and take pain. Here now would I see, if any man dare to
be so bold as to compare with this equity the justice of
other nations; among whom, I forsake God if I can find
any sign or token of equity and justice. For what justice is
this, that a rich goldsmith, or an usurer, or to be short, any
of them which either do nothing at all, or else that which
they do is such that it is not very necessary to the commonwealth, should have a pleasant and a wealthy living, either
by idleness, or by unnecessary business; when in the mean-
time poor labourers, carters, ironsmiths, carpenters and
ploughmen, by so great and continual toil as drawing and
bearing beasts be scant able to sustain, and again so necessary toil that without it no commonwealth were able to
continue and endure one year, should yet get so hard and
poor a living, and live so wretched and miserable a life,
that the state and condition of the labouring beasts may
seem much better and wealthier? For they be not put to so
continual labour, nor their living is not much worse, yea to
them much pleasanter, taking no thought in the mean
season for the time to come. But these silly poor wretches
be presently tormented with barren and unfruitful labour.
And the remembrance of their poor indigent and beggarly
old age killeth them up. For their daily wages is so little,
that it will not suffice for the same day, much less it yield-
eth any overplus, that may daily be laid up for the relief of
old age. Is not this an unjust and an unkind public weal,
which giveth great fees and rewards to gentlemen, as they
call them, and to goldsmiths, and to such other, which be
either idle persons, or else only flatterers, and devisers of
vain pleasures; and of the contrary part maketh no gentle
provision for poor ploughmen, colliers, labourers, carters,
ironsmiths, and carpenters: without whom no commonwealth can continue? But after it hath abused the labours
of their lusty and flowering age, at the last when they be
oppressed with old age and sickness, being needy, poor,
and indigent of all things, then forgetting their so many
painful watchings, not remembering their so many and so
great benefits, recompenseth and acquitteth them most un-
kindly with miserable death. And yet besides this the rich

men not only by private fraud, but also by common laws, do every day pluck and snatch away from the poor some part of their daily living. So whereas it seemed before unjust to recompense with unkindness their pains that have been beneficial to the public weal, now they have to this their wrong and unjust dealing (which is yet a much worse point) given the name of justice, yea and that by force of a law. Therefore when I consider and weigh in my mind all these commonwealths, which nowadays anywhere do flourish, so God help me, I can perceive nothing but a certain conspiracy of rich men procuring their own commodities under the name and title of the commonwealth.]

CHAPTER V

Machiavelli

THOMAS CROMWELL, WHO, AS WE HAVE SEEN, SUCCEEDED
More and brought into being the modern centralized state,
brought to England the first manuscript copy of Machiavelli's *Prince*. This was a fateful succession, and its dramatic character is heightened by the time coincidence of
the actual writing of the book with the issuing of More's
Utopia (1516). The Middle Ages with their dreamers
and martyrs were yielding to the cold inquisitive gaze of
science. It is the turning point inside the Renaissance.

Pious souls gave the name of Old Nick to the Devil
himself. Later statesmen and monarchs wrote against
Machiavelli and called him a master of evil, but it was, as
Voltaire said, because he had given away their trade
secrets. Thus, we are dealing not only with a thinker on
history, but with one whose thought played a role in shaping it. He has influenced Marlowe and Shakespeare as well
as Hobbes and Spinoza. Karl Marx derived fundamental
ideas from him, and the dictators of our day thought they
could derive from him their justification.

Niccolò Machiavelli (1469-1527) was Assistant Secretary of State of the Republic of Florence from 1498 to
1512. When the Republic fell and the Medicis came back to
power, he was compelled to retire to private life on his
little farm. It was there that he wrote *The Prince* and the
Discourses. In 1518 the Medicis relented and commis-
sioned him to write the *History of Florence*. He was also
called in by them to advise about the policy to be followed
with the city, which was proving difficult to hold. He suggested, quite correctly as it turned out, that it would be
impossible to hold unless it were given a republican form

of government, and he even drafted a constitution, which
was never applied.

In 1527, Florence did regain her liberty, albeit for a
brief time. Machiavelli's name was seconded in Council for
his old post as Secretary, but it was passed up in favor of
a nonentity. "It was commonly imagined," writes a contemporary, "that the Duke had learned from the *Prince*
how to despoil the rich of their wealth, and the poor of
their freedom. To the pious people he appeared heretical;
to the good, wicked; to the evil ones, far too knowledge-
able in their ways." A few weeks later, Machiavelli was
dead at the age of fifty-nine. There is a fitting tragic irony
in the end of this dedicated statesman who had incapaci-
tated himself for statesmanship by becoming a thinker.

Such would not have been his fate, needless to say, if
his philosophy had been of the traditional sort that "adorns
the mind and moves it on to higher things." But Machiavelli had tried at his own risk to explore reality in a field
where reality becomes explosive. In him there appears for
the first time a new and modern type of theorist. He is
conscious of being a pioneer quite as much as the men
who were opening up new continents.

Two great events had shaped his thinking while he was
still in his early twenties. The first one was the French
invasion of Charles VIII, which, although carried out with
a small army, had succeeded in toppling the Italian system
of principalities like a house of cards. This taught the
young politician to look beneath the appearance of power.
"Our Italian rulers," he was to write later, "thought it
sufficed a prince to know how, from his desk, to make a
smart retort and to indite an elegant letter, to be subtle
in argument and quick at repartee; know how to contrive
a fraud, to bedeck himself with jewels and gold, to sleep
and eat with greater splendor than his neighbors, and to
lead a life of unmitigated lasciviousness; how to behave
with avarice and arrogance towards his subjects, . . . to
believe the sound of his words as the response of an oracle.
Whence in 1494 the great fright, and the sudden flights, and
the well-nigh incredible losses."

In other words, Machiavelli had learned to distinguish,

as we would say today, between the facts of power and the superstructure.

The other experience was that of the greatness and downfall of Savonarola. He had seen Florence go through a passionate religious revival, which went so far as to cast out the achievements of arts and letters. It had been a political and social upheaval, and then in a minute the wind had turned, and the populace had jeered at the great reformer as he was led to the stake in 1498. He had refused to incite the mob to violence when he could have removed his rivals; whereby, remarked Machiavelli, "he ruined the new order of things; for, when the multitude no longer believed in him, he had no means of keeping those steadfast who did believe or of instilling belief in the unbeliever." Conclusion: "unarmed prophets have always been destroyed, whereas armed prophets have succeeded."

These are clarifying experiences for a man with a scientific turn of mind. And Machiavelli happened to be the earliest scientific mind of the modern type. In fact, a very modern operationist type, as we shall see. While the political thinkers of his day still worried old clichés, like the community as the body and the ruler as the head and so on—a simile so instinctive that it is still rehearsed in our day by technocrats who ought to know better—Machiavelli puts the problem thus: Nothing happens except by way of power. Hence, what is the mechanism of power?

He inaugurates thus the "tough-minded" school of political thought, as opposed to the "tender-minded," which believed that sweet reasonableness, plus "authority which comes from God," would bring about the Good Society.

To him, man is a natural reality which has to be defined through its behavior. Machiavelli treats of him as a modern biologist would treat of a living system with respect to output. The definition of man is purely physical: active matter, as it were, which will always behave thus and so under given circumstances. What Machiavelli seeks to discover in history are correlations of cause and effect of permanent validity. He takes his examples indifferently from the classical past and from the present. But he expects of course the classical past to teach him most, through the thought of its mature historians, Polybius and Livy. Thus he, too, falls under the spell of antiquity. The Romans are the unapproachable model; they are also the skyline of his intellectual world.

But then he is of the Roman tradition. His scientific aim is not theoretical and contemplative; he wants to work out a set of rules for further action, a way for the will to power to unfold itself. The art and poetry that have made his city great he seems to take for granted: they simply tend to show, in his mind, that the times are not unfavorable for the achieving of excellence. His own very great and poetic imagination he considers only a political capacity deprived of action.

Thus also, Machiavelli is a strong and clear moralist, but within the frame of the interests of the state, which are the only imperative he is willing to consider. This is where "virtue" has to come in. The best thinking, he remarks, is of no avail if the leaders do not know how to take responsibilities, if the citizens are not willing to stand up when the time comes. His style takes on the ring of those ancient orators of the Roman Senate:

[For when on the decision to be taken wholly depends the survival of one's country [*la salute della patria*], no consideration should be given either to justice or injustice, to kindness or cruelty, or to its being praiseworthy or ignominious, but rather, any other thought being set aside, that alternative should be followed utterly which will save its existence and preserve its freedom.]

This is clearly where the ultimate meanings of life lie for Machiavelli.

In a letter written to Francesco Vettori from his enforced and penurious retreat, he describes his daily life on the farm as that of a peasant, and he tells of mornings spent in trying to run it and not to be cheated by woodcutters, carters and dealers. "Then," he goes on,

[I seat myself along the road, by the tavern, I talk to those passing by, I ask news of their own parts. I hear many things, and take note of sundry ways and diverse fancies

of men. Thus comes time for dinner, and with my family
I eat of such fare as this my poor farm and minute patrimony consent. Then back to the tavern, where I find per
usual the owner, a butcher, a miller, a couple of brick-
makers. With these I go their loutish way, playing check-
ers all afternoon, whence spring up a thousand quarrels
and numberless insulting spites, and as we argue about a
farthing you might hear us shout as far as San Casciano.
Thus involved among these lice I keep my mind from
going sour, and I yield myself to the malice of this beastly
fate of mine, not minding that it should tread me in the
mire in this fashion, so haply it might be driven to shame.

When evening comes, I go home and enter my study;
at the door I discard these daily clothes full of dirt and
dust, and put on regal and curial robes, and thus condignly
clad I enter the ancient courts of ancient men, where I am
received by them lovingly, and partake of that nourish-
ment which alone is mine, and for it was I born. Then I
am bold to converse with them, and question them as to
the reasons of their actions, and they out of their courtesy
willingly answer me; and during those four hours I am
above any trouble, I fear not poverty, nor does death ap-
pal me; I utterly become one with them. . . .]

HERE WE HAVE THE WHOLE MAN AS HE WAS. TECHNICAL
remarks that we find in his writings, such as that the enemy
should be either reconciled or destroyed, or that if the ruler
decides to kill an opponent he must beware of also con-
fiscating his estate, because that is what his sons will not
forgive, have earned Machiavelli the fame of a cynic. Yet
it is the kind of worldly knowledge Raleigh found it natural
to recall to Cecil in urging him to have Essex executed
quickly: "As for after-revenges, fear them not; for your
own father Lord Burleigh was esteemed to be the contriver
of Norfolk's ruin, yet his son followeth your father's son
and loveth him. . . ."

Machiavelli invents no new trick, he exposes old ones:
he is taking his material from the actual stock-in-trade of
political practitioners, past and present, the kind of thing
they all know and would never entrust to writing: the

"political behavior of the human male." In the cold light of
the theoretical inquiry, the subject loses its shuffling and
hyprocritical connotations, and the hope emerges that
scientific objectiveness and clarity of design might prove
merciful alternatives to mediocrity and good intentions,
which merely perpetuate the messy and bloody nonsense
that most of history actually is.

Machiavelli may see a certain "distinction in evil"
achieved by a well-devised murder, and be ranked by
Donne among the counselors of the Devil (together, it
should be noted, with Copernicus). But we notice (p. 122)
that when he has to mention mass deportations and liquida-
tions, such as have become the small change of present-day
policy, it is to consider them as unthinkable and beyond
the pale of humankind. And if he was so detested, it was,
as Boccalini said, because he was caught trying to put
dog's teeth in the mouth of sheep.

As a responsible statesman, Machiavelli showed that he
believed in the old-fashioned virtues. His treatment of Pisa
after her rebellion was strikingly mild and conciliatory. It
helped only for a short while. The notorious eighteenth
chapter of the *Prince,* in which he discusses whether and
when it pays to keep one's promises, is a rueful after-
thought on his own experience as secretary of state. During
that time, all the powers of Italy changed sides several
times except Florence, which remained steadfast in her
French alliance and in consequence was undone. In the
same old-fashioned way Machiavelli personally remained
faithful to his friend the chancellor Pier Soderini, who
refused to betray the Republic to the Medicis; and as a
consequence both men went ultimately into exile.

Rather, if Machiavelli deserves criticism, it is because,
for such a "modern" mind, he was singularly unreceptive
to modern possibilities. The new weapon of artillery he
tends to dismiss as a noisy toy. But neither, it should be
remembered, did Napoleon pay any attention to the steam-
boat, or Foch to the airplane. More serious is his un-
awareness of the great geopolitical changes of his time,
which were reducing the Mediterranean world to insignif-

icance as they opened up the ocean routes. With the wisdom of hindsight, one wonders why he did not advise Venice and Genoa, the threatened powers, to join forces and seize the Rock of Gilbraltar.—But Machiavelli's geographic horizon was bounded by the Roman past, and Gibraltar was still to him the Pillars of Hercules.

Machiavelli is in the Roman tradition also in that he is a natural and unencumbered pagan. God, he remarks wryly, does not seem to disapprove of the strong, or he would not cause them to prosper. (An idea which was to be taken up with infinite soul-searchings by the Calvinists unaware of such a dangerous precedent, and brought to fruition by skillfully combining it with the other principle that the meek shall inherit the earth.) For him who had spent his youth amid the emotions of a Christian revival, the value of such emotions is discounted. Christianity, in his mind, cannot work as an established religion because it is outside the natural laws of society from the start, and the waverings and contradictions it imposes between the claims of spiritual authority and those of the temporal are the seeds of confusion, hypocrisy, and, finally, decay. "Thus the world has fallen a prey to scoundrels, who can rule it in all impunity, because people, in order to go to heaven, prefer to bear and bewail their abuses rather than punish them."

Man and his fate have lost for him any supernatural connotation. Man is a force inside nature, and the same through time. "Things have always been the same way." There is no City of God, no goal, no Higher Design. Effort and luck are the factors in the same sense in which the atomists spoke of Chance and Necessity. What, then, is history? It expresses the varying distribution of man's free energy. A high potential of available free energy in men or communities, which can be expended in great deeds, he calls *virtù* or excellence. Led by statesmanlike excellence, it founds great empires. When the free energy in a society is fallen very low, it is "corrupt." Then the only way to raise it is for powerful individuals to force themselves to the top, and from there, so to speak, work against entropy or decay in building up a new state.

We have used the modern word "entropy" in what is a much older context, but this *rapprochment* is not arbitrary. Machiavelli's thought has its closest parallel in that of the modern biophysicist, for whom a living system builds itself up by developing a network of communications of commands which work against the random uniformization, or entropy, which would prevail otherwise.

The parallel, of course, should not be pushed too far. The "potential" of Machiavelli's thought is not the abstract notion of modern physics. The force that is in man is conceived, as in Leonardo, to be a vital force which goes directly into the creation of form, indeed of high intelligent form, which is the single object of interest. It is only from there that the "randomizing" process goes to work. That fully realized thing called "man" is taken as an absolute, he is not an item in the scale of nature: it is, much rather, nature which is seen through him.

Yet, to apply such "physicalist" concepts boldly to social reality is bound to lead a man astray. An experienced statesman like Francesco Guicciardini, Machiavelli's younger successor, was to advert to the difficulty of applying the theory to any given political situation. In Machiavelli's thought itself, the dramatic tension is only too clear between the Florentine citizen and the theorist of national or supranational power. As the adviser to statesmen that he wanted to be, he is too often unsound. But Machiavelli's theoretical approach could be proven sound, as Napoleon was to show, himself a fairly consistent Machiavellian. It proves intrinsically more valid than that of Hobbes, who came a century later; for it is not a philosophical doctrine but a working hypothesis, and as such open to continuous correction.

It has been the fate of Machiavelli to be known almost exclusively through the *Prince,* which is strictly speaking a *pièce d'occasion.* We have based our selections on the *Discourses,** which show much more clearly the course of his thought, and also—what he had to omit in the *Prince*—his considered philosophical judgment.

*Christian E. Detmold (trans.). New York: The Modern Library, 1940.

Although the envious nature of men, so prompt to blame and so slow to praise, makes the discovery and introduction of any new principles and systems as dangerous almost as the exploration of unknown seas and continents, yet, animated by that desire which impels me to do what may prove for the common benefit of all, I have resolved to open a new route, which has not yet been followed by any one, and may prove difficult and troublesome, but may also bring me some reward in the approbation of those who will kindly appreciate my efforts.

When we consider the general respect for antiquity, and how often—to say nothing of other examples—a great price is paid for some fragments of an antique statue, which we are anxious to possess to ornament our houses with, or to give to artists who strive to imitate them in their own works; and when we see, on the other hand, the wonderful examples which the history of ancient kingdoms and republics presents to us, the prodigies of virtue and of wisdom displayed by the kings, captains, citizens, and legislators who have sacrificed themselves for their country,—when we see these, I say, more admired than imitated, or so much neglected that not the least trace of this ancient virtue remains, we cannot but be at the same time as much surprised as afflicted. The more so as in the differences which arise between citizens, or in the maladies to which they are subjected, we see these same people have recourse to the judgments and the remedies prescribed by the ancients.

. . . Yet to found a republic, maintain states, to govern a kingdom, organize an army, conduct a war, dispense justice, and extend empires, you will find neither prince, nor republic, nor captain, nor citizen, who has recourse to the examples of antiquity. This neglect, I am persuaded, is due less to the weakness to which the vices of our education have reduced the world, than to the evils caused by the proud indolence which prevails in most of the Christian states, and to the lack of real knowledge of history, the true sense of which is not known, or the spirit of which they do not comprehend. Thus the majority of those who read it take pleasure only in the variety of the events which history relates, without ever thinking of imitating the noble actions, deeming that not only difficult, but impossible; as though heaven, the sun, the elements, and men had changed the order of their motions and power, and were different from what they were in ancient times.

*   *   *   *   *   *   *   *   *

OF THE EVENTS THAT CAUSED THE CREATION OF TRIBUNES IN ROME; WHICH MADE THE REPUBLIC MORE PERFECT

All those who have written upon civil institutions demonstrate (and history is full of examples to support them) that whoever desires to found a state and give it laws, must start with assuming that all men are bad and ever ready to display their vicious nature, whenever they may find occasion for it. If their evil disposition remains concealed for a time, it must be attributed to some unknown reason; and we must assume that it lacked occasion to show itself; but time, which has been said to be the father of all truth, does not fail to bring it to light. After the expulsion of the Tarquins the greatest harmony seemed to prevail between the Senate and the people. The nobles seemed to have laid aside all their haughtiness and assumed the popular manners, which made them supportable even to the lowest of the citizens. The nobility played this role so long as the Tarquins lived, without their motive being divined; for they feared the Tarquins, and also lest the ill-treated people might side with them. Their party therefore assumed all possible gentleness in their manners towards the people. But so soon as the death of the Tarquins had relieved them of their apprehensions, they began to vent upon the people all the venom they had so long retained within their breasts, and lost no opportunity to outrage them in every possible way; which is one of the proofs of the argument we have advanced, that men act right only upon compulsion; but from the moment that they have the option and liberty to commit wrong with impunity, then they never fail to carry confusion and disorder everywhere. It is this that has caused it to be said that poverty and hunger make man industrious, and that the law makes men good; and if fortunate circumstances cause good to be done without constraint, the law may be dispensed with. But when such happy influence is lacking, then the law immediately becomes necessary. Thus the nobles, after the death of the Tarquins, being no longer under the influence that had restrained them, determined to establish a new order of things, which had the same effect as the misrule of the Tarquins during their existence; and therefore, after many troubles, tumults, and dangers occasioned by the excesses which both the nobles and the people committed, Rome came, for the security of the people, to the creation of the Tribunes, who were endowed with so many prerogatives, and surrounded with so much respect, that they formed a powerful barrier between the Senate and the people, which curbed the insolence of the former.

THE DISUNION OF THE SENATE AND THE PEOPLE RENDERS THE REPUBLIC OF ROME POWERFUL AND FREE

It cannot be denied that the Roman Empire was the result of good fortune and military discipline; but it seems to me that it ought to be perceived that where good discipline prevails there also will good order prevail, and good fortune rarely fails to follow in their train. Let us, however, go into details upon this point. I maintain that those who blame the quarrels of the Senate and the people of Rome condemn that which was the very origin of liberty, and that they were probably more impressed by the cries and noise which these disturbances occasioned in the public places, than by the good effect which they produced; and that they do not consider that in every republic there are two parties, that of the nobles and that of the people; and all the laws that are favorable to liberty result from the opposition of these parties to each other, as may easily be seen from the events that occurred in Rome. From the time of the Tarquins to that of the Gracchi, that is to say, within the space of over three hundred years, the differences between these parties caused but very few exiles, and cost still less blood; they cannot therefore be regarded as having been very injurious and fatal to a republic, which during the course of so many years saw on this account only eight or ten of its citizens sent into exile, and but a very small number put to death, and even but a few condemned to pecuniary fines. Nor can we regard a republic as disorderly where so many virtues were seen to shine. For good examples are the result of good education, and good education is due to good laws; and good laws in their turn spring from those very agitations which have been so inconsiderately condemned by many. . . .

And if it be said that these are strange means,—to hear constantly the cries of the people furious against the Senate, and of a Senate declaiming against the people, to see the populace rush tumultuously through the streets, close their houses, and even leave the city of Rome,—I reply, that all these things can alarm only those who read of them, and that every free state ought to afford the people the opportunity of giving vent, so to say, to their ambition; and above all those republics which on important occasions have to avail themselves of this very people. Now such were the means employed at Rome; when the people wanted to obtain a law they resorted to some of the extremes of which we have just spoken, or they refused to enroll to serve in the wars, so that the Senate was obliged to satisfy them in some measure. The demands of a free people are rarely pernicious to their liberty; they are generally inspired by oppressions, experienced or apprehended; and if their fears are ill founded, resort is had to public assemblies where the mere eloquence of a single good and respectable man will make them sensible of their error. "The people," says Cicero, "although ignorant, yet are capable of appreciating the truth, and yield to it readily when it is presented to them by a man whom they esteem worthy of their confidence."

*   *   *   *   *   *   *   *   *   *   *

TO WHOM CAN THE GUARDIANSHIP OF LIBERTY MORE SAFELY BE CONFIDED, TO THE NOBLES OR TO THE PEOPLE? AND WHICH OF THE TWO HAVE MOST CAUSE FOR CREATING DISTURBANCES, THOSE WHO WISH TO ACQUIRE, OR THOSE WHO DESIRE TO CONSERVE?

All the legislators that have given wise constitutions to republics have deemed it an essential precaution to establish a guard and protection to liberty; and according as this was more or less wisely placed, liberty endured a greater or less length of time. As every republic was composed of nobles and people, the question arose as to whose hands it was best, to confide the protection of liberty. The Lacedæmonians, and in our day the Venetians, gave it into the hands of the nobility; but the Romans intrusted it to the people. We must examine, therefore, which of these republics made the best choice. There are strong reasons in favor of each, but to judge by the results, we must incline in favor of the nobles, for the liberties of Sparta and Venice endured a longer space of time than those of Rome. But to come to the reasons, taking the part of Rome first, I will say, that one should always confide any deposit to those who have least desire of violating it; and doubtless, if we consider the objects of the nobles and of the people, we must see that the first have a great desire to dominate, whilst the latter have only the wish not to be dominated, and consequently a greater desire to live in the enjoyment of liberty; so that when the people are intrusted with the care of any privilege or liberty, being less disposed to encroach upon it, they will of necessity take better care of it, and being unable to take it away themselves, will prevent others from doing so.

On the contrary, it is said in favor of the course adopted by Sparta and Venice, that the preference given to the nobility, as guardians of public liberty, has two advantages: the first, to yield something to the ambition of those who, being more engaged in the management of public affairs, find, so to say, in the weapon which the office places in their hands, a means of power that satisfies them; the other, to deprive the restless spirit of the masses of an authority

calculated from its very nature to produce trouble and dissensions, and apt to drive the nobles to some act of
desperation, which in time may cause the greatest misfor-
tunes. Rome is even aduced as an example of this; for
having confined, it is said, this authority to the Tribunes
of the people, these were seen not to be content with having only one Consul taken from this class, but wanted
both to be plebeians. They afterwards claimed the Censure, the Prætorate, and all the other dignities of the
republic. And not satisfied with these advantages, and
urged on by the same violence, they came in the end to
idolize all those whom they saw disposed to attack the
nobles, which gave rise to the power of Marius and to the
ruin of Rome.

And, truly, whoever weighs all these reasons accurately
may well remain in doubt which of the two classes he
would choose as the guardians of liberty, not knowing
which would be least dangerous,—those who seek to acquire an authority which they have not, or those who desire
to preserve that which they already possess. After the
nicest examination, this is what I think may be concluded
from it. The question refers either to a republic that desires
to extend its empire, as Rome, or to a state that confines
itself merely to its own preservation. In the first case Rome
should be imitated, and in the second the example of Sparta
and Venice should be followed; and in the next chapter we
shall see the reasons why and the means by which this is
to be done. . . .

*   *   *   *   *   *   *   *   *

OF THE RELIGION OF THE ROMANS

. . . Doubtless, if any one wanted to establish a republic at the present time, he would find it much easier with
the simple mountaineers, who are almost without any civilization, than with such as are accustomed to live in cities,
where civilization is already corrupt; as a sculptor finds it
easier to make a fine statue out of a crude block of marble
than out of a statue badly begun by another. Considering
then, all these things, I conclude that the religion introduced by Numa into Rome was one of the chief causes

of the prosperity of that city; for this religion gave rise to good laws, and good laws bring good fortune, and from good fortune results happy success in all enterprises. And as the observance of divine institutions is the cause of the greatness of republics, so the disregard of them produces their ruin; for where the fear of God is wanting, there the country will come to ruin, unless it be sustained by the fear of the prince, which may temporarily supply the want of religion. But as the lives of princes are short, the kingdom will of necessity perish as the prince fails in virtue. . . .

The welfare, then, of a republic or a kingdom does not consist in having a prince who governs it wisely during his lifetime, but in having one who will give it such laws that it will maintain itself even after his death. And although untutored and ignorant men are more easily persuaded to adopt new laws or new opinions, yet that does not make it impossible to persuade civilized men who claim to be enlightened. The people of Florence are far from considering themselves ignorant and benighted, and yet Brother Girolamo Savonarola succeeded in persuading them that he held converse with God. I will not pretend to judge whether it was true or not, for we must speak with all respect of so great a man; but I may well say that an immense number believed it, without having seen any extraordinary manifestations that should have made them believe it; but it was the purity of his life, the doctrines he preached, and the subjects he selected for his discourses, that sufficed to make the people have faith in him. Let no one, then, fear not to be able to accomplish what others have done, for all men (as we have said in our Preface) are born and live and die in the same way, and therefore resemble each other.

THE IMPORTANCE OF GIVING RELIGION A PROMINENT IN-
FLUENCE IN A STATE, AND HOW ITALY WAS RUINED
BECAUSE SHE FAILED IN THIS RESPECT THROUGH THE
CONDUCT OF THE CHURCH OF ROME

Princes and republics who wish to maintain themselves free from corruption must above all things preserve the purity of all religious observances, and treat them with proper reverence; for there is no greater indication of the

ruin of a country than to see religion contemned. . . .
It is therefore the duty of princes and heads of republics to uphold the foundations of the religion of their
countries, for then it is easy to keep their people religious,
and consequently well conducted and united. And therefore everything that tends to favor religion (even though
it were believed to be false) should be received and availed
of to strengthen it; and this should be done the more, the
wiser the rulers are, and the better they understand the
natural course of things. Such was, in fact, the practice
observed by sagacious men; which has given rise to the
belief in the miracles that are celebrated in religions, however false they may be. . . .

And certainly, if the Christian religion had from the beginning been maintained according to the principles of its
founder, the Christian states and republics would have
been much more united and happy than what they are.
Nor can there be a greater proof of its decadence than to
witness the fact that the nearer people are to the Church
of Rome, which is the head of our religion, the less religious are they. And whoever examines the principles upon
which that religion is founded, and sees how widely different from those principles its present practice and application are, will judge that her ruin or chastisement is near at
hand. But as there are some of the opinion that the well-
being of Italian affairs depends upon the Church of Rome,
I will present such arguments against that opinion as occur
to me; two of which are most important, and cannot according to my judgment be controverted. The first is, that
the evil example of the court of Rome has destroyed all
piety and religion in Italy, which brings in its train infinite
improprieties and disorders; for as we may presuppose all
good where religion prevails, so where it is wanting we
have the right to suppose the very opposite. We Italians
then owe to the Church of Rome and to her priests our
having become irreligious and bad; but we owe her a still
greater debt, and one that will be the cause of our ruin,
namely, that the Church has kept and still keeps our country divided. And certainly a country can never be united
and happy, except when it obeys wholly one government,
whether a republic or a monarchy, as is the case in France

and in Spain; and the sole cause why Italy is not in the same condition, and is not governed by either one republic or one sovereign, is the Church; for having acquired and holding a temporal dominion, yet she has never had sufficient power or courage to enable her to seize the rest of the country and make herself sole sovereign of all Italy. And on the other hand she has not been so feeble that the fear of losing her temporal power prevented her from calling in the aid of a foreign power to defend her against such others as had become too powerful in Italy. . . . The Church, then, not having been powerful enough to be able to master all Italy, nor having permitted any other power to do so, has been the cause why Italy has never been able to unite under one head, but has always remained under a number of princes and lords, which occasioned her so many dissensions and so much weakness that she became a prey not only to the powerful barbarians, but of whoever chose to assail her. This we other Italians owe to the Church of Rome, and to none other. And any one, to be promptly convinced by experiment of the truth of all this, should have the power to transport the court of Rome to reside, with all the power it has in Italy, in the midst of the Swiss, who of all peoples nowadays live most according to their ancient customs so far as religion and their military system are concerned; and he would see in a very little while that the evil habits of that court would create more confusion in the country than anything else that could ever happen there.

*   *   *   *   *   *   *   *   *   *

WHOEVER WISHES TO REFORM AN EXISTING GOVERNMENT IN A FREE STATE SHOULD AT LEAST PRESERVE THE SEMBLANCE OF THE OLD FORMS

He who desires or attempts to reform the government of a state, and wishes to have it accepted and capable of maintaining itself to the satisfaction of everybody, must at least retain the semblance of the old forms; so that it may seem to the people that there has been no change in the institutions, even though in fact they are entirely different from the old ones. For the great majority of mankind are satisfied with appearances, as though they were realities, and are often even more influenced by the things that seem than by those that are. The Romans understood this well, and for that reason, when they first recovered their liberty, and had created two Consuls in place of a king, they would not allow these more than twelve lictors, so as not to exceed the number that had served the king. Besides this, the Romans were accustomed to an annual sacrifice that could only be performed by the king in person; and as they did not wish that the people, in consequence of the absence of the king, should have occasion to regret the loss of any of their old customs, they created a special chief for that ceremony, whom they called the king of the sacrifice, and placed him under their high priest; so that the people enjoyed these annual sacrificial ceremonies, and had no pretext, from the want of them, for desiring the restoration of the kings. And this rule should be observed by all who wish to abolish an existing system of government in any state, and introduce a new and more liberal one. For as all novelties excite the minds of men, it is important to retain in such innovations as much as possible the previously existing forms. . . . This, as I have said, should be observed by whoever desires to convert an absolute government either into a republic or a monarchy; but, on the contrary, he who wishes to establish an absolute power, such as ancient writers called a tyranny, must change everything, as we shall show in the following chapter.

A NEW PRINCE IN A CITY OR PROVINCE CONQUERED BY HIM SHOULD ORGANIZE EVERYTHING ANEW

Whoever becomes prince of a city or state, especially if the foundation of his power is feeble, and does not wish to establish there either a monarchy or a republic, will find the best means for holding that principality to organize the government entirely anew (he being himself a new prince there); that is, he should appoint new governors with new titles, new powers, and new men, and he should make the poor rich, as David did when he became king, "who heaped riches upon the needy, and dismissed the wealthy empty-handed." Besides this, he should destroy the old cities and build new ones, and transfer the inhabitants from one place to another; in short, he should leave nothing unchanged in that province, so that there should be neither rank, nor grade, nor honor, nor wealth, that should not be recognized as coming from him. He should take Philip of Macedon, father of Alexander, for his model, who by proceeding in that manner became, from a petty king, master of all Greece. And his historian tells us that he transferred the inhabitants from one province to another, as shepherds move their flocks from place to place. Doubtless these means are cruel and destructive of all civilized life, and neither Christian nor even human, and should be avoided by every one. In fact, the life of a private citizen would be preferable to that of a king at the expense of the ruin of so many human beings. Nevertheless, whoever is unwilling to adopt the first and humane course must, if he wishes to maintain his power, follow the latter evil course. But men generally decide upon a middle course, which is most hazardous; for they know neither how to be entirely good or entirely bad, as we shall illustrate by examples in the next chapter.

SHOWING THAT MEN ARE VERY RARELY EITHER ENTIRELY GOOD OR ENTIRELY BAD

When Pope Julius II. went, in the year 1505, to Bologna to expel the Bentivogli from that state, the government of which they had held for a hundred years, he wanted also to remove Giovanpaolo Baglioni from Perugia, who had made himself the absolute master of that city; for it was the intention of Pope Julius to destroy all the petty tyrants that occupied the possessions of the Church. Having arrived at Perugia with that purpose, which was well known to everybody, he did not wait to enter the city with his army for his protection, but went in almost alone, although Giovanpaolo had collected a large force within the city for his defence. And thus, with the customary impetuosity which characterized all his acts, Julius placed himself with only a small guard in the hands of his enemy Baglioni, whom he nevertheless carried off with him, leaving a governor in his stead to administer the state in the name of the Church. Sagacious men who were with the Pope observed his temerity and the cowardice of Baglioni, and could not understand why the latter had not by a single blow rid himself of his enemy, whereby he would have secured for himself eternal fame and rich booty, for the Pope was accompanied by all the cardinals with their valuables. Nor could they believe that he had refrained from doing this either from goodness or conscientious scruples; for no sentiment of piety or respect could enter the heart of a man of such vile character as Giovanpaolo, who had dishonored his sister and murdered his nephews and cousins for the sake of obtaining possession of the state; but they concluded that mankind were neither utterly wicked nor perfectly good, and that when a crime has in itself some grandeur or magnanimity they will not know how to attempt it. Thus Giovanpaolo Baglioni, who did not mind open incest and parricide, knew not how, or, more correctly speaking, dared not, to attempt an act (although having a justifiable opportunity) for which every one would have admired his courage, and which would have secured him eternal fame, as being the first to show these prelates how little esteem those merit who live and govern as they do; and as having done an act the greatness of which would have overshadowed its nefariousness and all the danger that could possibly result from it.

*   *   *   *   *   *   *   *   *

THE PEOPLE ARE WISER AND MORE CONSTANT THAN PRINCES

Titus Livius as well as all other historians affirm that nothing is more uncertain and inconstant that the multitude; for it appears from what he relates of the actions of men, that in many instances the multitude, after having condemned a man to death, bitterly lamented it, and most earnestly wished him back. This was the case with the Roman people and Manlius Capitolinus, whom they had condemned to death and afterwards most earnestly desired him back, as our author says in the following words: "No sooner had they found out that they had nothing to fear from him, then they began to regret and to wish him back." And elsewhere, when he relates the events that occurred in Syracuse after the death of Hieronymus, nephew of Hiero, he says: "It is the nature of the multitude either humbly to serve or insolently to dominate." I know not whether, in undertaking to defend a cause against the accusations of all writers, I do not assume a task so hard and so beset with difficulties as to oblige me to abandon it with shame, or to go on with it at the risk of being weighed down by it. Be that as it may, however, I think, and ever shall think, that it cannot be wrong to defend one's opinions with arguments founded upon reason, without employing force or authority.

I say, then, that individual men and especially princes may be charged with the same defects of which writers accuse the people; for whoever is not controlled by laws will commit the same errors as an unbridled multitude. This may easily be verified, for there have been and still are plenty of princes, and a few good and wise ones, such, I mean, as needed not the curb that controlled them. Amongst these, however, are not to be counted either the kings that lived in Egypt at that ancient period when that country was governed by laws, or those that arose in Sparta; neither such as are born in our day in France, for that country is more thoroughly regulated by laws than any other of which we have any knowledge in modern times. And those kings that arise under such constitutions are not to be classed amongst the number of those whose individual nature we have to consider, and see whether it resembles that of the people; but they should be compared with a people equally controlled by law as those kings were, and then we shall find in that multitude the same good qualities as in those kings, and we shall see that such a people neither obey with servility nor command with insolence. Such were the people of Rome, who, so long as that republic remained uncorrupted, neither obeyed basely nor ruled insolently, but rather held its rank honorably, supporting the laws and their magistrates. And when the unrighteous ambition of some noble made it necessary for them to rise up in self-defence, they did so, as in the case of Manlius, the Decemvirs, and others who attempted to oppose them; and so when the public good required them to obey the Dictators and Consuls, they promptly yielded obedience. And if the Roman people regretted Manlius Capitolinus after his death, it is not to be wondered at; for they regretted his virtues, which had been such that the remembrance of them filled every one with pity, and would have had the power to produce the same effect upon any prince; for all writers agree that virtue is to be admired and praised, even in one's enemies. And if intense desire could have restored Manlius to life, the Roman people would nevertheless have pronounced the same judgment against him as they did the first time, when they took him from prison and condemned him to death. And so we have seen princes that were esteemed wise, who have caused persons to be put to death and afterwards regretted it deeply. . . .

Therefore, the character of the people is not to be blamed any more than that of princes, for both alike are liable to err when they are without any control. Besides the examples already given, I could adduce numerous others from amongst the Roman Emperors and other tyrants and princes, who have displayed as much inconstancy and recklessness as any populace ever did. Contrary to the general opinion, then, which maintains that the people, when they govern, are inconsistent, unstable, and ungrateful, I conclude and affirm that these defects are not more natural to the people than they are to princes. To charge the people and princes equally with them may be the truth, but to except princes from them would be a great mistake. For a people that governs and is well regulated by laws will be stable, prudent, and grateful, as much so, and even more, according to my opinion, than a prince, although he be esteemed wise; and, on the other hand, a prince, freed from the restraints of the law, will be more ungrateful, inconstant, and imprudent than a people similiarly situated. The difference in their conduct is not due to any difference in their nature (for that is the

same, and if there be any difference for good, it is on the
side of the people); but to the greater or less respect they
have for the laws under which they respectively live. And
whoever studies the Roman people will see that for four
hundred years they have been haters of royalty, and lovers
of the glory and common good of their country; and he
will find any number of examples that will prove both the
one and the other. And should any one allege the ingrati-
tude which the Roman people displayed towards Scipio,
I shall reply the same as I have said in another place on
this subject, where I have demonstrated that the people
are less ungrateful than princes. But as regards prudence
and stability, I say that the people are more prudent and
stable, and have better judgment than a prince; and it is
not without good reason that it is said, "The voice of the
people is the voice of God"; for we see popular opinion
prognosticate events in such a wonderful manner that it
would almost seem as if the people had some occult virtue,
which enables them to foresee the good and the evil. As to
the people's capacity of judging of things, it is exceedingly rare that, when they hear two orators of equal talents
advocate different measures, they do not decide in favor
of the best of the two; which proves their ability to discern the truth of what they hear. And if occasionally they
are misled in matters involving questions of courage or
seeming utility, (as has been said above,) so is a prince
also many times misled by his own passions, which are
much greater than those of the people. We also see that
in the election of their magistrates they make far better
choice than princes; and no people will ever be persuaded
to elect a man of infamous character and corrupt habits
to any post of dignity, to which a prince is easily influenced
in a thousand different ways. When we see a people take
an aversion to anything, they persist in it for many centuries, which we never find to be the case with princes. . . .
We furthermore see the cities where the people are masters make the greatest progress in the least possible time,
and much greater than such as have always been governed
by princes; as was the case with Rome after the expulsion
of the kings, and with Athens after they rid themselves

of Pisistratus; and this can be attributed to no other cause than that the governments of the people are better than those of princes.

It would be useless to object to my opinion by referring to what our historian has said in the passages quoted above, and elsewhere; for if we compare the faults of a people with those of princes, as well as their respective good qualities, we shall find the people vastly superior in all that is good and glorious. And if princes show themselves superior in the making of laws, and in the forming of civil institutions and new statutes and ordinances, the people are superior in maintaining those institutions, laws, and ordinances, which certainly places them on a par with those who established them.

And finally to sum up this matter, I say that both governments of princes and of the people have lasted a long time, but both required to be regulated by laws. For a prince who knows no other control but his own will is like a madman, and a people that can do as it pleases will hardly be wise. If now we compare a prince who is controlled by laws, and a people that is untrammelled by them, we shall find more virtue in the people than in the prince, and if we compare them when both are freed from such control, we shall see that the people are guilty of fewer excesses than the prince, and that the errors of the people are of less importance, and therefore more easily remedied. For a licentious and mutinous people may easily be brought back to good conduct by the influence and persuasion of a good man, but an evil-minded prince is not amenable to such influences, and therefore there is no other remedy against him but cold steel. We may judge then from this of the relative defects of the one and the other; if words suffice to correct those of the people, whilst those of the prince can only be remedied by violence, no one can fail to see that where the greater remedy is required, there also the defects must be greater. The follies which a people commits at the moment of its greatest license are not what is most to be feared; it is not the immediate evil that may result from them that inspires apprehension, but the fact that such general confusion might afford the opportunity for a tyrant to seize the government. But with evil-disposed princes the contrary is the case; it is the immediate present that causes fear, and there is hope only in the future; for men will persuade themselves that the termination of his wicked life may give them a chance of liberty. Thus we see the difference between the one and the other to be, that the one touches the present and the other the future. The excesses of the people are directed against those whom they suspect of interfering with the public good; whilst those of princes are against apprehended interference with their individual interests. The general prejudice against the people results from the fact that everybody can freely and fearlessly speak ill of them in mass, even whilst they are at the height of their power; but a prince can only be spoken of with the greatest circumspection and apprehension. . . .]

CHAPTER VI

Erasmus, Luther and Dürer

IN TRYING TO PRESENT IN ONE EPISODE THE IMMENSELY important and still living conflict between humanistic thought and the Reformation, we would like to give one of its spectators the voice which belonged to the chorus in ancient drama. Albrecht Dürer is then going to speak in this triptych for simple Christendom. Dürer the artist (1471-1528) could not be called a simple man by far. Many traits in him remind us of Leonardo; he was indeed in one way more of a modern than Leonardo himself in that he grasped the importance of the new medium of copperplate engraving, which was the artistic equivalent of printing. In his geometric books on perspective, in his conception of painting and in his theory of it, Dürer shows himself a full worthy member of the group of Nuremberg humanists headed by his friend Willibald Pirkheimer. We need only think of his three most famous etchings (1513-1514) to grasp something of the range of his perception. "The Knight, the Death and the Devil" takes up an old motif of medieval death dances, but transmutes it to express the victorious power of man: The old theme of the Pilgrim's quest is there in the central figure, but clearly it carries also the inspiration of Erasmus's Christian knight. Erasmian, too, in its glorification of peaceful learning is his "St. Jerome," another medieval theme transfigured; the traditional dog and lion are sitting at the old man's feet, but they are taken up in the serenity of the marvelous play of varied surface and checkered light on the floor and ceiling and furnishings of the cell. Finally, the strange Pythagorean-inspired "Melancholia," with its brooding winged genius sitting meditatively amidst a litter of scientific in-

struments and symbols, is the mysterious wondering pause
of the Renaissance mind at the threshold of the as-yet-
only-dreamt-of powerhouse of Science. Yet Dürer—and
we can see that from much of his art—remained a straight
and true medieval Christian, a Gothic-inspired soul. Only
from his faith did he expect the higher context for his life
and work.

Dürer the good burgher of Nuremberg can be seen in
the simplicity of his letters and in his Diary from the
Netherlands. He shows in action what Machiavelli had
just been writing admiringly about, the uncorrupted *virtù*
of the Germans of his time. The Diary from which we are
going to quote is otherwise a quaint itemized list of small
daily transactions: "Two florins for a hat; Item, painted
right carefully Master Lorenz Sterck in oils, 25 florins.
Gave 1 florin to Suzanna the maid for help. Dined with
the rich Canon. Item, to the doctor, 8 pennies . . ." Then,
abruptly, under the shock of news which seemed to pur-
port Luther's death (it was actually his successful escape
under the protection of the Count Palatine) Dürer gives
way to a passionate outbreak of grief, a sobbing implora-
tion to God and all the Christian people. He begs Erasmus
to come out for the good cause. But his prophetic lament
conveys far more; it conveys the whole world of his time
as felt through his candid soul, with its wonderful confusion of new factors and ancient emotions:

⟦ Item This Friday before Pentecost, 1521, came the news
that Martin Luther had been treacherously abducted near
Eisenach, and some say he has been killed; if he was, he
will have suffered for the truth and because he has scourged
that unchristian Papacy, which resists so the setting free of
Christ among us with its great afflictions and so that we
should be robbed and despoiled of our sweat and blood
and have them shamelessly wasted by lazy goodfornothings
so sinfully while poor thirsty sick people must die of hunger because of it. And the hardest for me is, that perhaps
God does intend to leave us still under their blind false
teaching, that has been invented and set up by the men
whom they call Fathers, so that the divine word is falsely

set forth in many ways or not considered at all. O God in heaven, have pity on us, O Lord Jesus Christ, pray for your people, free us in time, preserve us in the true Christian faith. . . . call back the sheep to your pasture, of which too many are still to be found in that of the Roman Church, together with the Indians, Muscovites, Russians and Greeks. . . . O God, you have never so afflicted a people with harsh laws as us poor ones under the Roman throne, we who should fittingly through your blood be free redeemed Christians. . . . O Lord, give us the new Jerusalem that comes down from heaven, of which is written in Revelation, the holy clear Gospel, not darkened with human errors. Hence anyone can see who reads the books of Martin Luther how clear his teaching is, because he teaches the Holy Gospel. Hence they are to be kept in great honor and not to be burned unless so be that we should have his enemies' works thrown into the fire too, with all their opinions which want to make gods out of men, then have more Lutheran books printed. O God, what he would not have writ yet in ten or twenty years more! Oh good Christians all, help me to earnestly lament the passing of this God-inspired man and pray that we may be sent another one. O Erasmus Roderadamus, where are you? Don't you see what unjust tyranny and the powers of darkness can do? Listen, you good knight of Christ, come forth riding at the side of our Lord Christ, defend the truth, win the crown of martyrdom! You are a little old man anyway, I heard it said that you gave yourself only a couple of years that you could still be any good, use those well for the Gospel and true faith, let yourself be heard, and the gates of Hell, the throne of Rome, as Christ says, shall not prevail against you. And even if you had to go the way of your master Christ and die at the hands of the liars a little earlier, so you would yet come from death unto life and be clarified by Christ. O Erasmus, stand up that God may be glad of you, as is written of David, and in truth well you may down Goliath. Oh good Christians all, pray to God for help, for his judgment neareth and his justice becometh manifest. Then shall we see the innocent blood spilt by the Pope and the priests and the monks, receive justice and retribution. Apocalypse. These are the slaughtered ones lying at the foot of God's altar and they cry for vengeance, whereupon the voice of God replieth: wait for the accomplished number of innocent dead, then I shall do justice.

Item, I have changed 1 florin for food. Item to the Doctor 8 pennies. Item twice dined with Ruderigo. To the apothecary 12 pennies. Dined with the rich Canon. Changed 1 florin. Have had as a guest Master Conrad sculptor in Malines. Item paid 18 pennies for Italian art. Lost 4 pennies at game. Drawn 3 Depositions from the Cross and 2 Mounts of Olives on 5 half-sheets. Item to the Englishman painted his arms in color, gave me 1 florin. Jan the goldsmith in Brussels, his likeness drawn in charcoal, gave me 1 florin. Went to the horse market in Antorff where they had a great many fine stallions, and two of them sold for 700 florins. Item lost 4 pennies gambling. . . .]

Erasmus

LUTHER WAS NOT KILLED, BUT WENT ON TO HURL INKPOTS at the Devil and invectives at the "whore of Babylon." Nor did Erasmus, the good Christian knight, come out riding in the lists for him, for his early reforming sympathies had been antagonized by Luther's excesses. Three years after Dürer's desperate appeal, in 1524, when he did enter the struggle at last, it was against Luther.

Desiderius Erasmus of Rotterdam (1466-1536) is the man who held sway over the minds for two generations and led the fight against the intellectual domination of the Church. He is the Voltaire of the sixteenth century. From his childhood on, he had experienced only deceit and oppression at the hands of the monks, who had cheated him out of his family inheritance entrusted to their care: later he learned to know them better in the monastery, and to dislike them no less. This initial motive in his thinking cannot be denied. As Fuller says, he was like the badger, he never did bite but he made his teeth meet. From his impressively erudite beginnings, he turned to larger literary activity: poetry or prose, treatise, dialogue, pamphlet or epistle, there is hardly a form that he did not turn to use, always lightly, with the improvising temper of the born journalist. He handled the Latin of the humanists with ease and charm and a superior sense of language, and made it respond to all the moods of his time. He reflected, indeed, all of its drives and contradictions: the rough play of a vigorous age with sensual images, the joy at the dawning of science, the hatred of an independent mind against the unworthy representatives of spiritual power, and yet an earnest, even passionate, concentration on theological problems. He was, as Dilthey says, a kind of hundred-faced daemon capable of a bewildering variety of expressions, and that was not the least reason of his fascination of his contemporaries. What he stood for, however, always and unequivocally, was religious tolerance. The frail little man with the tight lips and the half-closed blue eyes that Holbein has imprinted forever on our consciousness never yielded in his faith that the word alone should be used as a weapon in religious quarrels. In this he was a true philosopher, in that he did not recognize any domain that should not submit to the intellect; it gave gravity and penetration to his critique however lightly handled.

In his most famous pamphlet, the *Praise of Folly,* he reminds us that it is only irrational and foolish desires which make the wheels of the world go around; he can thus display in a pageant of weaknesses not only the recognized ones, but the unrecognized in Church and learning, with the same bold and reckless irony.

A brief passage will give us the tone of the satire:

[. . . Now next unto the felicity of these master doctors such do approach as people call religious men and monks, that is to say, solitary livers, but by both names evil applied, seeing the greatest part of them are most far from religion, and none so commonly shall you meet roving abroad, even in every alehouse. Whose trade and observance surely were most miserable and abject unless that I (i.e. Folly) did many ways relieve them. For though this kind of men be commonly so abhorred as even to meet

with them at unawares or next a body's rising it is taken
for a sign of evil luck all day after, yet Lord! how they
make themselves to be more than cherubyms. For first
they hold it a great holiness to meddle so little with books
and learning as scarce they know how to read their own
names. And when they roar forth (like a meny of asses)
in their monasteries a number of psalms not understood,
then they ween verily to feed saints' ears with a marvelous
melody. Moreover, some orders of them—namely friars—
do take a pride in their beggary, in going from door to door
to ask their bread with a great lowing voice, pest'ring
men everywhere, both in inns, in wagons, and in pas-
sengers, not a little (I promise you) to the hindrance of
other begsters. And thus, lo, the blind minions, what with
their greasiness, doltishness, rudeness and shameless
hanging on men, do represent unto us (as themselves say)
the life of the Apostles.]

In a more serious vein, but in a spirit of reform not very
different, Erasmus, taking up from Valla, established the
critical historical method in the study of Scripture. His
most important scientific work is his edition of the New
Testament. His aim was clear: he wanted to recapture
the true and genuine Gospel. Its spirits as he understood
it he set forth in his "Manual of the Christian Knight,"
which became a great devotional text. "You should hold
Christ not for an empty invocation, but for nothing else
than love, simplicity, patience, purity, in a word, for whatever He did actually teach."

Now, thinks Erasmus, some of this teaching we find in
the great classics; hence they, too, must be divinely inspired
in a way; they are also much better reading than certain
Fathers; yet it is clear they proceed according to reason.
This touchstone of reason can then be applied to those
parts of Scripture which seem contrary to it, like the
threat of the fire of Hell, and it will show that they
ought to be considered allegoric. In this way Erasmus is
quietly preparing the way for a universal rational religion.

Challenged by Luther's sharpened paradoxes which
made Christianity not only irrational but anti-rational,

Erasmus wrote at last his pamphlet on *Free Will*. We may note that he does not voice the criticism in his own person, but suggests that "the ignorant might be scandalized if, etc." This was a transparent dodge but respectful of forms: the Catholic authorities did not take it amiss, and offered Erasmus high dignities and preferments, including a cardinalship, if he would put his time at their service. He quietly refused and went his way to the last—a correct model of the liberal mind. True, he did not choose to be a hero, but then the liberal mind believes, more than in heroism, in respect for the rules of the game.

The following sections from *De libero arbitrio* (of Free Will) are from Mary Martin McLaughlin's translation.*

⟨ Among the difficulties which not infrequently arise in Holy Scriptures, there is perhaps no more inescapable labyrinth than the question of free will. For this problem has marvellously exercised the wits of theologians, both ancient and modern, as it once did those of the philosophers, but, it seems to me, with greater effort than results. In our day the controversy has been renewed by Carlstadt and by Eck, but in a moderate way; this question was soon agitated more violently by Martin Luther, one of whose theses concerns free will. Although his assertion has not been unanswered, I am intervening in my turn, at the urging of my friends, in the hope that my little work may contribute to the progress of truth.

Now I know that certain people will shut their ears and protest: "The world is turned upside down! Erasmus dares to oppose Luther! This is the mouse going into battle against the elephant!" To pacify them, if I may be allowed a moment's silence, I shall simply repeat by way of preface one single well-established fact: I have never accepted the doctrines of Luther. No one should then be shocked to see me affirm publicly a difference of opinion such as this which can divide one man and another; still less am I prevented from contesting one of his opinions and espe-

*Mary Martin McLaughlin and James Bruce Ross (eds.), *The Portable Renaissance Reader*. New York: The Viking Press, 1953. Copyright, 1953, by The Viking Press, Inc.

cially from engaging in a temperate discussion with him,
inspired only by a desire to seek out the truth. Certainly
I do not think that Luther can be scandalized if someone
disagrees with him, since he himself has not hesitated to
attack not only the opinions of all the doctors of the
Church, but the doctrines taught by all the schools, all the
councils, and all the popes. . . .

Let us then suppose that it is true in a certain sense,
as Wyclif has taught and as Luther has asserted, that
whatever is done by us is done not by free will but by
pure necessity; what is more inexpedient than to publish
this paradox to the world? Again, let us suppose that in
a certain sense it is true, as Augustine says somewhere,
that God works both good and evil in us, and rewards
His own works in us and punishes His own evil works.
What a door to impiety this pronouncement would open
to countless mortals, if it were spread abroad in the world,
especially in view of the great sloth, indifference, and wickedness of men, and their ineradicable proclivity to all kinds
of impiety! What weak man would keep up the perpetual
and weary struggle against the flesh? What evil man would
strive to amend his life? Who could persuade his soul to
love with all his heart a God who prepared a hell flaming
with eternal tortures where He may avenge on wretched
men His own misdeeds, as if He delighted in human tortures? . . .

Now I hear the objection: "What need is there for interpretation when Scripture is entirely clear?" But if it is
so clear, why have such eminent men groped so blindly
and for so many centuries in such an important matter,
as our adversaries claim? If there is no obscurity in the
Scriptures, what need was there for prophecies in apostolic
times? This, you may say, was a gift of the Holy Spirit.
But I hardly know whether, like the gift of healing and the
gift of tongues, this gift of prophecy has not also ceased.
If it has not ceased, it should be asked to whom it has
passed. If to everyone, then all interpretation is uncertain.
If it passed to no one, then today, when so many obscuri-
ties baffle learned men, no interpretation will be certain.
If I claim that it passed to those who succeeded the Apos-

tles, then some will protest that for many centuries the successors of the Apostles did not possess the apostolic spirit. Yet of these men we may very probably assume, other things being equal, that God infused His spirit into those to whom He entrusted His mission, just as we may believe it more probable that grace was given to the baptized, rather than to the unbaptized. . . .

So far we have confined ourselves to comparing the passages of the Scripture which support free will and those which, on the contrary, seem to suppress it entirely. But since the Holy Spirit, who is the author of the whole of Scripture, cannot contradict Himself, we are then constrained, whether we will or not, to seek some moderate conclusion. Since each of the two opposed opinions is based on the same Scripture, it is clear that the defenders of each have examined the Scripture from their own particular points of view, and have read it in the light of the end that they pursue. Some have considered how slothfully men strive for piety and then what a great evil is despair, and while they tried to find a remedy for these evils, they fell imprudently into another error, by granting too much to human free will. But other authors, considering how great an enemy of true piety is the confidence of man in his own powers and merits, and how intolerable is the pride of those who praise themselves for their good works, and who go so far as to sell them to others, according to measure, as one sells oil and soap; in their anxiety to avoid this evil, the opponents of this pride have cut free will in half, saying that a good work cannot be done, or they have killed it entirely by invoking the absolute necessity of all things. . . .

When I hear it said that human merit is so null that all works of men, however pious, are sinful; that our will has no more power than the clay in the hand of the potter; that everything we may do or will derives from an absolute necessity, my spirit is assailed by many scruples. First, how shall we understand all the texts in which we read that the saints, who were full of good works, observed justice, that they walked justly before God, that they turned neither to the right nor to the left,—if all the actions of even the most pious men are sinful, and so

sinful that without the divine mercy he for whom Christ
died would be plunged into hell? Why do we hear so often
of reward, if there is no merit? On what grounds would one
dare to praise the obedience of those who submit to divine
commands, and condemn the disobedience of those who
do not submit? Why does the Scripture so often mention
judgment, if no account is taken of our merits? Or why
are we obliged to present ourselves before the sovereign
Judge if everything is done in us by pure necessity and
nothing according to our free will?

And I repeat again this other thought: What is the
purpose then of all these warnings, precepts, threats, exhortations, and innumerable demands, if we do nothing,
but if God, according to His immutable will, works everything in us, wills it, and accomplishes it. God commands
us to pray without ceasing, to watch, to struggle, and to
contend for the reward of eternal life. Why does He wish
to be prayed to endlessly for that which He has already
decreed to grant or not to grant, since being immutable
He cannot change His decrees? Why does He command us
to seek by so many labours that which He has already
decided to grant us freely? We are afflicted, we are despised, we are mocked, we are put to death; it is thus
that the grace of God contends in us, it is thus that it
vanquishes, that it triumphs. The martyr suffers atrocities,
and yet no merit is imputed to him; still more, it is claimed
that he sins if he exposes his body to punishment in the
hope of heavenly life. But why would God, who is all
merciful, wish to deal thus with the martyrs? Would we
not consider a man cruel who, having decided to give
largess freely to a friend, would give it only after seeing
him tortured to the point of despair?

In my opinion, one could so define free will as to avoid
that abusive confidence in our merits, and the other difficulties which Luther avoids, and also those which I have
noted above, and all without losing those advantages which
Luther praises. This solution seems to me to be manifest
in the doctrine which attributes entirely to grace the first
impulsion which stimulates the soul, but which leaves to
the human will, when it does not lack divine grace, a

certain place in the unfolding of the act. . . . Grace is the principal cause, and the will is the secondary cause, which can do nothing without the principal cause, while this cause suffices in itself alone. . . .

On the other hand, those who deny absolutely the existence of free will, and claim that everything is done by pure necessity, assert that God produces in all men not only good works but also bad. It follows, then, that if man has no claims to be considered the author of his good works, he also cannot be regarded as the author of his bad works. This conclusion, which seems manifestly to attribute injustice and cruelty to God, which is most abhorrent to pious ears (for God would not exist if He had in Him anything vicious or imperfect), finds defenders nonetheless, who uphold this cause which is so little defensible. They say: "Since God is, what He does can only be the best and most beautiful. If you contemplate the order of the universe, even those things which are bad in themselves are good there, and show forth the glory of God. Nor does it pertain to any creature to judge the designs of the Creator, but he should on the contrary submit himself entirely to God; if he sees then that God condemns this one and that one, he should not murmur, but embrace that which is pleasing to God, and at the same time persuade himself that what He does is for the best and could only be for the best." On the other hand, who would support the man who says to God: "Why have you not made me an angel?" Would not God justly answer him: "Shameless one, if I had made you a frog, what would you have to complain about?" Similarly if a frog demanded of God: "Why am I not a peacock with many coloured plumage?"—would He not justly reply to him: "Ingrate, I could have made you a mushroom or an onion, while as it is, you jump, you drink, and you sing." Finally, if a basilisk or a viper would say: "Why have you made me an animal which no one can see and which is poisonous to everyone, instead of a sheep?"—what should God reply? Perhaps simply: "Because I have found it good and in accord with the beauty and harmony of the universe. There is no more injustice in your case than for the flies, mosquitoes, and other insects whose organization seems a great marvel to those who examine it. . . ."

But let us stop reasoning with these people who are deprived of reason, and take up our discussion of man, whom God has created in His image and likeness, whose goodness is the source of all creation. Yet we see that certain men are born with well-made bodies, or suffer from terrible maladies, and still others have minds so stupid that they are indistinguishable from animals, and that certain men surpass even the beasts in beastliness, and that some have souls so naturally inclined to evil that they seemed to be seized by a fatal power, and that others are completely mad and demoniac. How shall we in these circumstances explain the divine justice and mercy? Shall we repeat with Paul: "O the depths, etc."? This would be better, in my opinion, than to judge in bold and wicked fashion those counsels of God which are inscrutable to men. . . .

They most excessively exaggerate original sin, in which they claim that the most splendid powers of human nature have been so corrupted that of themselves they can do nothing but remain ignorant of God and hate Him, and that no one, even if he is justified by faith, can do anything that is not a sin. They claim that this very inclination to sin left in us by the sin of our first parents is already a sin, and that it is so invincible that not even the man justified by faith can fulfill any divine commandments, but that so many precepts of God have no other purpose than to magnify the divine grace which bestows salvation on man without regard to merits. . . . If God has burdened man with so many commandments which have no other purpose than to make him hate God the more and condemn Him more severely, do they not make God more unmerciful than Dionysius, the tyrant of Sicily, who purposely made many laws which he expected most persons would not observe, if no one compelled them, and for a while overlooked offences until he saw that almost everyone had violated his laws, and then he began to punish at his pleasure? Thus he made everyone hate him. . . .

Luther seems to delight in this kind of extravagance so

that he might, as the saying goes, split the evil knot of others' excesses with an evil wedge. The temerity of those who sell not only their merits but also those of all the saints is excessive. And for what kind of works? Incantations, the recitation of psalms, abstinences, fastings, vestments, and titles? But Luther only drove out this nail with another by asserting that there are no merits of the saints at all, and that all the works of pious men are sins leading to eternal damnation, unless faith and God's mercy come to the aid. Again one side makes a profit out of the confessions and reparations by which they have wonderfully ensnared the consciences of men, and also out of Purgatory, concerning which they hold some paradoxical notions. Their opponents correct this vice by claiming that confession is an invention of Satan (the more moderate deny that it should be enforced), and that no satisfaction for sins is necessary, since Christ has paid for the ransom for all our sins, and finally that there is no Purgatory. . . .

It is from the collision of such excesses that the lightnings and thunders arise which today violently shake the world. And if each side continues to defend its exaggerations so bitterly, I foresee such a struggle between them as that between Achilles and Hector, who since they were so equal in savagery could only be separated by death. There is a popular saying that in order to straighten a curved stick it is necessary to bend it to the other side; this is perhaps applicable in the reformation of morals, but I am not sure that it should be applied in the case of doctrine. In exhorting or dissuading men, I can see that there is sometimes a place for exaggeration, as, to give confidence to the timid, you might aptly say: "Never fear, God speaks and does all things in you." And on the other hand, to humble the wicked insolence of man, you might usefully say that man is nothing but sin; and against those who claim to make their teaching equal to the canonical Scriptures, you would doubtless profitably say that man is nothing but a lie.

But when axioms are proposed in the search for truth, I do not think that such paradoxes, which are not far from enigmas, should be used. For my part I prefer moderation.

Pelagius seemed to attribute too much to free will, and Scotus still more, but Luther first mutilated it by cutting off its right arm, then not content with this he throttled free will and destroyed it altogether. For myself, I prefer the doctrine of those who allow something to free will, and at the same time acknowledge the greater share of grace. For it does no good to avoid the Scylla of pride in order to fall into the Charybdis of despair or indifference; or to set a dislocated limb in such a way that you dislocate it on the other side, instead of putting it back in its proper place. . . .

One should then accept this moderate solution: that there may be some good works, although imperfect, but for them man cannot arrogate anything to himself; there will be some merit, but its achievement is owing to God. The life of man is so full of weakness, vice, and sin that if anyone contemplates it he will easily lose his conceit, even if we do not assert that man, however justified, can only be sinful, especially since Christ speaks of a rebirth, and Paul, of the "new man." But why, you say, should anything be allowed to free will? In order to charge with something by way of deserts the wicked who willingly reject the grace of God, in order to spare God the reproaches of cruelty and injustice, to deliver ourselves from despair, so that we may be incited to effort. Such are the reasons which have led almost all men to admit free will, but as inefficacious without the perpetual grace of God, so that we may not arrogate anything to ourselves. But someone may say: "Of what value is free will, if it is not efficacious?" And I answer: "Of what value is man as a whole, if God works in him as does the potter in clay, or as He would in stone?"

Now if this matter has now been sufficiently demonstrated to be such that it is not expedient, so far as piety is concerned, to investigate it more deeply than is necessary, especially among the unlearned; if I have shown that this opinion is based on more numerous and more evident texts of Holy Scripture than the other; if it is plain that Holy Scripture is obscure and figurative in many passages, or even at first glance seems to be in conflict with itself, and that, for this reason, whether we wish to or not, we must depart from it somewhat verbally and literally, and we must modify the sense by interpretation; and if, finally, there are set forth the many inconveniences, I will not say absurdities, which would follow if free will were once entirely taken away; and if it were openly brought about, by the acceptance of this doctrine of which I have spoken, that none of those things would be lost which Luther has discussed piously and in a Christian manner—supreme love of God, the abolition of confidence in our merits, works, and efforts, and the transference of these to God and His promises—I would now ask the reader to weigh this and say whether he would think it just to condemn this judgment of so many doctors of the Church, approved by the consent of so many ages and peoples, and to take in its place certain erroneous opinions which now convulse the Christian world? If these latter opinions are true, I candidly confess the slowness of my wits in not being able to understand them. Certainly I do not knowingly resist the truth, and from my heart I favour the true freedom of the Gospel, and I detest whatever is opposed to the Gospel. I do not here assume the role of a judge, as I have said, but that of one who discusses thoroughly, and yet I can truly affirm that in discussing this matter I have maintained the religious point of view, which was formerly required of judges appointed to consider these capital cases. Although I am an old man, it will not shame or anger me to learn from a young man, if he teaches me more evident doctrines with evangelical gentleness. Here I know that I shall hear: "Let Erasmus learn to know Christ and be strong; let him give up his human wisdom, for no one who does not have the Spirit of God understands these things." If I do not yet understand what Christ is, I have certainly wandered far afield up to now. . . .]

Luther

THAT MOST UNPHILOSOPHICAL OF CHARACTERS, MARTIN Luther (1483-1546) replied with a slashing counterattack, and the breach became irretrievable. Luther's

pamphlet was entitled *De servo arbitrio* (Of Unfree Will).
Doctrinally, it said nothing new, in fact, it simply reaffirmed
the late medieval position; but it drove home the incom-
patibility between that doctrine and classicistic humanism.
If any change can be detected, it must be admitted it had
been rather on the part of the powerful ecclesiastical
sponsors of Erasmus, who were willing to ease Catholic
doctrine somewhat in order to align it with his type of
humanism. Against them, Luther aroused the fighting
younger generation of German humanists, with Philip
Melanchthon at their head.

For although a "barbarian," as he liked to call himself,
Luther was not wholly unaware of the intellectual needs of
the epoch. He might have quoted the words that Erasmus
was said to have spoken years before in his defense: "God
in these last times, in which great and terrible diseases
have prevailed, has given the world also a sharp physician."
Having reasserted, however, with all his intransigence, the
metaphysical servitude of the will, Luther sends the wheel
spinning full circle and comes out passionately for the
"freedom of the Christian man." It is indeed not his
theology, but his conception of freedom that rings new:

[This is a spiritual power, which rules in the midst of
enemies, and is powerful in the midst of distresses. And
this is nothing else than that strength is made perfect in
my weakness, and that I can turn all things to the profit
of my salvation; so that even the cross and death are compelled to serve me. This is a lofty and eminent dignity, a true
and mighty dominion, in which there is nothing so good,
nothing so bad, as not to work together for my good, if
only I believe. . . . Nor are we only kings and the freest
of all men, but also priests for ever, a dignity higher than
kingship. . . . From this any man may clearly see how a
Christian man is free from all things; that he needs no
works in order to be justified and saved, but receives these
gifts in abundance from his faith alone.]

THERE IS IN LUTHER A COLOSSAL SIMPLICITY AND DIRECT-
ness. "I never work better," he used to say, "than when
I am inspired by anger. Those who condemn the movement

of anger against antagonists are theologians who deal in mere speculations." This made him, like Savonarola, into a great tribune, but, unlike the Italian, he was addressing a people ready to explode. He does not waste his time preaching abstinence and moral betterment; he is a political mind: "Our manner of life is as evil as that of the papists. But what I affirm roundly and plainly is that they preach not the truth. To this I am called: I take the goose by the neck, and set the knife in its throat. When I can show that the papists' doctrine is false, then I can easily prove that their manner of life is evil." In most other things, he remains a mind of true medieval naïveté: "I am persuaded," he muses, "that it costs God, yearly, more to maintain only the sparrows, than the revenue of the French king amounts to. . . . Scarcely a small proportion of the earth bears wheat, I verily believe that there grow not as many sheaves of wheat as there are people in the world, and yet we are all fed, yea, there remains a good surplus of wheat at the year's end. This is a wonderful thing." All is still miracle and providence, and all of truth is in the literal word of Scripture. This goes for Calvin too, and it accounts for the medieval level of argumentation in the furious controversy which filled the presses and occupied the minds for the next century and a half.

Yet Protestantism as a force is philosophically modern. The strong words on freedom quoted above show no longer the medieval longing of man to escape the worldly part of his being, and create for himself a new life in renunciation and "imitation of Christ." Gone, too, are the medieval humility and tenderness. The new doctrine involves much rather the full operation of faith inside a toughly accepted worldly activity. As a political mind, Luther is instinctively close to Machiavelli. He, too, intends to do away with the equivocation and insincerity that went with the struggle between spiritual and temporal power. The state is for him "sinful power to curb sin" and its primacy in this world is undisputed: the Reformed pastor becomes its chaplain.

Luther's denial of merit for good work is really a breaking loose from the controlled, institutional direction of life; it is or intends to be an acceptance of the normal free business of man on earth, which comes to be sanctified in that he lives in the light of saving grace. "Every man his own priest." In Melanchthon's doctrine the intellectual liberation from dogmatic structure is perilously visible. Luther himself has told the sorrow and anguish it cost him to tear himself loose from the mystery of the Mass. Religiously he was abandoning the sacramental and symbolic togetherness which makes the City of God, the directed and organized "Christian life." Each man for himself, in the sovereign solitude of his conscience. Philosophically, he was abandoning, almost unawares, the cosmological premises, the structural connection of man with a universe of harmonized Being. This explains why Copernicianism, so roundly condemned in the beginning, became rapidly acceptable in Protestant Germany. But the ontological crisis goes farther and deeper. Man's specific "existence" becomes a "just-being-there" or "standing-out," as it were, which poses a weirdly problematic issue. It is not by chance that modern existentialist philosophy was born on sternly Lutheran ground from the Lutheran soul of Kierkegaard. Aristotelian and Thomistic "being" had been a simple positive good, a cosmic endowment. The new connotations of man's own strange being will gradually emerge, under intensive metaphysical introspection, to imply "cleavage," "anguish," "tending-away-from," "tending-beyond," "being-locked-up-in-oneself," "no exit."

The following passages are from *The Bondage of the Will*.*

{ I openly concede that to you, which I never did to anyone before: that you not only by far surpass me in the powers of eloquence, and in genius (which we all concede to you as your desert, and the more so as I am but a barbarian and do all things barbarously), but that you have damped my spirit and impetus, and rendered me languid before the battle; and that by two means. First, by art: because, that is, you conduct this discussion with a most specious and uniform modesty, by which you have met and

*Henry Cole (trans.). Grand Rapids, Michigan: The Zondervan Publishing House, 1931.

prevented me from being incensed against you. And next, because, on so great a subject, you say nothing but what has been said before. . . .

The "form" of Christianity set forth by you, among other things, has this: "that we should strive with all our powers, have recourse to the remedy of repentance, and in all ways try to gain the mercy of God; without which, neither human will nor endeavor is effectual"; also, "that no one should despair of pardon from a God by nature most merciful."

These statements of yours are without Christ, without the Spirit, and more cold than ice, so that the beauty of your eloquence is really deformed by them. Perhaps a fear of the popes and those tyrants extorted them from you, their miserable vassal, lest you should appear to them a perfect atheist. . . .

Are you not then the person, friend Erasmus, who just now asserted that God is by nature just and by nature most merciful? If this be true, does it not follow that He is *immutably* just and merciful? That as His nature is not changed to all eternity, so neither His justice nor His mercy? And what is said concerning His justice and His mercy must be said also concerning His knowledge, His wisdom, His goodness, His will, and His other attributes. If therefore these things are asserted religiously, piously, and wholesomely concerning God, as you say yourself, what has come to you that, contrary to your own self, you now assert that it is irreligious, curious, and vain to say that God foreknows of necessity? You openly declare that the immutable *will* of God is to be known, but you forbid the knowledge of His immutable *prescience*. Do you believe that He foreknows against His will or that He wills in ignorance? If, then, He foreknows, willing, His will is eternal and immovable, because His nature is so; and, if He wills, foreknowing, His knowledge is eternal and immovable, because His nature is so. . . .

How copious an orator! And yet you understand nothing of what you are saying. . . .

For, by the grace of God, I am not so great a fool or madman as to have desired to sustain and defend this cause

so long, with so much fortitude and so much firmness
(which you call obstinacy), in the face of so many
dangers of my life, so much hatred, so many traps
laid for me; in a word, in the face of the fury of men
and devils—I have not done this for money, for that I
neither have nor desire; nor for vainglory, for that, if I
wished, I could not obtain in a world so enraged against
me; nor for the life of my body, for that cannot be made
sure of for an hour. Do you think, then, that you only have
a heart that is moved by these tumults? Yet I am not made
of stone, nor was I born from the Marpessian rocks. But
since it cannot be otherwise, I choose rather to be battered
in temporal tumult, happy in the grace of God, for God's
Word's sake, which is to be maintained with a mind in-
corrupt and invincible, than to be ground to powder in
eternal tumult, under the wrath of God and torments intolerable! . . .

"Who," you say, "will endeavour to amend his life?" I
answer, "No man! No man can!" For your self-amenders
without the Spirit, God regardeth not, for they are hypo-
crites. But the Elect, and those that fear God, will be
amended by the Holy Spirit; the rest will perish un-
amended. Nor does Augustine say that the works of *none,*
nor that the works of *all,* are crowned, but the works of
some. Therefore there will be *some* who shall amend their
lives.

"Who will believe," you say, "that he is loved of God?"
I answer, "No man will believe it! No man can!" But the
Elect shall believe it; the rest shall perish without believing
it, filled with indignation and blaspheming, as you here
describe them. Therefore there will be *some* who shall
believe it. . . .

God has promised certainly His grace to the humbled:
that is, to the self-deploring and despairing. But a man
cannot be thoroughly humbled until he comes to know
that his salvation is utterly beyond his own powers, counsel,
endeavours, will, and works, and absolutely depending on
the will, counsel, pleasure, and work of another, that is,
of God only. For if, as long as he has any persuasion that
he can do even the least thing himself towards his own

salvation, he retain a confidence in himself and do not utterly despair in himself, so long he is not humbled before God; but he proposes to himself some place, some time, or some work, whereby he may at length attain unto salvation. But he who hesitates not to depend wholly upon the good will of God, he totally despairs in himself, chooses nothing for himself, but waits for God to work in him; and such a one is the nearest unto grace. . . .

This is the highest degree of faith—to believe that He is merciful, who saves so few and damns so many; to believe Him just, who according to His own will makes us necessarily damnable, that He may seem, as Erasmus says, "to delight in the torments of the miserable, and to be an object of hatred rather than of love." If, therefore, I could by any means comprehend how that same God can be merciful and just who carries the appearance of so much wrath and iniquity, there would be no need of faith. But now, since that cannot be comprehended, there is room for exercising faith, while such things are preached and openly proclaimed: in the same manner as, while God kills, the faith of life is exercised in death.]

CHAPTER VII

Michelangelo

WHAT WE SAID ABOUT THE POETIC ELEMENT, THAT IS, thought searching for a truer definition through the image, may be shown by way of the poetry of Michelangelo Buonarroti (1475-1564). Michelangelo's imagination is essentially plastic rather than verbal, but his few sonnets (to which he used to refer disdainfully), such as they stand, tight, rugged, contrary and flinty at times like the stone of which they speak, may reveal more of their author's nature than Shakespeare's do. Their occasional obscurity is not an involvement in conceits. It comes from the fundamental ambiguity that was Michelangelo's experience of the creative effort. Strange it is that the man who was renowned for bringing forth "the most incredibly difficult pieces with the easiest of ease" should have been the one to express dramatically the struggle of the mind with the matter that it molds; stranger still that, notwithstanding the reassurance, the understanding, the admiration, nay adulation, that he received from pontiff after worldly pontiff, he should never have tried to reconcile his Christian feelings with his humanistic philosophy as Ficino and Erasmus and so many others had done, and should have lived forever in religious dread of his own irresistibly pagan and dramatically overreaching creativeness.

That he was a Platonist with the Platonic conception of beauty as leading to the Good, the first of these sonnets will show. It is the song of his moments of joy. The second sonnet is that of Michelangelo's suffering and despair, coming, as he feels, from the essential ambiguity of reality. What faces him is at once life-giving and life-destroying, carrying within itself the powers of both Mercy and Death. It is to the inspiration coming to him from his lady that he transfers the image of the unhewn stone on which his artistry fails; but the idea comes full circle to cast doubt on the meaning of his whole work; the dragon is biting its own tail. Platonic dualism has yielded here to a deeper dialectical insight.

The poem is a philosophically considered statement. The first quatrain, oft-cited, expresses Michelangelo's idea of creation. Literally translated, it says this: "The excellent artist has no conception that a single marble does not circumscribe in itself with its excess; it is attained only by the hand which obeys the intellect." Leonardo's fragment, discussed previously in Chapter III, "be content to know the end of such things as your own mind designs." With Michelangelo the statement is more extreme: art seems to take over the abstract intellectual function; and in fact he said once: "I sometimes set myself thinking and imagining that I find amongst men but one single art or science, and that is drawing, all others proceeding therefrom." There are here none of the overtones of the physicist. The "concept" is the accomplished form—an end in itself. Michelangelo has explained it further. "Sculpture," he used to say, "is achieved by way of removing. What is done by way of adding belongs to painting." For him, modeling a figure out of clay is not true sculpture, because it starts, as it were, from nothing. The real relationship of the sculptor to his matter starts from the massive unhewn block out of which the intellect's conception has to be "extracted" by sheer force of chisel. We are far from Platonism here. In another simile, related by Vasari, he thinks of the figure as still invisible, and emerging out of the still surface of the deep under the sculptor's hammer. This is indeed what even the Sistine frescoes convey. One cannot help being reminded of a much later description of the scientist's labor, hammering out truth "in the teeth of irreducible stubborn facts." It is not by chance that Galileo will repeat Michelangelo's definition of sculpture in rehearsing the highest achievements of man.

We can see thus how Michelangelo's Platonism and "metaphysics of light" are only part of his thought: they are an echo of the *amour courtois* and a holdover from a happier era. Leonardo is still of that era, although only by a few years his senior. There is no greater contrast than in the life and style of these two men so close to each other in their culture and in their birth from the same Tuscan countryside. Leonardo's trust in impartial cosmic harmony and mathematical rightness, in divine proportion and intellectual contemplation, appears now as archaic as the calm, almost pre-Socratic impersonality of his writing, in contrast with Michelangelo's tormented fire and his universe dark to the soul, except, as he repeats desperately, for Grace. Michelangelo's anguish at facing divine judgment with his own irreducible nature would sound, if stripped of the conventional pious language, even closer to Calvinism than it does.

> Now hath my life across a stormy sea
> > Like a frail bark reached that wide port where all
> > Are bidden, ere the final reckoning fall
> > Of good and evil for eternity.
> Now know I well how that fond phantasy
> > Which made my soul the worshipper and thrall
> > Of earthly art, is vain . . . *

He had never forgotten Savonarola "and kept always in mind the memory of his living voice," but his thought he had transposed out of its medieval setting and medieval hopes into a new irreversible loneliness.

Pico della Mirandola, the young genius who had sought universal concordance in the deeper doctrine of all civilizations, had come, a generation earlier, to feel the perils and paradoxes of his adventure. Not out of any failure of nerve, for he stood up for his famous unorthodox "900 theses" with considerable courage, but out of a sudden change of heart, he embraced Savonarola's somber revivalism and was planning to go forth as an itinerant preacher of the Gospel when death cut him short. Yet, if he had been overreaching or "hyperbolic," it was in a naïve, generous and

* Michelangelo, *Sonnets,* trans. J. A. Symonds. New York: Irving Ravin, 1950; London: Vision Press Ltd., 1951.

utterly confident way. Michelangelo's attempt at "going beyond" is in a way more self-conscious, and also irretrievable, since there is no clear-cut intellectual orthodoxy for him to go back to, and he himself is forging his metaphysics through his work as it goes on to the end. His former Platonism obscured, he has also severed the tie with non-human nature and the multiple world of sensuous perception which had inspired Aristotle as well as Titian. There is a revealing remark in his conversations with Francisco d'Ollandia:

"A painting made up of draperies and little houses, of rural verdure, shadows of trees, bridges and brooks, what they call a landscape, with certain little figures here and there . . . will appeal much to women, especially to those who are very old or very young, as well as to some gentlemen who are devoid of the musical sense of true harmony . . . but in reality it is all without reason and without art or discernment, or design, in a word without substance and without strength. As for true painting, it is a music and a melody that the intellect alone can perceive, and not without difficulty."

It is impossible not to see here the artistic intellect moving towards higher abstraction in its own sphere. It was to drive Michelangelo gradually from sculptural into gigantic architectural design. It is in its way a kind of permanent warfare with reality in a direction which tends to go above human dimensions. In Michelangelo as in Marlowe, the Renaissance has become conscious of its tragedy. After him, art will go on to the irresponsible exaggerations of mannerism, until it finds a new creative level in the Baroque.

In thinking of Leonardo, one instinctively places him against a landscape in daylight, forever observing. Even his *Last Supper* is thus open to nature. Of Michelangelo, the image that remains in mind is that of his somber old age in a closed and dusty room, with "death graven in each and every one of his thoughts." He worked nights, says Condivi, with the help of a candle that he had fitted into a helmetlike cap. The slivers of stone flew from under his chisel "with such violence that it looked as if the whole work were going to be shattered." Thus we see him close to his eightieth year, still hammering away in the dim shifting and flickering light at his last *Deposition from the Cross*. The gathered mourners bend over the dead Christ, and Joseph of Arimathea, a hooded old figure which stands by "stricken with dread," is slowly taking on the features of the artist himself. This is truly the aftermath of the *Last Supper*. The universe has lost its light.

There might be found a certain strange irony in a judgment uttered once by Pope Julius II. Michelangelo had defied him and gone home to Florence over an imagined slight. For a long time he would not budge, notwithstanding the pope's imperious briefs and his ultimatums to the Florentine Chancellery to deliver up the truant under threat of war. He was even talking of offering his services to the Grand Turk. Then at last he regained his composure, went back and apologized. "The Pope kept his head lowered, saying nothing, and looked exceeding troubled. Then Cardinal Soderini, trying to intercede for Michelangelo, broke in, saying: 'Please it your Holiness not to consider his fault, for he has erred through ignorance. These painters in things outside their art are all like this.' Then the Pope retorted in sudden anger: 'You are insulting him, not We. It is you who are a wretch and don't know what you are talking about, not he. Take yourself out of here to the devil." And as he did not move fast enough, recounted Michelangelo later, the cardinal was thrown out bodily by the pope's guard.

Poetic translations ought never to be attempted. Poetry is indissolubly tied to its own language. Yet, since distinguished writers have tried their hand again and again at Michelangelo's sonnets, it seems unfair to disregard their achievements. We have chosen here some versions which seem to come closest to the original, and we have ventured also to introduce some changes in order to restore the author's meaning. The changes have been put between square brackets.

La forza d'un bel volto al ciel mi sprona

The pow'r of one fair face spurs me to heaven—
    For such delight the world can nowhere show—
    And I rise, living, and with angels go,
    A gift to man still mortal rarely given.
So with its maker does the work accord
    That my conceptions high become divine
    And they inspire each thought and word of mine
    While burning in the love such beings afford.

If then from those two eyes I cannot turn
    My own regard, I find in them the light
    Which shows the way to God that I employ,
And if, in kindling at their fire I burn,
    In my proud flame there gloweth sweet and bright
    The heavens' laughter of eternal joy.

                    Translated by W. C. GREENE *

II

Non ha l'ottimo artista alcun concetto

No concept that the artist apprehends
    But marble in itself will circumscribe
    With its excess; and thereto may arrive
    Alone the hand that intellect attends.
The evil that I flee, what good portends
    In you, fair lady, proud and heavenly,
    Are likewise hid; but bringing death to me
    My art goes counter to its wished-for ends.
Love bears not then—nor does your beauty's grace
    Your great disdain nor your severity—
    Blame for my pain, nor chance nor fortune's breath,
If in your heart both death and pity's place
    At one I find and my poor talent free,
    In burning, from that marble only death.

                    Translated by W. C. GREENE

* As we had to discard Wordsworth's version as painfully ornate
and bowdlerized, we had recourse to the courtesy of Prof.
William C. Greene of M.I.T., and he gave us the above, as well
as the next version, which are remarkably faithful to the original.

Sì amico al freddo sasso è il fuoco acerbo *

So friendly is the fire to flinty stone,
>   That, struck therefrom and kindled to a blaze,
>   It burns the stone, and from the ash doth raise,
>   What lives thenceforward binding stones in one;
Kiln-hardened this resists both frost and sun,
>   Acquiring higher worth for endless days—
>   As the purged soul from hell returns with praise,
>   Amid the heavenly host to take her throne.
E'en so the fire struck from my soul, that lay
>   Close-hidden in my heart, may temper me,
>   Till burned and slaked to better life I rise.
If made mere smoke and dust I live today,
>   Fire-hardened I shall live eternally;
>   Such gold, not iron, my spirit strikes and tries.

Carico d'anni e di peccati pieno

Burdened with years and full of sinfulness,
>   With evil custom grown inveterate,
>   Both deaths I dread that close before me wait,
>   Yet feed my heart on poisonous thoughts no less.
No strength I find in mine own feebleness
>   To change or life or love or use or fate,
>   Unless thy heavenly guidance come, though late,
>   Which only helps and stays our nothingness.
'Tis not enough, dear Lord, to make me yearn
>   [For heaven, if you need to have my soul
>   Made out again, as erst it was, of nought]
Nay, ere though strip her mortal vestment, turn
>   My steps toward the steep ascent, that whole
>   And pure before thy face she may be brought.

* This and the following sonnet are from Michelangelo, *op. cit.*

CHAPTER VIII

Copernicus

NIKLAS KOPPERNIGK (1473-1543) WAS A GERMAN ECCLE-
siastic from the Polish border regions. He studied first in
Cracow, then at length in Italy, and came home, much like
Cusanus, if almost a century later, an international mind
and an Italianate humanist. It is he, as everyone knows,
who worked out the idea that the sun, and not the Earth, is
at the center of the celestial orbs. Being a modest man and
a classicist, he did not try to present himself as the origi-
nator of the theory, but insisted that the idea of a motion
of the Earth had already been advanced by certain Pythagoreans in the fifth century B.C., as indeed it had; but this
in no way detracts from the greatness of his achievement.
It took extraordinary intellectual audacity for a man to
free himself thus from the whole philosophical conditioning
of his education and go against what seemed to be the very
foundations of the world order; the more so as the prevail-
ing theories were based not only on what appeared to be
common sense, but also on much careful observation and
reasonable inference. Galileo, who was a good judge, wrote
later: "Those experiences which overtly contradict the annual motion of the Earth have so much more of the appearance of convincingness, that I cannot find any bounds for
my admiration how reason was able in Aristarchus and
Copernicus to commit such a rape upon their senses as, in
despite thereof, to make herself mistress of their belief."

Galileo is right in coupling thus the two names, for they
stand across the gulf of twenty centuries for the same type
of mathematical rationalism which will not be unduly
impressed by sensible reality but will strive rather to
submit it to its canons. Copernicus was a scientist in that

he undertook the great labor of careful repetitive computation which made his system technically plausible, but he would never have carried it through if he had not been quasi-mystically convinced as a philosopher that this was the right scheme according to the aesthetic criteria of geometry. The "lamp of the universe" could be nowhere except in the center. Nor was he concerned with the physical difficulties to which he had no satisfactory answer. Now that we have a heavy body like the Earth (and not only the stars, shapes of some spiritual quintessential fire) placed in heaven, what force will keep it moving and following exactly its orbit? Nothing, said Copernicus; perfect spheres and circles have a virtue of rotating by themselves. This was truly, as Galileo had to admit, the insouciance of genius. It was his absolute Pythagorean faith which made Copernicus insist that what he presented was not merely an abstract model such as mathematics was supposed to provide, but a true physical system.

We shall see (p. 188) the cold skepticism that the enlightened mind of Montaigne opposes to such ideas. But even in the seventeenth century, after Galileo's telescopic discoveries had brought weighty confirmation, men like Francis Bacon refused to be budged. "I shall not stand upon that piece of mathematical elegance," writes the Lord Chancellor, "the reduction of motion to perfect circles." Hence why replace one set of them with another? A teacher of the more modern empirical approach, he does not see the need for such subversive imaginings. Both the old and the new system, he remarks, "are equally and indifferently supported by the phenomena." He himself prefers to retain the idea of the Earth as stationary "for that I now think the truer opinion."

To most of the educated people of his own time, Copernicus's ideas made no sense at all. The man himself was respected as a distinguished astronomer, and a consultant on the Gregorian calendar reform; but his theory not only looked irresponsible, it looked almost naïvely reactionary, a return to "primitive" Pythagorean conceptions, and to a curious kind of sun worship. Also, it was said, he seemed to have forgotten in his geometrical infatuation that mathematics provided abstract schemes of computation, but could lay no claim to explaining physical reality. That could be accounted for only starting from "the good" of each thing combining towards the good of the all, and mathematics simply does not deal with the good.

The attitude of ruling orthodoxies does not change through time. Today, Copernicus would have been described very similarly by the new orthodoxy of the East as a "formalist-idealist-reactionary"—which is indeed the official reproof handed down against moderns like Eddington who are akin to Copernicus in spirit. Luther went farther; he called Copernicus "an ass who wants to pervert the whole art of astronomy and deny what is said in the book of Joshua, only make a show of ingenuity and attract attention."

Copernicus himself was fully aware of the audacity of his suggestion and of its revolutionary consequences, to the point that he would not bring himself to state the most serious one: if the world machine as a whole does not revolve in twenty-four hours, why then there is no reason for imagining the fixed stars as placed on a sphere, driven in its turn by an outer "prime mover" sphere. It might very well be unlimited space itself that we are looking up to, with stars distributed in it at such enormous distances that they might be really suns like ours. This was a fearsome idea. "I must leave it," says Copernicus, "to the philosophers to decide." But as things stand, philosophy is fast running out of decisions. Science has decided for her invisibly.

It was indeed only twenty years after writing his book that Copernicus yielded to the entreaties of his friends and superiors, and gave it to the press. But in his dedicatory letter to Pope Paul III, he spelled out the reasons which made science, in his opinion, a reserved activity, to be carried on only in a restricted circle. It is not so much, he intimates, the fear of being derided by the vulgar, or criticized by the intellectual "lower middlebrow" which has invaded the universities, or even attacked by theologians, which restrains him. No, his contention is that science is intrinsically a delicate and dangerous activity, to be reserved to those fully prepared for it. Thus he comes out in the end quite candidly for a revival of the Pythagorean school secret.

The original manuscript shows that he came back to the subject in the conclusion of the First Book, to state his position unequivocally. Philolaus and the other Pythagoreans, he remarked, had never entrusted their ideas to writing, and we happen to know of them only through later references. To justify and confirm this attitude, Copernicus translated this time in full the text he had only mentioned in the Preface, viz., the reproachful letter of Lysis, one of the early disciples of Pythagoras, to "Hipparchos" (i.e., Hippasos) who had first dared to publish the mathematical discoveries. The letter is, of course, apocryphal, but philological criticism was as yet in its infancy, and Bessarion himself had considered it genuine. It was felt to be part of "perennial philosophy" even to its symbolism, which is a prelude to Dante's Dark Forest. (See p. 165.)

Many years later, Rheticus having already broadcast the new theory, Copernicus was moved, as we saw, by the entreaties of his superiors to publish his book. At this point, however, as he entrusted his ideas to the new and revolutionary medium of print, he felt it would be slightly absurd to insist on his stand for privacy, and he accordingly struck out this section. But we can still read it in the facsimile edition, as the evidence of a dramatic conflict in his mind, and of his firm original intention to have the text only privately circulated.

The following selections from *On the Revolutions of the Heavenly Spheres* are from C. G. Wallis's translation.*

[PREFACE AND DEDICATION TO POPE PAUL III

I can foresee easily enough, Most Holy Father, that as soon as certain people learn that in these books of mine which I have written about the revolutions of the spheres

* In *Great Books of the Western World,* Vol. 16. Chicago: The Encyclopaedia Britannica, 1952. Copyright, 1939, by Encyclopaedia Britannica, Inc.

of the world, I attribute certain motions to the terrestrial globe, they will immediately shout to have me and my opinion hooted off the stage. For my own works do not please me so much that I do not weigh what judgments others will pronounce concerning them. And although I realize that the conceptions of a philosopher are placed beyond the judgment of the crowd, because it is his loving duty to seek the truth in all things, in so far as God has granted that to human reason; nevertheless I think we should avoid opinions utterly foreign to common sense. And when I considered how absurd my suggested theory would be held by those who know that the opinion that the Earth rests immovable in the middle of the heavens had been confirmed by the judgments of many ages—if I were to assert to the contrary that the Earth moves; for a long time I was in great difficulty as to whether I should bring to light my commentaries written to demonstrate the Earth's movement, or whether it would not be better to follow the example of the Pythagoreans and certain others who used to hand down the mysteries of their philosophy not in writing but by word of mouth and only to their relatives and friends—witness the letter of Lysis to Hipparchus. They seem to me to have done that not, as some judge, out of a jealous unwillingness to communicate their doctrines but in order that things of very great beauty which have been investigated by the loving care of great men should not be scorned by those who do not care to spend much study on letters—except on the money-making variety—or who are provoked by the exhortations and examples of others to the liberal study of philosophy but on account of the dullness of their minds hold the position among philosophers that drones hold among bees. Therefore, when I weighed these things in my mind, the scorn which I had to fear on account of the newness and absurdity of my opinion almost drove me to abandon a work already undertaken.

But my friends made me change my course in spite of my long-continued hesitation and even resistance. First among them was Nicholas Schönberg, Cardinal of Capua, a man distinguished in all branches of learning; next to him was my devoted friend Tiedemann Giese, Bishop of Culm, a man filled with zeal for the divine and liberal arts: for he in particular urged me frequently and even spurred me on by added reproaches into publishing this book and letting come to light a work which I had kept hidden among my things for not merely nine years, but for almost four times nine years. Not a few other learned and distinguished men demanded the same thing of me, urging me to refuse no longer—on account of the fear which I felt—to contribute my work to the common utility of those who are really interested in mathematics: they said that the absurder my teaching about the movement of the Earth now may seem, the more wonder and thanksgiving will it be the object of, when after the publication of my commentaries those same persons see the fog of absurdity dissipated by my luminous demonstrations. Accordingly I was led by such persuasion and by that hope finally to permit my friends to undertake the publication of a work which they had long sought from me.

But perhaps Your Holiness will not be so much surprised at my publishing the results of my nights of study, in which I did not hesitate to put in writing my conceptions as to the movement of the Earth—as you will desire to hear from me what came into my mind that in opposition to the general opinion of mathematicians and almost in opposition to common sense I should dare to imagine some movement of the Earth. And so I am unwilling to hide from Your Holiness that nothing except my knowledge that mathematicians have not agreed with one another in their researches moved me to think out a different scheme of drawing up the movements of the spheres of the world. . . . . For some make use of homocentric circles only, others of eccentric circles and epicycles, by means of which, however, they do not fully attain what they seek and have in the meanwhile admitted a great deal which seems to contradict the first principles of regularity of movement. Moreover, they have not been able to discover or to infer the chief point of all, i.e., the form of the world and the certain commensurability of its parts. But they are in exactly the same predicament as someone taking from different places hands, feet, head, and the other limbs—shaped very beautifully but not with reference to one body and without correspondence to one another—so that such parts made up a monster rather than a man. And so, in the process of demonstration which they call "method," they are found either to have omitted something necessary or to have admitted something foreign which by no means pertains to the matter; and they would by no means have been in this predicament, if they had followed sound principles. For if the hypotheses they assumed were not false, everything which followed from the hypotheses would have been verified without fail; and though what I am saying may be obscure at this point, nevertheless it will become clearer in the proper place.

Accordingly, when I had meditated upon this lack of certitude in the traditional mathematics concerning the composition of movements of the spheres of the world, I found it disturbing that the philosophers, who in other respects had scrutinized the world in detail, had discovered no sure scheme for the movements of the machinery of the world, which has been built for us by the Best and Most Orderly Workman of all. Wherefore I undertook to reread all the books by philosophers which I could get hold of, to see if any of them even supposed that the movements of the spheres of the world were different from those laid down by those who taught mathematics in the schools. And as a matter of fact, I found first in Cicero that Nicetas {i.e., Hiketas the Pythagorean} thought that the Earth moved. And afterwards I found in Plutarch that there were some others of the same opinion: I shall quote his words here, so that they may be known to all:

"Some think that the Earth is at rest; but Philolaus the Pythagorean says that it moves around the central fire with an obliquely circular motion, like the sun and moon. Herakleides of Pontus and Ekphantus the Pythagorean do not give the Earth any movement of locomotion, but rather a limited movement of rising and setting around its center, like a wheel."

Therefore I also, having found occasion, began to meditate upon the mobility of the Earth. And although the

opinion seemed absurd, nevertheless because I knew that
others before me had been granted the liberty of construct-
ing whatever circles they pleased in order to demonstrate
astral phenomena, I thought it legitimate to test whether
or not, by the laying down that the Earth had some movement, demonstrations less shaky than those of my predecessors could be found for the revolutions of celestial
spheres.

And so, having laid down the movements which I
attribute to the Earth, I finally discovered by the help of
long and numerous observations that if the movements of
the other wandering stars are correlated with the circular
movement of the Earth, and if the movements are com-
puted in accordance with the revolution of each planet,
not only do all their phenomena follow from that but also
this correlation binds together so closely the order and
magnitudes of all the planets and of their spheres or orbital
circles and the heavens themselves that nothing can be
shifted around in any part of them without disrupting the
remaining parts and the universe as a whole.

I have no doubt that talented and learned mathematicians will agree with me, if—as philosophy requires—
they are willing to give not superficial but profound thought
and effort to what I bring forward in this work in demon-
strating these things. And in order that the unlearned as
well as the learned might see that I was not seeking to flee
from the judgment of any man, I preferred to dedicate
these results of my nights of study to Your Holiness rather
than to anyone else; because, even in this remote corner of
the earth where I live, you are held to be most eminent
both in the dignity of your order and in your love of letters
and even of mathematics; hence, by the authority of your
judgment you can easily provide a guard against the bites
of slanderers, despite the proverb that there is no medicine for the bite of a sycophant.

But if perchance there are certain idle talkers who take
it upon themselves to pronounce judgment, although wholly
ignorant of mathematics, and if by shamelessly distorting
the sense of some passage in Holy Writ to suit their purpose, they dare to reprehend and to attack my work; they

worry me so little that I shall even scorn their judgments as foolhardy. For it is not unknown that Lactantius, otherwise a distinguished ecclesiastical writer but hardly a mathematician, speaks in an utterly childish fashion concerning the shape of the Earth, when he derides those who have affirmed that the Earth has the form of a globe. And so the studious need not be surprised if such people deride us. Mathematics is written for mathematicians; and among them, if I am not mistaken, my labours will be seen to contribute something to the ecclesiastical commonwealth, the principate of which Your Holiness now holds. For not many years ago under Leo X when the Lateran Council was considering the question of reforming the Ecclesiastical Calendar, no decision was reached, for the sole reason that the year and the months and the movements of the sun and moon had not yet been measured with sufficient accuracy. From that time on I gave attention to making more exact observations of these things and was encouraged to do so by that most distinguished man, Paul, Bishop of Fossombrone, who had been present at those deliberations. . . .

WE ADD HERE A (SLIGHTLY CONDENSED AND PARAPHRASED) version of the "Letter of Lysis to Hipparchos" as Copernicus translated it into Latin for a conclusion to the First Book of *De Revolutionibus*. It seems to express his genuine feelings about science.

[After Pythagoras departed from us I would never have believed that his group of disciples would come asunder. But since we are now shipwrecked, as it were, and dispersed in many parts, it would be well for you to remember his divine precepts, and not to communicate the gifts of philosophy to those who have never even dreamt of a purification of the soul. Think of what a long time it took us disciples to become spiritually prepared: after five years, we were still judged barely able to receive the teachings of the Master. As dyers prepare the material with certain astringents, so that it imbibes the color indelibly, thus that divine man prepared his disciples to philosophy.

For he was not a teacher of mercenary doctrine, but he taught human and divine truth. As to those who try to impart those doctrines in the wrong order and without preparation, they are like people who should pour pure water into a muddy cistern; they can only stir up the mud and lose the water. For a deep and dense tangle [of passions and prejudices] obscures the minds of such as were not rightly initiated, and it stands in the way of gentleness and reason entering the soul. Incontinence and avarice hold the first place, and learning can only help them spawn a prodigious number of evils, not only in the form of lust and wrong pleasures, but also in contempt of the city's laws and love of tyranny. Such and more evils are to be found in the recesses of that forest, that have to be destroyed with steel and fire before reason can sow her seed. These things, my friend, you learned from the Master; yet, carried away by your taste for Sicilian luxuries, you have taken to teaching philosophy in public, what Pythagoras had ordered you never to do. . . .]

CHAPTER IX

Montaigne

MICHEL EYQUEM, SEIGNEUR DE MONTAIGNE IN GASCONY (1533-1592) came of a family which had grown rich in business in the course of the preceding century. He frequented the court of the Valois kings, was a councillor in the Bordeaux parliament and later mayor of Bordeaux. He acquitted himself with distinction on several delicate assignments in that troubled period of the wars of religion which was to end with the accession of Henry IV, whom he greatly favored. At the age of thirty-eight, he elected to retire to a studious leisure in his castle of Montaigne. The notes that he took in the course of his readings became gradually the *Essays,* a classic of French literature. They are really a way of musing, as it were, aloud and in a style rather spoken than written, about everything under the sun. "What a wonderful neighbor to have," Madame de Lafayette remarked wistfully two centuries later. Montaigne is still everybody's good neighbor.

Intellectually, Montaigne is the man of the world who appraises critically all that the culture and history accessible to a man of his time may have brought of solid acquisition, and then tests these results on his own life experience. His conclusion is that they are very uncertain, except as woven into the substance of life itself. On theory he is a skeptic. He lists the contradicting opinions of the ancient philosophers, "who knew so much more than we ever may," as well as of their modern followers, very much in the spirit of the early Christian apologists, to show that they lead nowhere. But he is not led thereby to seek again the only certainty in revealed Truth. That he takes for granted, as a dutiful believer, but it seems not to concern him overmuch. The sole knowledge that he finds to be both relevant and indubitable is knowledge of himself. Hence a singularly defiant reasoning in such a skeptic, hence confidence and assurance once he is on his own ground, the ground of himself: "To be sincerely true is the beginning of a great virtue."

He is the ancestor of a very modern intellectual trend; but his ways and instincts are rooted in the times of feudal simplicity, independence and self-reliance. A gentleman living on his land, he wrote, provided he conformed to the customs of his equals, "need hardly be aware of the existence of the king." Such perfect freedom and self-assurance allowed him to forge one of the most accomplished instruments of good sense the world has ever known, and to apply it unerringly to his own experience. "This, dear reader," he announces in his preface, "is a book about myself." And it is, to a degree utterly unprecedented. He is all there, carefully self-scrutinized: his own tastes, foibles, passions, conflicts, quirks and limits; even what we would call his own conditioning, with the quiet assurance that in the end it will all cohere into the portrait of a real man and not of an idealized personage—a man no more consistent than need be, but completely at ease in this uncertain, contradictory and fragmentary world of ours.

"Others," he says, "fashion man, I repeat him." He is quite aware of the novelty of this departure. He is not interested in what he *ought* to be, or to think, or to feel; he will not allow any theoretical or dogmatic certainty, however august, to define him or guide him from the outside; for he knows himself to be undefinable: "I have seen no such monster, or more express wonder in this world, than myself." And he means, himself as the *normal* man, for "every man bears the whole stamp of human condition (*l'humaine condition*)." All the more will he be skeptical about knowledge and its foundations: "All universal judgments are treacherous and dangerous." He will not even stay within the limits of his own wisdom, which he largely identifies with a sensible conformism, but sees himself as thriving on contradictions, a swaying, moving, undulating form, at once yielding and resistant, shaping itself on the arts and institutions yet wrestling with them, even as he steers wide of the force of his own passions which are contrary unto him.

With a mind as inexhaustibly curious as it is unconventional and compassionate, Montaigne remains nonetheless a careful conservative; hardly a Christian, he likes to consider himself a good Catholic and dislikes the Protestants as subversive: "The ancientest evil, if it be known to us, bears always lighter upon us than a new one of which we know but little." He is representative of the best judgment of his own times in seeing in the quest for knowledge an appealing quality, no doubt, but mostly a disordered enthusiasm. Even the new discoveries on earth and in the skies lead him to wonder whether they will only increase the confusion. The Copernican system he discusses as one more mathematical fad which shows how little we may really know about the skies. We realize through him what a miserable forecaster good judgment can be. His evaluations of theoretical possibilities are wrong almost at every turn. Montaigne has no vision of the future. He may have been spared some gloomy moments thereby.

His motto was "Que sçais-je?" (What do I know?) But the critics sometimes forget that it was shown engraved on a balance. Actually, Montaigne was quite sure of a number of things: of his good judgment first of all, which was the balance itself on which he weighed all things; of the need for fairness and tolerance; of the value of friendship, which caused his tie with Etienne de la Boëtie to become the central fact of his life; of his passionate admiration for greatness under any form, which he worshipped in the exemplary ancients but knew how to recognize in his own world, and more frequently among the lower orders than among the rulers; and, lastly, of his own conception of happiness, which would have been inconceivable to a man of the Age of Belief: "It is an absolute perfection, and as it were divine for a man to know how to enjoy his own being loyally." Four centuries before Wittgenstein, and in his own casual way, he does provide an early cure for metaphysical puzzlement and perplexity.

His language is a faithful mirror of his being, as it flows

unaffectedly from the old French source, with its inex-
haustible richness of words and homely turns, much akin
to that of the Elizabethans. He is the last classic, in fact,
to write that French, for it was soon to undergo a fearful
cutting and paring at the hands of the writers of Louis
XIV, to emerge as the elegant but scant and linear precision instrument we know today.

Montaigne's skepticism is the high point of troubled
French Renaissance thought; it tends inevitably to degen-
erate into harsher and cruder forms, as in his successor
Charron. But within four years of the death of Montaigne,
Descartes was born, and with him French philosophy was
going to grapple decisively with doubt, first driving it as
far as conceivable in its "hyperbolic form" in order to build
up a new certainty on an unassailable basis. Yet intelligent
doubt is not easy to allay. Pascal was again to confront
Montaigne, in fact his whole thinking has been called "a
dialogue with Montaigne," a dialogue which reached the
deepest depths just because Montaigne had become part of
his being.

The passages that we give here are mainly from Montaigne's *Essays,* Chapter XII, Book II, the "Apology of
Raymond of Sebonde."

[Learning is a great ornament, and an instrument of marvelous service; such as despise it merely discover their
own folly: but yet I do not prize it at the excessive rate
some others do; as Herillus the philosopher for one, who
therein places the sovereign good, and maintained that it
was merely in her to render us wise and contented, which
I do not believe; no more than I do what others have
said, that learning is the mother of all virtue, and that all
vice proceeds from ignorance. If this be true, it is subject to
a very long interpretation. My house has long been open
to men of knowledge and is very well known to them; for
my father, who governed it fifty years and more, inflamed
with the new ardour with which Francis I embraced letters
and brought them into esteem, with great diligence and
expense hunted after the acquaintance of learned men,
receiving them at his house as persons sacred, and who

had some particular inspiration of divine wisdom; collecting their sayings and sentences as so many oracles, and with so much the greater reverence and religion, as he was the less able to judge; for he had no knowledge of letters, no more than his predecessors. For my part I love them well, but I do not worship them.

*   *   *   *   *   *   *   *   *

Every one, as Pliny says, is a good doctrine to himself, provided he be capable of discovering himself near at hand. Here, this is not my doctrine, 'tis my study; and is not the lesson of another, but my own; and if I communicate it, it ought not to be ill taken, for that which is of use to me, may also, peradventure, be useful to another. As to the rest, I spoil nothing, I make use of nothing but my own. . . . We hear but of two or three of the ancients, who have beaten this road, and yet I cannot say if it was after this manner, knowing no more of them but their names. No one since has followed the track: 'tis a rugged road, more so than it seems, to follow a pace so rambling and uncertain, as that of the soul; to penetrate the dark profundities of its intricate internal windings; to choose and lay hold of so many little nimble motions; 'tis a new and extraordinary undertaking, and that withdraws us from the common and most recommended employments of the world.

'Tis now many years since that my thoughts have had no other aim and level than myself: or, if I study any other thing, 'tis to apply it to or rather in myself. And yet I do not think it a fault, if, as others do by other much less profitable sciences, I communicate what I have learned in this, though I am not very well pleased with my own progress. There is no description so difficult, nor doubtless of so great utility, as that of a man's self: and withal, a man must curl his hair and set out and adjust himself, to appear in public; now I am perpetually tricking myself out, for I am eternally upon my own description. Custom has made all speaking of a man's self vicious, and positively interdicts it, in hatred to the boasting that seems inseparable from the testimony men give of themselves. . . . I believe such rules are bits for calves, with which neither the saints whom we hear speak so highly of themselves, nor the philosophers, nor the divines, will be curbed; neither will I, who am as little the one as the other. If they do not write of it expressly, at all events, when the occasions arise, they don't hesitate to put themselves on the public highway. Of what does Socrates treat more largely than of himself? To what does he more direct and address the discourses of his disciples, than to speak of themselves, not of the lesson in their book, but of the essence and motion of their souls? . . .

My trade and art is to live; he that forbids me to speak according to my own sense, experience, and practice, may as well enjoin an architect not to speak of building according to his own knowledge, but according to that of his neighbour; according to the knowledge of another, and not according to his own. . . .

I seek, in the reading of books, only to please myself, by an honest diversion; or, if I study, 'tis for no other science than what treats of the knowledge of myself, and instructs me how to die and how to live well. I do not bite my nails about the difficulties I meet with in my reading; after a charge or two, I give them over. Should I insist upon them, I should both lose myself and time; for I have an impatient understanding, that must be satisfied at first: what I do not discern at once, is by persistence rendered more obscure. I do nothing without gaiety; continuation and a too obstinate endeavour, darkens, stupefies, and tires my judgment. My sight is confounded and dissipated with poring; I must withdraw it, and refer my discovery to new attempts; just as to judge rightly of the lustre of scarlet, we are taught to pass the eye lightly over it, and again to run it over at several sudden and reiterated glances. If one book do not please me, I take another; and never meddle with any, but at such times as I am weary of doing nothing. I care not much for new ones, because the old seem fuller and stronger.

*   *   *   *   *   *   *   *   *

We ought to be ashamed that in all the human sects there never was sectary, what difficulty and strange novelty soever his doctrine imposed upon him, who did not, in some measure, conform his life and deportment to it; whereas so divine and heavenly an institution as ours only distinguishes Christians by the name.

Will you see the proof of this? compare our manners with those of a Mohammedan or Pagan; you will still find that we fall very short, whereas, having regard to the advantage of our religion, we ought to shine in excellence at an extreme, an incomparable distance, and it should be said of us, "Are they so just, so charitable, so good? Then they are Christians." All other signs are common to all religions; hope, trust, events, ceremonies, penance, martyrs; the peculiar mark of our Truth ought to be our virtue, as it is also the most heavenly and difficult mark, and the most worthy product of Truth. And therefore our good St. Louis was in the right, who when the king of the Tartars, who had become a Christian, designed to visit Lyons to kiss the Pope's feet, and there to be an eye-witness of the sanctity he hoped to find in our manners, immediately diverted him from his purpose, for fear lest our disorderly way of living should, on the contrary, put him out of conceit with so holy a belief. Yet it happened quite otherwise since, to him who going to Rome to the same end, and there seeing the dissoluteness of the prelates and people of that time, settled himself all the more firmly in our religion, considering how great the force and divinity of it must necessarily be that could maintain its dignity and splendour amongst so much corruption and in so vicious hands.

Some impose upon the world that they believe that which they do not believe; others, more in number, make themselves believe that they believe, not being able to penetrate into what it is to believe. . . .

I evidently perceive that we do not willingly afford to devotion any other offices but those that best suit with our own passions; there is no hostility so outstanding as the Christian; our zeal performs wonders when it seconds our inclinations to hatred, cruelty, ambition, avarice, detraction, rebellion: but moved against the hair towards goodness, benignity, moderation, unless by miracle some rare and virtuous disposition prompt us to it, we stir neither

hand nor foot. Our religion is intended to extirpate vices;
whereas it screams, nourishes, incites them. We must not
mock God. If we did believe in Him, I do not say by
faith, but with a simple belief, that is to say (and I speak
it to our great shame), if we did believe Him, or knew
Him as any other character of history, or as one of our
companions, we should love Him above all other things;
at least, He would go equal in our affections with riches,
pleasures, glory, and our friends. Whereas the best of us is
not so much afraid to offend Him, as he is afraid to offend
his neighbour, his kinsman, his master. . . .

All this is a most evident sign that we only receive our
religion after our own fashion, by our own hands, and no
otherwise than other religions are received. Either we are
in the country where it is in practice, or we bear a reverence to its antiquity, or to the authority of the men who
have maintained it, or we fear the menaces it fulminates
against unbelievers, or are allured by its promises. . . .
Another religion, other testimonies, the like promises and
threats, might in the same way imprint a quite contrary
belief. We are Christians by the same title that we are Peri-
gordins or Germans.

And what Plato says, that there are few men so obstinate in their atheism whom a pressing danger will not
reduce to an acknowledgment of the divine power, does
not concern a true Christian; 'tis for mortal and human
religions to be received by human recommendation. What
kind of faith can we expect that should be, that cowardice
and feebleness of heart plant and establish in us? A
pleasant faith, that does not believe what it believes, but
for want of courage to disbelieve it. Can a vicious passion,
such as inconstancy and astonishment, cause any regular
product in our souls?

What does Truth mean . . . when she so often in-
culcates to us, that our wisdom is but folly in the sight of
God; that the vainest of all vanities is man; that the man
who presumes upon his wisdom, does not yet know what
wisdom is; and that man, who is nothing, if he think himself to be anything, but seduces and deceives himself?
These sentences of the Holy Ghost so clearly and vividly
express that which I would maintain, that I should need

no other proof against men who would not, with all humility and obedience, submit to its authority; but these will be whipped at their own expense, and will not suffer a man to oppose their reason, except by itself, letting it run to the end of its tether.

Let us then now consider a man alone, without foreign assistance, armed only with his own proper arms, and unfurnished of the divine grace and wisdom, which is all his honour, strength, and the foundation of his being: let us see what certainty he has in this fine equipment. Let him make me understand by the force of his reason, upon what foundations he has built those great advantages he thinks he has over other creatures: what has made him believe, that this admirable movement of the celestial arch, the eternal light of those planets and stars that roll so proudly over his head, the fearful motions of that infinite ocean, were established, and continue so many ages, for his service and convenience? Can anything be imagined to be so ridiculous as that this miserable and wretched creature, who is not so much as master of himself, but subject to the injuries of all things, should call himself master and emperor of the world, of which he has not power to know the least part, much less to command it. And this privilege which he attributes to himself, of being the only creature in this grand fabric that has the understanding to distinguish its beauty and its parts, the only one who can return thanks to the architect, and keep account of the revenues and disbursements of the world; who, I wonder, sealed for him this privilege? Let us see his letters-patent for this great and noble charge; were they granted in favour of the wise only? few people would be concerned in that: are fools and wicked persons worthy so extraordinary a favour, and, being the worst part of the world, to be preferred before the rest? If we derive this little portion of reason we have from the bounty of heaven, how is it possible that reason should ever make us equal to it? how subject its essence and conditions to our knowledge? Whatever we see in these bodies astonishes us: What kind of machinery can it be? How is it built and maintained? "What kind of machinery can this be," says Cicero, "what engines, what structures were needed for it, and

who were the builders?" Why do we deprive it of soul, of
life, and reason? Have we discovered in it any immovable
and insensible stupidity, we who have no commerce with
the heavens but by obedience? Shall we say that we have
discovered in no other creature but man the use of a
reasonable soul? What! have we seen anything like the
sun? does he cease to be, because we have seen nothing
like him? and do his motions cease, because there are
no others like them? If what we have not seen is not,
our knowledge is wonderfully contracted. Are they not
dreams of human vanity, to make the moon a celestial
earth? there to fancy mountains and vales, as Anaxagoras
did there to fix habitations and human abodes, and plant
colonies for our convenience, as Plato and Plutarch have
done, and of our earth to make a beautiful and luminous
star? "We are not only bound to make mistakes, we seem
to love them once made."

Presumption is our natural and original disease. The
most wretched and frail of all creatures is man, and withal
the proudest. He feels and sees himself lodged here in
the dirt and filth of the world, nailed and riveted to the
worst and deadest part of the universe, in the lowest story
of the house, and most remote from the heavenly arch,
. . . and yet in his imagination will be placing himself
above the circle of the moon, and bringing heaven under
his feet. 'Tis by the vanity of the same imagination that he
equals himself to God, attributes to himself divine qualities, withdraws and separates himself from the crowd of
other creatures, cuts out the shares of animals his fellows and companions, and distributes to them portions
of faculties and force as himself thinks fit. How does
he know, by the strength of his understanding, the secret
and internal motions of animals? and from what comparison betwixt them and us does he conclude the
stupidity he attributes to them? When I play with my cat,
who knows whether I do not make her more sport than
she makes me? we mutually divert one another with our
monkey tricks: if I have my hour to begin or to refuse,
she also has hers. . . . The defect that hinders communication betwixt them and us, why may it not be on

our part as well as theirs? 'Tis yet to determine where the fault lies that we understand not one another; for we understand them no more than they do us.

*   *   *   *   *   *   *   *   *

As to what concerns fidelity, there is no animal in the world so treacherous as man. . . .

As to the rest, the very share that we allow to beasts of the bounty of nature, by our own confession, is very much to their advantage; we attribute to ourselves imaginary and fantastic goods, future and absent goods, for which human capacity cannot, of herself, be responsible; or goods that we falsely attribute to ourselves by the licence of opinion, as reason, knowledge and honour; and leave to them, for their share, essential, manageable and palpable goods, as peace, repose, security, innocence and health; health, I say, the fairest and richest present that nature can make us. . . .

We have had reason to magnify the power of our imagination, for all our goods are only in dream. Hear this poor calamitous animal huff: "There is nothing," says Cicero, "so charming as the occupation of letters; of those letters, I say, by means whereof the infinity of things, the immense grandeur of nature, the heavens, even in this world, the earth, and the seas are discovered to us. 'Tis they that have taught us religion, moderation, the grandeur of courage, and that have rescued our soul from obscurity, to make her see all things, high, low, first, middle, last, and 'tis they that furnish us wherewith to live happily and well, and conduct us to pass over our lives without displeasure and without offence." Does not this man seem to speak of the condition of the ever-living and almighty God? Yet, as to the effect, a thousand little country-women have lived more equal, more sweet and constant than his.

*   *   *   *   *   *   *   *   *

Should I examine, finally, whether it be in the power of man to find out that which he seeks, and if that quest wherein he has busied himself so many ages has enriched him with any new force or any solid truth: I believe he

will confess, if he speaks from his conscience, that all
he has got by so long an inquiry is only to have learned
to know his own weakness. We have only by long study
confirmed and verified the natural ignorance we were in before. The same has fallen out to men truly wise which befalls ears of wheat; they shoot and raise their heads high
and pert, whilst empty; but when full and swollen with
grain in maturity, begin to flag and droop; so, men having
tried and sounded all things, and having found in that accu-
mulation of knowledge and provision of so many various
things, nothing massive and firm, nothing but vanity, have
quitted their presumption and acknowledged their natural
condition.

Whoever goes in search of anything, must come to this,
either to say that he has found it, or that it is not to be
found, or that he is yet upon the quest. All philosophy is
divided into these three kinds: her design is to seek out
truth, knowledge, and certainty. The Peripatetics, Epicureans, Stoics, and others, have thought they had found
it: these have established the sciences that we have, and
have treated of them as of certainties. Clitomachus,
Carneades, and the Academics, have despaired in their
quest, and concluded that truth could not be conceived
by our capacity; the result with these is all weakness and
human ignorance; this sect has had the most and most
noble followers. Pyrrho and other sceptics (whose dogmas
were held by many of the ancients to have been taken from
Homer, the seven sages, Archilocus, Euripides, Zeno,
Democritus, and Xeńophanes) say, that they are yet upon
the search of truth: these conclude that the others who
think they have found it out are infinitely deceived; and
that it is too daring a vanity in the second sort to determine that human reason is not able to attain unto it;
for to establish the standard of our power, to know and
judge the difficulty of things, is a great and extreme knowledge, of which they doubt whether man is capable. . . .
The ignorance that knows itself, judges, and condemns
itself, is not an absolute ignorance: to be this, it must be
ignorant of itself; so that the profession of the Pyrrhonians is to doubt and inquire, not to make themselves

sure of or responsible to themselves for anything. . . .
Now this situation of their judgment, upright and inflexible,
receiving all objects without application or consent, led
them to their Ataraxy, which is a condition of life, peace-
able, temperate, and exempt from the agitations we receive by the impression of the opinion and knowledge that
we think we have of things; from which spring fear, avarice,
envy, immoderate desires, ambition, pride, superstition,
love of novelty, rebellion, disobedience, obstinacy, and
the greatest part of bodily ills; nay, by this they exempt
themselves from the jealousy of their discipline: for they
debate after a very gentle manner; they fear no rejoinder
in their disputes: when they affirm that heavy things descend, they would be sorry to be believed, and love to be
contradicted, to engender doubt and suspense of judgment,
which is their end. They only put out their propositions to
contend with those they think we have in our belief. If you
take their arguments, they will as readily maintain the contrary; 'tis all one to them; they have no choice. . . . And
by this extremity of doubt, which jostles itself, they
separate and divide themselves from many opinions, even
of those that have several ways maintained doubt and
ignorance. Why shall not they be allowed, say they, as well
as the dogmatists, one to say green, another yellow; why
may not they also doubt? Can anything be proposed to
us to grant or deny which it shall not be permitted to consider as ambiguous? And where others are carried away,
either by the custom of their country or by the instruction
of parents, or by accident, as by a tempest, without judging and without choice, nay, and for the most part before
the age of discretion, to such or such an opinion, to the sect
of the Stoics or Epicureans, to which they are enslaved
and fast bound, as to a thing they cannot shake off, . . .
why shall not these likewise be permitted to maintain their
liberty and to consider things without obligation or slavery?
. . . Is it not of some advantage to be disengaged from
the necessity that curbs others? is it not better to remain
in suspense than to entangle one's self in the innumerable
errors that human fancy has produced? is it not much better to suspend one's persuasion than to intermeddle with

these wrangling and seditious divisions? What shall I
choose? "What you please, provided you do choose." A
very foolish answer, but one, nevertheless, to which all
the dogmatists seem to point; by which we are not permitted to be ignorant of that of which we are ignorant.
Take the most eminent side, that of the greatest reputation;
it will never be so sure, that to defend it you will not be
forced to attack and contend with a hundred and a hundred adversaries; is it not better to keep out of this hurly-
burly? . . . The effect of it is a pure, entire, perfect, and
absolute suspension of the judgment: they make use of
their reason to inquire and debate, but not to fix and determine. Whoever shall imagine a perpetual confession of
ignorance, a judgment without bias or inclination, upon
any occasion whatever, conceives a true idea of Pyrrhonism. I express this fancy as well as I can, by reason that
many find it hard to conceive; and the authors themselves
represent it somewhat variously and obscurely.

As to what concerns the actions of life, they are in this
of the common fashion; they yield and lend themselves to
the natural inclinations, to the power and impulse of passions, to the constitutions of laws and customs, and to the
tradition of arts: . . . They suffer their ordinary actions
to be guided by these things without any dispute or judgment. . . .

How many arts are there that profess to consist more in
conjecture than in knowledge, that decide not upon true
and false, and only follow that which seems true? There
is, say they, true and false, and we have in us wherewith
to seek it, but not to fix it when we touch it. We are much
more prudent in letting ourselves be carried away by the
swing of the world without inquisition; a soul clear from
prejudice has a marvellous advance towards tranquillity
and repose. Men who judge and control their judges never
duly submit to them.

How much more docile and easy to be governed, both
in the laws of religion and civil polity, are simple and in-
curious minds, than those over-vigilant and pedagoguish
wits that will still be prating of divine and human causes?
. . . "Take in good part," says Ecclesiastes, "the things

that present themselves to thee, as they seem and taste from hand to mouth: the rest is out of thy knowledge.". . .

Thus we see that, of the three general sects of philosophy, two make open profession of doubt and ignorance; and in that of the Dogmatists, which is the third, it is easy to discover that the greatest part of them only assume a face of assurance that they may have the better air; they have not so much thought to establish any certainty for us, as to show us how far they have proceeded in their search of truth. . . .

Moreover, how many things are there in our own knowledge that oppose those fine rules we have cut out for and prescribed to nature? And yet we must undertake to circumscribe God Himself! How many things do we call miraculous and contrary to nature? this is done by every nation and by every man, according to the measure of their ignorance; how many occult properties and quintessences do we discover? For, with us, to go "according to nature," is no more but to go "according to our intelligence," as far as that is able to follow, and as far as we are able to see into it: all beyond that must be monstrous and irregular. Now, by this account, all things shall be monstrous to the wisest and most understanding men; for human reason has persuaded them that it has no manner of ground or foundation, not so much as to be assured that snow is white . . . or . . . if there be knowledge or ignorance, which Metrodorus of Chios denied that man was able to determine; or whether we live, as Euripides doubts, "whether the life we live is life, or whether that we call death be not life:" . . . and not without some appearance; for why do we, from this instant which is but a flash in the infinite course of an eternal night, and so short an interruption of our perpetual and natural condition, death possessing all that passed before and all the future of this moment, and also a good part of the moment itself, derive the title of Being?

Our speaking has its failings and defects, as well as all the rest: grammar is that which creates most disturbances in the world: our suits only spring from disputation as to the interpretation of laws; and most wars proceed from the inability of ministers clearly to express the conventions and treaties of amity among princes. How many quarrels, and those of how great importance, has the doubt of the meaning of this syllable *Hoc* created in the world? Let us take the conclusion that logic itself presents us as manifestly clear: if you say it is fine weather, and that you say true, it is, then, fine weather. Is not this a very certain form of speaking? and yet it will deceive us; that it will do so, let us follow the example: if you say, I lie, and that you say true, then you do lie. The art, reason and force of the conclusion of this are the same with the other; and yet we are gravelled. The Pyrrhonian philosophers, I see, cannot express their general conception in any kind of speaking; for they would require a new language on purpose: ours is all formed of affirmative propositions, which are totally hostile to them; insomuch that when they say, "I doubt," they are presently taken by the throat, to make them confess that at least they know and are assured of this, that they do doubt. And so they have been compelled to shelter themselves under this medicinal comparison, without which their humour would be inexplicable: when they pronounce, "I know not:" or, "I doubt;" they say that this proposition carries off itself with the rest, no more nor less than rhubarb that drives out the ill humours and carries itself off with them. This fancy is more certainly understood by interrogation: What do I know? as I bear it in the emblem of a balance. . . .

See what use we make of our irreverent way of speaking: in the present disputes about our religion, if you press the adversaries too hard, they will roundly tell you, "that it is not in the power of God to make it so that His body would be in paradise and upon earth, and in several places at once." And see what advantage the old scoffer [Pliny] makes of this! "At least," says he, "it is no little consolation to man to see that God cannot do all things; for he cannot kill himself though he would, which is the greatest privilege we have in our condition: he cannot make mortals immortal, nor revive the dead, nor make it so that he who has lived has not, nor that he who has had honours, has not had them, having no other power over the past than that of oblivion. And that the comparison of a man to God may yet be made out by pleasant examples, he cannot order it so that twice ten shall not be twenty." This is what he says, and what a Christian ought to take heed shall not escape his lips; whereas, on the contrary, it seems as if all men studied this impudent kind of blasphemous language, to reduce God to their own measure. . . .

This arrogance of attempting to discover God with our weak eyes has been the cause that an eminent person of our faith [Tertullian] has attributed to the divinity a corporeal form; and is the reason of what happens amongst us every day of attributing to God important events, by a special appointment: because they sway with us, they conclude that they also sway with Him, and that He has a more intent and vigilant regard to them than to others of less moment, or of ordinary course: "The gods take care of important things only:" observe [Cicero's] example; he will clear this to you by his reason: "For kings, too, do not attend to all the small details of their kingdom;" as if to that King of kings it were more and less to subvert a kingdom or to move the leaf of a tree: or as if His providence acted after another manner in inclining the event of a battle than in the leap of a flea.

*   *   *   *   *   *   *   *   *   *

If you ask philosophy of what matter is heaven, of what the sun, what answer will she return, but that it is of iron, with Anaxagoras of stone, or some other matter that she makes use of? If a man inquire of Zeno what nature is? "A fire," says he, "artisan, proper for generation, proceeding regularly." Archimedes, master of that science which attributes to itself the precedence before all others for truth and certainty: "the sun," says he, "is a god of red-hot iron." Was not this a fine imagination, extracted from the beauty and inevitable necessity of geometrical demonstrations? yet not so inevitable and useful, but that Socrates thought it was enough to know so much of geometry only as to measure the land a man bought or sold; and that Polyænus, who had been a great and famous master in it, despised it, as full of falsity and manifest vanity, after he had once tasted the delicate fruits of the garden of Epicurus. Socrates in Xenophon concerning this proposition of Anaxagoras, reputed by antiquity learned above all others in celestial and divine matters, says that he had cracked his brain, as all men do who too immoderately search into knowledges which nothing appertain unto them: when he made the sun to be a burning stone, he did not consider that a stone does not shine in the fire; and which is worse, that it will there consume; and in making the sun and fire one, that fire does not turn complexions black in shining upon them; that we are able to look fixedly upon fire: and that fire kills herbs and plants. 'Tis Socrates' opinion, and mine too, that it is best judged of heaven not to judge of it at all.

Let us see if we have a little more light in the knowledge of human and natural things. Is it not a ridiculous attempt for us to devise for those, to whom by our own confession our knowledge is not able to attain, another body, and to lend a false form of our own invention: as is manifest in the motion of the planets, to which, seeing our wits cannot possibly arrive nor conceive their natural conduct, we lend them material, heavy and substantial springs of our own, by which to move: . . . you would say that we had had coach-makers, wheelwrights, and painters that went up on high to make engines of various movements, and to range the wheels and interlacings of the heavenly bodies of differing colours about the axis of Necessity, according to Plato: these are all dreams and fantastic follies. Why will not Nature please, once for all, to lay open her bosom to us, and plainly discover to us the means and conduct of her movements, and prepare our eyes to see them? Good God, what blunders, what mistakes should we discover in our poor science!

Have I not read in Plato this divine saying, that "Nature is nothing but an enigmatic poesy?" as if a man might, peradventure, say, a veiled and shaded picture, breaking out here and there with an infinite variety of false lights to puzzle our conjectures. . . . And certainly philosophy is no other than a sophisticated poesy. Whence do the ancient writers extract their authorities but from the poets? and the first of them were poets themselves, and wrote accordingly. Plato himself is but a disconnected poet: Timon injuriously calls him the great forger of miracles. All super-human sciences make use of the poetic style. Just as women for themselves make use of teeth of ivory where the natural are wanting, and instead of their true complexion make one of some foreign matter; legs of cloth or felt, and plumpness of cotton, and in the sight and knowledge of every one paint, patch, and trick up themselves with false and borrowed beauty: so does science (and even our law itself has, they say, legal fictions whereon it builds the truth of its justice); she gives us, in presupposition and for current pay, things which she herself informs us were invented: for these epicycles, excentrics and concentrics, which astrology makes use of to carry on the motions of the stars, she gives us as the best she could contrive upon that subject; as also, in all the rest, philosophy presents us, not that which really is or what she really believes, but what she has contrived with the most plausible likelihood and the fairest aspect.

'Tis not to heaven only that she sends her ropes, engines, and wheels; let us consider a little what she says of ourselves and of our contexture: there is not more retro-gradation, trepidation, accession, recession, aberration, in the stars and celestial bodies than they have found out in this poor little human body. Truly they have good reason upon that very account to call it the Little World, so many tools and parts have they employed to erect and build it. To accommodate the motions they see in man, the various functions and faculties that we find in ourselves, into how many parts have they divided the soul? in how many places lodged, into how many orders have they divided, to how many stories have they raised this poor creature man, besides those that are natural and to be perceived? and how many offices and vocations have they assigned him? They make of him an imaginary public thing; 'tis a subject that they hold and handle; and they have full power granted to them to rip, place, displace, piece, and stuff it, every one according to his own fancy, and yet to this day they possess it not.

*   *   *   *   *   *   *   *   *

Every science has its principles presupposed, by which human judgment is everywhere limited. If you drive against the barrier where the principal error lies, they have presently this sentence in their mouths; "that there is no disputing with persons, who deny principles"; now men can have no principles, if not revealed to them by the Divinity; of all the rest, the beginning, the middle and the end are nothing but dream and vapour. To those who contend upon presupposition, we must, on the contrary, presuppose to them the same axiom upon which the dispute is: for every human presupposition, and every declaration, has as much authority one as another, if reason do not make the difference. Wherefore they are all to be put into the balance, and first the general and those that tyrannise over us. The persuasion of certainty is a certain testimony of folly and extreme uncertainty; . . . Now 'tis very likely, that if the soul knew anything, it would in the first place know itself; and if it knew anything out of itself, it would be its own body and case, before anything else: if we see the gods of physic, to this very day, debating about our anatomy, when are we to expect that they will be agreed? We are nearer neighbours to ourselves than the whiteness of snow or the weight of stones are to us: if man does not know himself, how should he know his functions and powers? It is not, peradventure, that we have not some real knowledge in us, but 'tis by chance; and forasmuch as errors are received into our soul by the same way, after the same manner and by the same conduct, it has not wherewithal to distinguish them, nor wherewithal to choose the truth from falsehood.

As to what remains, this malady does not very easily discover itself, unless it be extreme and past remedy; forasmuch as reason goes always lame and halting, and that as well with falsehood as with truth; and therefore 'tis hard to discover her deviations and mistakes. I always call that appearance of meditation which every one forges in himself, reason: this reason, of the condition of which there may be a hundred contrary ones about the same subject, is an instrument of lead and wax, ductile, pliable, and accommodable to all sorts of biasses and to all measures, so that nothing remains but the knowledge how to turn and mould it. How uprightly soever a judge may resolve to act, if he do not well look to himself, which few care to do, their inclination to friendship, to relationship, to beauty or revenge, and not only things of that weight, but even the fortuitous instinct that makes us favour one thing more than another, and that, without the reason's leave, puts the choice upon us in two equal subjects, or some other shadowy futility, may insensibly insinuate into his judgment the recommendation or disfavour of a cause, and make the balance dip.

I, who watch myself as narrowly as I can, and who have my eyes continually bent upon myself, like one that has no great business elsewhere to do, dare hardly tell the vanity and weakness I find in myself; my foot is so unstable and stands so slippery, I find it so apt to totter and reel, and my sight so disordered, that fasting I am quite another man than when full; if health and a fair day smile upon me, I am a very good fellow; if a corn trouble my toe, I am sullen, out of humour, and inaccessible. The same pace of a horse seems to me one while hard and another easy; the same way, one while shorter and another while longer; the same form, one while more and another while less, taking. Now I am for doing everything and then for doing nothing at all; what pleases me now would be a trouble to me at another time. I have a thousand senseless and casual humours within myself; either I am possessed by melancholy, or swayed by choler; now, by its own private authority, sadness predominates in me, and, by and by, I am as merry as a cricket. When I take a book in hand, I have discovered admirable graces in such and such passages, and such as have struck my soul: let me light upon them at another time, I may turn and toss, tumble and rattle the leaves to much purpose; 'tis then to me a shapeless and unrecognizable mass. Even in my own writings, I do not always find the air of my first fancy: I know not what I meant to say; and am often put to it to correct and pump for a new sense, because I have lost the first that was better. I do nothing but go and come: my judgment does not always advance; it floats and wanders. . . .

Now, from the knowledge of this volubility of mine, I have accidentally begot in myself a certain constancy of opinion, and have not much altered those that were first and natural in me: for what appearance soever there may be in novelty, I do not easily change, for fear of losing by the bargain: and since I am not capable of choosing, I take other men's choice, and keep myself in the state wherein God has placed me; I could not otherwise prevent myself from perpetual rolling. Thus have I, by the grace of God, preserved myself entire, without anxiety or trouble of conscience, in the ancient belief of our religion, amidst so many sects and divisions as our age has produced.

*   *   *   *   *   *   *   *   *   *

The facility that good wits have of rendering everything they would recommend likely, and that there is nothing so strange to which they will not undertake to give colour enough to deceive such a simplicity as mine, this evidently shows the weakness of their testimony. The heavens and the stars have been three thousand years in motion; all the world were of that belief, till Cleanthes the Samian, or, according to Theophrastus, Nicetas of Syracuse, bethought him to maintain that it was the earth that moved, turning about its axis by the oblique circle of the zodiac; and in our time Copernicus has so grounded this doctrine, that it very regularly serves to all astrological consequences: what use can we make of this, except that we need not much care which is the true opinion? And who knows but that a third, a thousand years hence, may overthrow the two former? . . . So that when any new doctrine presents itself to us, we have great reason to mistrust it, and to consider that before it was set on foot, the contrary had been in vogue; and that as that has been overthrown by this, a third invention, in time to come, may start up which may knock the second on the head. Before the principles that Aristotle introduced were in reputation, other principles contented human reason, as these satisfy us now. What letters-patent have these, what particular privilege, that the career of our invention must be stopped by them, and that to them should appertain for all time to come the possession of our belief? They are no more exempt from being thrust out of doors than their predecessors were.

When any one presses me with a new argument, I ought to consider that what I cannot answer, another may: for to believe all likelihoods that a man cannot himself confute, is great simplicity; it would by that means come to pass, that all the vulgar, and we are all of the vulgar, would have their belief as turnable as a weathercock: for the soul, being so easily imposed upon and without resisting power, would be forced incessantly to receive other and other impressions, the last still effacing all footsteps of that which went before. He that finds himself weak, ought to answer as in law questions, that he will speak with his counsel; or will refer himself to the wise from whom he received his teaching. How long is it that physic has been practised in the world? 'Tis said that a new comer, called Paracelsus, changes and overthrows the whole order of ancient rules, and maintains that till now it has been of no other use but to kill men. I believe that he will easily make this good; but I do not think it were wisdom to venture my life in making trial of his new experiments. . . .

I have been told that in geometry, which pretends to have gained the highest point of certainty among all the sciences, there are found inevitable demonstrations that subvert the truth of all experience: as Jacques Peletier told me at my own house, that he had found out two lines stretching themselves one towards the other to meet, which, nevertheless, he affirmed, though extended to all infinity, could never reach to touch one another. And the Pyrrhonians make no other use of their arguments and their reason than to ruin the appearance of experience; and 'tis a wonder how far the suppleness of our reason has followed them in this design of controverting the evidence of effects. . . .

Ptolemy, who was a great man, had established the bounds of this world of ours: all the ancient philosophers thought they had the measure of it, excepting some remote isles that might escape their knowledge; it would have been Pyrrhonism, a thousand years ago, to doubt the science of cosmography, and the opinions that every one had

thence received; and behold! in this age of ours there is an
infinite extent of *terra firma* discovered, not an island or a
particular country, but a part very nearly equal in greatness
to that we knew before. The geographers of our times stick
not to assure us, that now all is found, all is seen. . . . But
the question is whether, if Ptolemy was therein formerly deceived, upon the foundations of his reason, it were not
very foolish to trust now in what these later people say:
and whether it is not more likely that this great body,
which we call the world, is not quite another thing than
what we imagine.]

CHAPTER X

Paracelsus, Kepler and Boehme

PHILIPP THEOPHRASTUS BAUMAST OR BOMBAST VON HOH-
enheim (1493?-1541), a great Swiss physician from Ein-
siedeln, who translated his name into Paracelsus, is the
most famous representative of the occult philosophy of the
Renaissance. His name has remained surrounded by legend; it was, strictly speaking, one to conjure with. He was
said to have converse with spirits at will, to have had a
pact with the devil, and he was one of the prototypes for
the composite character of Dr. Faustus, whereas in fact
it happened that he himself had been quite aware of the
growing "Faust" current and strove to redeem occult science from its disreputable associations with black magic.
He got justice in a way, for his fame remained essentially
that of a sage and a healer. His grave was to become a
place of pilgrimage to the sick for centuries. His real life
was that of an unhappy and lonely man, wandering rest-
lessly, and dispensing medical help with selfless gener-
osity. He died, poor and worn out, at the age of forty-eight.

Although he came of a noble family and had a good education in the universities of Italy, at nearly the same time
as Copernicus, Paracelsus seems to have been a rough-
hewn character proud of his peasant traits, unversed in
the ways of the world, and an adept at the easy art of
making enemies. "By nature," he writes, "I am not subtly
spun. . . . I am a philosopher in the German manner."
An adequate sense of his own importance was a necessary
part of a scholar's equipment in those days, but Paracelsus
swung it at times like a sledgehammer:

"From the middle of this Age the Monarchy of all the
Arts has been at length derived and conferred on me,

191

Theophrastus Paracelsus, Prince of Philosophy and of
Medicine. For this purpose I have been chosen by God to
extinguish and blot out all the fantasies of elaborate sophis-
try, of delusive and presumptuous works. My doctrine,
proceeding as it does from the light of nature, can never,
through its consistency, pass away or be changed; but in the
fifty-eighth year after the millennium and a half, it will then
begin to flourish. . . . Avicenna, Galen, Rhases, Mon-
tagnana, Mesua and other, after me, and not I after you!
. . . I shall put forth leaves, while you will be dry fig trees."*

This style helped fix the meaning of the word "bombast"
in the English language. But then, wonder-working physi-
cians have often had recourse to a haughty style, witness
Empedocles. Paracelsus is a sincere and passionately religious soul, an authentic reformer, the "Luther of medicine." He is the man who wrote:

"The art of medicine is rooted in the heart. If your heart
is just, you will also be a true physician . . . one for
whom the ultimate instance is man's distress. Privilege and
lineage pale to nothingness, only distress has meaning."

Paracelsus is acquainted with the formal philosophy of
his time. But he proclaims himself an initiate to a higher
philosophy, one whose aim is not merely cognitive but
operative. Like his distinguished predecessor Agrippa von
Nettesheim, he would gladly insist on "the uncertainty
and the vanity of the [verbal] sciences," for to him truth
is that which, once grasped, allows us to transmute nature
and heal men. Such a truth is perforce "occult," for it is
not for everyone; but not in the sense of trade secrets and
magic formulas confined to jealously guarded books, or of
a riddle of undecipherable obscurity. Occult means simply
what looks insignificant, paradoxical or commonplace to
the vulgar, but will be intuitively understood by such as
have reached a sufficiently high degree of spiritual preparation and attunement to the cosmic order. To any mind
thus constituted, it becomes the "light of nature" itself, the

*This and the following selections are from Paracelsus, *Selected
Writings*, ed. by Jolande Jacobi, trans. by Norbert Guterman.
New York: Pantheon Books (Bollingen Series), 1951; London:
Routledge and Kegan Paul, 1951. Copyright 1951 by Bollingen
Foundation Inc., New York, N. Y.

voice of the universe, which dictates its further thought. "It is understood by the eye, it roars like the falls of the Rhine, it is the sound of philosophy which is like that of the strong wind from the sea." This is no theosophy or mysteriosophy meant only for a small circle of adepts. It is there for the transformation of mankind, for visible results, a working truth, as we would say.

"That is complete understanding when the hand can grasp, the eye can see, what is comprehended inside the head. For what is secretly understood gives belief alone; the result and the completion are given by the works, and the works are visible. Thus, the visible and the invisible in one and not in two [realms], the whole achieved consoling realization, in which is happiness, and [from which] comes all good work, doctrine and teaching."

This is a pregnant announcement of what the new science of nature would aim at. This kind of science he names philosophy, and under it come medicine and also alchemy:

"An alchemist is the baker too who bakes bread, and the vintner who makes wine; what comes of nature that is of use to man, he who brings it to the end ordained by nature, he is the alchemist."

The proper object of knowledge has to be redefined. It is no longer purely intellectual knowledge by way of abstraction and classification as the Schools offered: it has to come intuitively, when you ask, as it were, a thing what it stands for, and it answers by revealing to you its signature or "seal," whereby its true properties will be known. Real knowledge, in the light of nature, is intuitive and operative.

Needless to say, the whole of this philosophy is vitalistic, and indeed animistic in a very archaic sense. It is both irrational and anti-mathematical; it conceives of reality as not spatially located at all but interpenetrating at all levels, articulated and defined only in time. The religious emotion of Paracelsus centers on growth and delicate unfolding from the womb of time; he teaches "respect for the divinely appointed moment," for the "hour of God" that the physician-alchemist alone can discern.

It is only in such a scheme, on the other hand, that

things can be conceived as really independent beings, having their reason and their principle of growth in themselves. Gone is the neat hierarchy of intelligible causes, ending up in the already achieved design in the mind of the Unmoved Mover. There is here a true "becoming" and also protean metamorphosis.

In the great Chain of Being, God and Man are mystically equivalent. "I under God in his office, God under me in mine." This might sound like satanic pride, but it is a mystical intuition which is to be more strongly and paradoxically expressed later by Angelus Silesius in many of his doggerel couplets: "I know that without me God could not live a second— Turned if I were to nothing, He'd give up the ghost in despair."

All this by itself is not Renaissance and it is not new. It is a variant strain of that timeless mystical thought which had been more powerfully expressed long before by Meister Eckhart, combined with equally timeless animistic ideas from primitive religions.

Paracelsus is, even in temperament, a man from the waning Middle Ages——he is that in his love of poverty and in his tender perception of beings, in his almost morbid awareness of inner life, his torn and anxious and tormented soul——but he is "renascent" in his certainty that something great and new can be drawn from all this. A mind like Donne's, so flamboyant otherwise, is still medieval in its appalled meditation of death in its intellectual resignation: "Poor soule, in this thy flesh what wouldst thou know?" Paracelsus' saving force is in his faith in universal life and in his intellectual boldness.

The idea on which he centers is this: man and heaven are one and the same, not by way of the Earth being in heaven as Copernicus is going to suggest a few years later, but because it is the same understanding that reveals to us the law of both: "that it is one firmament, one starry nature, one earthly nature, and one being present in divided and multiple form." This is for him the principle of medicine: it consists "in turning the greater world in onto the little one." Hence also, there should be no limitations to the power of the physician; there is only a limitation in his own knowledge. . . .

Nature is so complete in herself that she is not to be apprehended idealistically by way of concepts and formal truths but much rather, "she will help us only if we struggle with her." "It is a great blindness and a great temptation to follow our own minds, our plain senses, which are no masters: it is the light of nature which is the master." But what is that "light of nature" if not the reflection of the divine spirit that is in it? It is the same reflection that we find in us, if our disposition (*Gemüt*) has been made right. The worn idea of a correspondence between Macrocosm and Microcosm is presented here in an original new twist. In the classic conception, coming all the way from the Stoics, man was a kind of receiving station, on which converged all the transmitted impulses and forces of the universe in the order and timing of the stars, and who therefore "reflected" in himself the greater order. In Paracelsus, this pseudo-physical conception is transformed into metaphysical equivalence. Man cannot be said to receive influxes nor to be acted on: the stars and he are in perfect correspondence, that is all. "Two twins that look alike, which of the two has the likeness from the other?" We have here a first idea of Leibniz's "pre-established harmony." And the result is that the conventional idea of astrology is gone: "Stars force us to nothing, they influence not, nor do they incline us; they are free on their own and so are we."

The basic components, too, are the same above and below. To the traditional four elements of earthly change, air, water, earth, and fire, the Greeks had added a fifth element of "celestial fire" of which the heavens alone are made. In Paracelsus' new alchemy, the old elements are themselves composite, and the new basic principles are three: sulphur, salt and mercury; not the ordinary bodies that go under that name, but metaphysical principles. One might almost call them, in the old Chinese terminology, "the harsh," "the subtle," "the stable." They are, of course, chemical too: what burns and attacks, what flows and volatilizes, what stays and carries. It is to this change that John Donne refers in his famous line: "the new philosophy puts all in doubt," for, in fact, the special element of celestial fire "is quite put out." All three of them are also sidereal principles, and also principles of the soul. The ancient alchemic art has been freed of its perpetual confusion in which rough chemistry was equivocally mixed up with animism and black magic: it has been declared to be essentially a science of psychic events, and only on a second level a tentative theory of matter.

"Let no one fancy that the wisdom, reason, ruse and strife which we have received from heaven, come directly from God! They do not come directly from him, but exist in us men as a reflection of the corresponding qualities of the macrocosm, the Great Creature. But the wisdom which comes to us from God Himself stands above the other and is stronger than heaven and the stars. . . . Though I myself often write in the manner of the heathen, I am a Christian and know that the truth of Christ is more profound than that of nature."

Here we see two elements not quite reconciled in Paracelsus' mind: his Christian belief and his mystical naturalism; but the way he has set for himself will lead him to an assertive conclusion: "Man is so noble and so high in the sight of God, that his image is reproduced in heaven with his own limits, with his good and bad." At which point it becomes clear that this refers in no way to man as he exists individually and empirically, but to his consciousness. The universe itself is a magnified reflection of that consciousness. And God beyond the world has become in truth more rather than less mysterious in that, without explicitly denying him all the Christian attributes, he is no longer seen as a fatherly image but essentially as the mystery of that consciousness.

In contrast with the prosy orderliness of scholastic exposition, Paracelsus' writing is willfully obscure and fantastic. The cosmological process of separation from the first substance, as he sees it would be, is complex enough by itself. The primal substance he calls "Yliaster" (*hyle* and *aster,* matter plus sidereal force) on which acts a higher individualizing principle called the Archeus, the alchemical force of nature which brings forth individual forms. Then there are Limus and Limbus, Leffas and Evestrum and Arcanum, and so on, through a bewildering variety of names that Paracelsus coins with unconcern, often without bothering to explain. (One of these names has remained in our language: it is that of "gas," which he invented for a certain air-like quality.)

Here comes also the idea of "mothers" or matrices for all being, the secret origin of things, that Goethe has used with such mysterious overtones in *Faust*. And as the alchemist strives to accomplish the transmutation into higher things, by way of the Great Art, come the quintessences and elixirs. They are alchemically obtained but also metaphysical; an extract is also the idea of a thing as well as its soul.

All this curiously materialistic machinery, largely inherited from the Stoic tradition, comes now into meaning with Paracelsus, insofar as he is first and last a physician intent on healing. We have seen how his correspondence theory between heaven and earth is no longer materially expressible. Under the name of a science of nature he is shaping a symbolic theory of psychic events, and the modern psychology of the unconscious (as represented by C. G. Jung) has recently come forth to claim him as a master. What content there may be in this claim only time will show.

In the last years of his life, with his immense hopes and defiant affirmations and sorry defeats left behind, Paracelsus does indeed enter a world of meditation and experience hardly communicable. After the lifelong, headlong and feverish writing which ends up in sibylline works like *Philosophia sagax* and *Archidoxis magica,* there are only a few friendly letters from that period. It is the quietness of "evening, when the faces of people at the window become indistinct." His work is ended, he says. "The snow of my misery has melted, what was meant to grow has come out . . . he who comes up to you and says the truth, he must die."

Paracelsus does not lend himself to extensive quotation. But even a few fragments will give us the temper of his mind:

[Everything that comes from the flesh is animal and follows an animal course; heaven has little influence on it. Only that which comes from the stars is specifically human in us; this is subject to their influence. But that which comes from the spirit, the divine part of man, has been formed in us in the likeness of God, and upon this neither earth nor heaven has any influence.

Hidden things (of the soul) which cannot be perceived by the physical senses, may be found through the sidereal body, through whose organism we may look into Nature in the same way as the sun shines through a glass. The inner nature of everything may therefore be known through Magic in general, and through the powers of the inner (or second) sight.

Magic power alone (that can neither be conferred by the universities nor created by the awarding of diplomas, but which comes from God) is the true teacher and preceptor, to teach the art of curing the sick.

As the physical forms and colors of objects, or as the letters of a book can be seen with the physical eye, so the essence and the character of all things may be recognized and become known by the inner sense of the soul. . . . *Magia inventrix* finds everywhere what is needed, and more than will be required. The soul does not perceive the external or internal physical construction of herbs and roots, but it intuitively perceives their powers and virtues, and recognizes at once their *signatum*. . . .

At the beginning of each birth stood the birth-giver and begetter—separation. It is the greatest wonder of the philosophies. . . . When the *mysterium magnum* in its essence and divinity was full of the highest eternity, *separatio* started at the beginning of all creation. And when this took place, every creature was created in its majesty, power, and free will. And so it will remain until the end, until the great harvest when all things will bear fruit and will be ready for gathering.

Man is like the image of the elements in a mirror; if the elements fall apart, man is destroyed. If that which faces the mirror is at rest, then the image in the mirror is at rest too. And so philosophy is nothing other than the knowledge and discovery of that which has its reflection in the mirror. And just as the image in the mirror gives no one any idea about his nature, and cannot be the object of cognition, but is only a dead image, so is man, considered in himself; nothing can be learned from him alone. For knowledge comes only from that outside being whose mirrored image he is.

Know that our world and everything we see in its compass and everything we can touch constitute only one half of the cosmos. The world we do not see is equal to ours in weight and measure, in nature and properties. From this it follows that there exists another half of man in which this invisible world operates. If we know of the two worlds, we realize that both halves are needed to constitute the whole man; for they are like two men united in one body.

Thoughts are free and are subject to no rule. On them rests the freedom of man, and they tower above the light of nature. For thoughts give birth to a creative force that is neither elemental nor sidereal. . . . Thoughts create a new heaven, a new firmament, a new source of energy, from which new arts flow. . . . When a man undertakes to create something, he establishes a new heaven, as it were, and from it the work that he desires to create flows into him. . . . For such is the immensity of man that he is greater than heaven and earth.

Know that man makes great discoveries concerning future and hidden things, which are despised and scoffed at by the ignorant who do not realize what nature can accomplish by virtue of her spirit. . . . Thus, the uncertain arts are in such a state that a new generation must come, full of prophetic or sibylline spirit, which will awaken and direct the skills and arts. The arts of this kind . . . are quite old, and enjoyed great reputation among the ancients. They were kept secret and taught secretly. For the students of these arts devoted their time to inner contemplation and faith, and by such means they discovered and proved many great things. But the men of today have no longer such capacity for imagination and faith. . . . These arts are uncertain today because man is uncertain in himself. For he who is not certain of himself cannot be certain in his actions; a sceptic can never create anything enduring. . . .

Magic has power to experience and fathom things which

are inaccessible to human reason. For magic is a great
secret wisdom, just as reason is a great public folly. Therefore it would be desirable and good for the doctors of
theology to know something about it and to understand
what it actually is, and cease unjustly and unfoundedly to
call it witchcraft.

It is a naïve philosophy that puts all blessedness and
eternity in the elements of our earth, and it is a foolish
opinion that looks on man as the noblest of creatures, since
there are more worlds than ours alone. . . . But doubt
will be impossible in the end, when all things are gathered
together in their eternal aspects. . . .

And it is contrary to true philosophy to affirm that the
little flowers do not partake of eternity; although they
wither away, they will nevertheless appear in the assembly
of all the generations. And nothing has been created in
the *mysterium magnum,* in God's great marvellous world,
that will not also be represented in eternity.]

Kepler

The second name in this constellation of what we might
call the great mystic-magical minds is Johann Kepler himself (1571-1630), the chief astronomer of the Renaissance
and the direct predecessor of Newton. A Protestant from
Wurttemberg, Kepler led, like Paracelsus, the life of the
poor and the persecuted. He was first persecuted by the
Protestant Faculty of Tubingen for his Copernican opinions, was offered in 1596 a haven in Austria by the Jesuits,
who did not think those opinions very dangerous at the
time—but once he had become the Catholic emperor's
court astronomer (i.e., astrologer) he found himself again
in difficulties because he would not change his faith, and
spoke the truth uprightly. A generous selfless soul, he was
unable to bear any grudge against those who embittered
his life.

In Prague, it was his good fortune to become associated
with old Tycho Brahe, the master of precise observation,
from whom he inherited his data. It is well known how he
used these to show that the orbit of Mars was elliptical

instead of circular, and how this led him in turn to the formulation of his famous three laws of planetary motion, which were to provide Newton with his starting point in 1666.

Kepler's philosophy, however, which is all one with his science, is like Paracelsus' that of an intellectual mystic. It is the merit of Wolfgang Pauli, the great physicist, to have made it clear how Kepler's fateful conversion to Copernicanism was not the result of scientific reasoning, but of a symbolic analogy that he saw between the role of the sun in the universe and that of the divine mind.

The following translations are from Pauli's "The Influence of Archetypal Ideas on the Scientific Theories of Kepler." *

[First of all the nature of every thing was bound to represent God its creator as far as it was able to do so within the condition of its being. For when the all-wise Creator sought to make everything as good, beautiful, and excellent as possible, he found nothing that could be better or more beautiful or more excellent than himself. Therefore when he conceived in his Mind the corporeal world he chose for it a form that was as similar as possible to himself. Thus originated the entire category of the quantities, and within it the differences of the curved and the straight, and the most excellent figure of all, the spherical surface. For in forming this the most wise Creator created playfully the image of his venerable Trinity. Hence the centre point is, as it were, the origin of the spherical body; the outer surface the image of the innermost point, as well as the way to arrive at it; and the outer surface can be understood as coming about by an infinite expansion of the point beyond itself until a certain equality of all the individual acts of expansion is reached. The point spreads itself out over this extension so that point and surface are identical, except for the fact that the ratio of density and extension is re-

* C. G. Jung and W. Pauli, *The Interpretation of Nature and the Psyche*, trans. R.F.C. Hull and Priscilla Silz, New York: Pantheon Books (Bollingen Series) 1955. Copyright 1955 by Bollingen Foundation Inc., New York, N. Y.

versed. Hence there exists everywhere between point and surface the most absolute equality, the closest unity, the most beautiful conspiring of parts, connection, relation, proportion, and commensurability. And although Centre, Surface, and Distance are manifestly Three, yet are they One, so that no one of them could be even imagined to be absent without destroying the whole.

This, then, is the genuine and most suitable image of the corporeal world, and every being among those physical creatures that aspire to perfection assumes it [viz. the spherical shape] either absolutely or in a certain respect. Therefore the bodies themselves which, as such, are confined by the limits of their surfaces and thus unable to expand into spherical form, are endowed with various powers, nesting in the bodies, which are somewhat freer than the bodies themselves, possessing no corporeal matter but consisting of a particular matter of their own that assumes geometrical dimensions; which powers flow out from them and aspire to the circular form—as can be clearly seen, especially, in the magnet but also in many other things. Is it any wonder, then, if the principle of all beauty ["let there be light"], which the divine Moses introduces into scarcely created matter, even on the first day of creation, as (so to speak) the Creator's instrument, by which to give visible shape and life to all things—is it any wonder, I say, if this primary principle and this most beautiful being in the whole corporeal world, the matrix of all animal faculties, and the bond between the physical and the intellectual world, is submitted to those very laws by which the world was to be formed? Hence the sun is a body in which [resides] that faculty of communicating itself to all things which we call light. For this reason alone its rightful place is the middle point and centre of the whole world, so that it may diffuse itself perpetually and uniformly throughout the universe. All other beings that share in light imitate the sun.]

ONE MIGHT FANCY THIS IS NICHOLAS OF CUSA HIMSELF, speaking two centuries after. It is a Neoplatonic line of speculation profoundly different from that of Paracelsus, however Paracelsian Kepler's ideas may be otherwise about the soul of the Earth and the planets, the terrestrial spirit or "Archeus" which contains the Earth's formative virtues, the signature of things and their occult correspondences. Kepler himself has indicated the point of distinction. The first property of things, he says, is undoubtedly Quality, but only insofar as we can extract quantitative elements out of it can we establish intellectual connections. "As the eye for colors, as the ear for sounds, so the mind is made for understanding not qualities but quantities." Here is no *a priori* refusal, but a clarification: the truth that we can grasp is to be found specifically in lines and numbers, and on that level we can deal with it. Galileo will say: "The book of Nature is written in mathematical characters." The idea itself is Pythagorean, but it leads forward to physical science. The "light of nature" shines intelligibly on the mathematical plane. There, entities are characterized and related univocally, the mind find its bearings and is able to consolidate one discovery after another.

These ideas may seem fairly obvious to us who are used to thinking of mathematics as the backbone of science. But Kepler's contemporaries found it hard to understand what he hoped for. Let us deal with the issue once more explicitly, at the risk of repeating things already said, since it concerns the most momentous of issues. It is a profound change in the very canons of relevance. Conventional philosophers, and educated people generally, had been taught that mathematics concerns "what can be made more and less." Hence, it appeared that it can have little to do with the objects of true philosophy, which are the real and irreducible substances and essences. A man is a man, a duty is a duty, and wood is wood, regardless of quantitative data. Substance and essence do not fall under number, weight and measure; they are all and indivisibly in every part of the thing. Nature herself displays a notable casualness as to measure: a Toy Poodle is every whit as much a dog as a Great Dane. Any kind of numerical data about the behavior of beings will hardly be relevant; wherever there is life there is individuality and growth, only in freeze and death does geometry dominate, as in the crystal. Or, of course, in the heavens, which have nothing to do with our condition. Philosophy tries to do justice to order and purpose, to the many aspects of being, their substance, behavior and change: how could we imagine to constrain the prodigious variety of being in the narrow category of the more and less? Such an extreme and arbitrary reductionism, even if it succeeded, would be the opposite of comprehensive knowledge. We shall never find there the reason and the secret of motion, which is life and spontaneity. Thus spoke the reasonable-minded. Plato himself—remarked the learned among them—when he tried to join the two realms and to construe metaphysical meaning into mathematical entities, wandered off into the more fanciful ranges of his system, which had to be abandoned by sober-minded successors. Let mathematics stay remote from all "real" sciences and be content with providing intellectual exercise.

There is an analogy which ought to be not entirely a matter of chance between this type of thinking and certain social criteria as expressed by the law. "Fungible" goods are the simplest kind of goods, they are those which can be indicated by weight and measure alone, like coal, gravel or potatoes, which go by the carload. More intrinsically valuable goods go by formal specifications. Such echoes of worldly value are not extraneous to so-called pure thought, and we shall find Galileo having to cope with them (p. 226). Be that as it may, it was commonly felt that mature metaphysics had once and for all gone beyond the Pythagorean fancy of explaining things by way of numbers. This point of view has been voiced closer to our own time and in more elaborate language by Hegel and others, for philosophy is still and forever on the quest for the true objects of knowledge.

Kepler himself was on none too firm ground in his own contentions, for after all he had nothing to show except fragmentary evidence from astronomy, music and optics. It was only his passionate divination—other people would have said, a streak of Paracelsus in him—that the truth at the core of things must have the simplicity and necessity of mathematical law: but the grounds for his belief were essentially mystical and aesthetic, as he was willing to admit. Francis Bacon, with his experience of the world, felt that the causes of real events must be more complicated than that. It is only with Galileo that the proper and operative point of junction is found between mathematics and physics, and the scientific revolution is accomplished. Of that revolution Kepler could only be the prophet, talking in riddles.

In the days of his telescopic discoveries (1610), Galileo felt them as a vindication of Kepler's lonely stand. "I am anxiously waiting," he wrote to the ambassador in Prague, "for what il Signor Keplero may have to say about the new marvels. . . . He may well state now that he has shown himself an excellent philosopher; however much it has been his lot, and may be hereafter, to be regarded by the philosophers of our time, who philosophize on paper, as a man of no intellect and little better than a fool." Kepler's response was characteristically enthusiastic and generous. But notwithstanding this brief exchange of signals, the two men were fated to be as ships that pass in the night.

"I have confessed to the truth of the Copernican view," wrote Kepler, "and contemplate its harmonies with incredible ravishment." He had in mind not the true laws he was discovering, but what he thought to be his chief contribution: the "Cosmographic Mystery" in which he explained the planetary distances starting from the five regular polyhedra of geometry, and the *Harmonice Mundi* in which he revived the Pythagorean "harmony of the spheres" and even wrote down its musical canon based on the actual planetary distances and angular velocities. This is far, indeed, from what Bacon is already suggesting at the time, that thought should take its start from things to modify the order of ideas. Geometry, for Kepler, is not only a logical system and a tool, it is the "archetype of the world," and it should shine forth as the "light of nature" did for Paracelsus.

This is clearly not scientific method as it will be defined, for Kepler promptly transmuted every new "harmony" that he thought he had discovered into an essential feature of the cosmos. The mind of this mystical rationalist, so brilliantly creative in pure astronomy, remained entangled in a web of far-reaching but unclear intuitions concerning the role of attraction, magnetism and planetary influences (it was all linked in his mind with a belief in astrology), whereas a true physicist like Galileo had the cold strength to discard even essential ideas like that of gravitation in order to construct a first scheme of dynamics that made sense. Conversely, Galileo gained the freedom thereby of speculating philosophically on the infinity of the universe, a freedom precluded to Kepler who conceived of the world as an organism enclosed by limits.

Notwithstanding his many romantic confusions, Kepler knew what he wanted, and still more what he did not want. The power of abstraction inherent in mathematics carried him invincibly beyond the circle of magic fancies. We have already mentioned in the Introduction the difference between two types of cosmology, the Platonic one based on "design" and the Stoic one, based on "begetting." In Kepler himself, the conflict between those views comes to a head. His archaic and half-animistic physics is still tied to the idea of the world as an organism, the parts of which can only be explained from the whole: but the word *soul* is mostly replaced by *force* in his language; the belief in number and design brings him to a parting of the ways from the traditional initiates. Robert Fludd, the alchemist and Hermetic theosophist, challenges him to abandon the "quantitative shadows," as he calls them: "Kepler excogitates the exterior movement of the thing once brought forth (*naturata*), whereas I behold the internal and essential impulses that issue from nature herself: he has hold of the tail, I grasp the head; I perceive the first cause, he its effects." And he refers mysteriously to a hidden science of numbers which has nothing to do with "ordinary" mathematics. Kepler replies that there is only one kind of mathematics, that which makes proper sense: "I reflect on the visible movements determinable by the senses themselves, you may consider the inner impulses and endeavor to distinguish them. . . . I hold the tail, but I hold it in my hand; you may grasp the head mentally, though only

I fear, in your dreams. I am content with the effects, that is, the movements of the planets. If you shall have found in the very causes harmonies as limpid as are mine in the movements, then it will be proper for me to congratulate you on your gift of invention and myself on my gift of observation—that is, as soon as I shall be able to observe anything."

We have here, in its clearest form, a distinction which will take on further importance; that between *natura naturans* and *natura naturata,* nature as the begetter and nature as the accomplished product. Mathematics is in the role of the true "signature"; the *formula* takes the place of the Aristotelian *forms,* of which Bacon did not know how to rid himself. It does so at a price. In this world there is no longer the heartbeat of becoming, the continuous passing of form from potency to act: the new form, as formula, is perpetually actualized. Like the formula itself, reality becomes analytical. The Aristotelian form *was* life, and could withstand analysis. How to derive analytically life from the formula is still a problem for future ages. Meanwhile, as he leaves to others the speculation on "essences, virtues and seeds," and states his concern with the accomplished and measurable "design," Kepler sets out, in the Platonic spirit, on the way of what might be called objective idealism, where his endeavor will ultimately rejoin that of Galileo.

Boehme

Kepler is a manifest sign of things to come. Yet, quietly aside from the main endeavor, there is another line of thought that goes on and should not be forgotten, however strange it may look, for it will come to fruition only much later.

Jakob Boehme, the shoemaker and prophet of Görlitz (1575-1624), might be considered the last original effort of the Renaissance against the scientific doom.

Boehme is an exact contemporary of Kepler, Galileo and Bacon. He lives at the beginning of the scientific era; but his thought branches out in an utterly different direction,

his universe is the antithesis of theirs, and he would have
been even more disturbed than we are at Newton's famous
definition of God that was to come, in the second edition
of the *Principia:*

". . . The Supreme God is a Being eternal, infinite, absolutely perfect; but a being, however perfect, without dominion, cannot be said to be Lord God. . . . It is the
dominion of a spiritual being which constitutes a God: a
true, supreme, or imaginary dominion makes a true, supreme or imaginary God. And from his true dominion it
follows that the true God is a living, intelligent, and powerful Being; and from his other perfections, that he is supreme, or most perfect. . . . We know him only by his
most wise and excellent contrivances of things, and final
causes; we admire him for his perfections; but we reverence
and adore him on account of his dominion; for we adore
him as his servants; and a god without dominion, providence, and final causes, is nothing else but Fate and Nature.
. . . And thus much concerning God; to discourse of
whom from the appearances of things does certainly belong
to natural philosophy."

His credentials duly checked, the scientific mind can
thus only acknowledge the authority of the universal mon-
arch, who is clearly not one to be troubled by such details
as the existence of Tyburn. He turns out to be concerned
exclusively with the enjoyment and upkeep of his costly
mechanical toy, viz., the gravitational universe. In fact one
suspects that the cosmic order of masses in motion is in
itself, and for him too, the final good. Newton himself, to
be sure, had loftier metaphysical ideas at the back of his
mind, but they were derived from his religious faith. We
have evidence of them even in the definition we just
quoted, which implies a subordination of the divine intellect to absolute Will. But that statement is as far as he can
go, philosophically, with "Nature's God," and out of it
can come only the ephemeral structure of Deism. Man
has no place in that universe, except as a computing intellect. The end of the road is given by a remark of Whitehead: "The Protestant Calvinism and the Catholic
Jansenism exhibited man as helpless to cooperate with

Irresistible Grace; the eighteenth-century scheme of science exhibited man as helpless to cooperate with the irresistible mechanism of nature. The mechanism of God and the mechanism of matter were the monstrous issues of limited metaphysics and clear logical intellect." In fact since the Deists were quite pleased with having delivered the proof of the existence of God by way of that mechanism, it became natural for Hume to point out that the God whom you will find will be the sort of God who made the mechanism.

With these sobering thoughts in mind, we may be better able to grant Boehme the attention he deserves. He has been given by a later age the name of *Philosophus Teutonicus*. Teutonic he certainly was in his abstruseness, but also in his peasantlike directness and simplicity. He could use German as beautifully as Luther in his devotional meditations; his philosophical thinking comes out as best it can "in the most uncouth and original Behmenese," as a translator complained. But Schelling was to say: "As the mythologies and theogonies preceded science, so does his thought foreshadow the advent of all the logical systems of the new philosophy." The not-so-illogical Boehme, and the not-so-logical Spinoza have indeed been the shaping influences of German Romantic philosophy. As "Behmen the Man of God," the former entered English thought, too, and wherever there are still "Brethren of the Free Spirit" such as Quaker thinkers, they will acknowledge him as a master.

Boehme's thought is undeniably part of the anarchic fermentation which came in with Lutheranism. His only real protectors were Saxon noblemen who had sympathized with Schwenkfeld's heretical sect. He was persecuted all his life by the local Lutheran pastors with abuse which today would be unprintable. The town authorities did little to safeguard him: "Jocken Boehme the cobbler, the confusionist enthusiast and fantast, has been invited to go and raise his tent elsewhere." Such things were written in the town register time and again. Actually, Boehme did manage, in his own sober and quiet way, to stay in or near Görlitz all his life.

Boehme does deal with cosmology and natural philosophy. The true way to external knowledge he will pronounce, like Paracelsus, to be by way, not of concept, but of the "signature of things." He is speaking, however, really of nothing but the inner experience. "The visible world is a manifestation of the inner world of Light and Darkness." This would define him in modern terms as an absolute idealist; yet he is far from being that. Nor, on the other hand, is he simply a mystical visionary. By "manifestation" Boehme means, as a medieval would, that the world is entirely real and wholly symbolic at the same time. Knowledge is not detachment from the world, it is a "gnosis," an enlightenment taking place within man. The Paracelsian identification of the *Mysterium Magnum* of the universe with the mystery of consciousness is here worked out to a conclusion.

The striking thing about this enlightenment is that it could by no means, even by the critical-minded, be called an escape into metaphysical harmonies. It expresses a profound experience of life. Boehme's idea of truth was far from sentimental: it was bitter and hard. A truly good soul, he was perplexed and tormented by the existence of evil; nor did he content himself with staring at it fixedly, like the Calvinist hypnotized by the *Gloria Dei,* brooding upon predestination. On the other hand, the Platonic doctrine of "God's non-responsibility" made no sense at all to him. How could an omniscient creator not foresee evil and suffering? What was wrong with him? "The learned," he writes, "have rigged up a great quantity of monstrosities concerning the origin of sin, and have scratched themselves therewith. . . . People seem to think that God has willed the bad, since he has created such a lot of it." The chief monstrosity for him is that God should have designedly chosen some men for blessedness and others for eternal condemnation. Even if the Apostles had written this he would not believe it; still less if it is Augustine. In the same way, the account of Genesis does seem to him "quite contrary to philosophy and reason"; on which account, too, he cannot bring himself to believe that "that worthy man Moses was its author."

He was "sore troubled and in despair." For a while it would seem that Boehme made up for himself an answer in the ancient gnostic manner: God has turned his face away from the world. Maybe there is an evil God, too. Was there then another God nearer to the heart, that may still save us?

But his strong philosophical instinct would not let him take this path of escape. There had been Copernicus, of whom he knew dimly, whom he could not deny, as Bacon was doing, and who dismayed him: man seemed very much of a small displaced person in the universe. But there was also Paracelsus, who gave him ideas and the alchemical symbolism; there were the mystics, Valentin Weigel and Sebastian Franck. These men provided a frame for his insight, which at last came to him, as though "life had pierced into the heart of death."

This insight he described many years later in his first work. *Aurora or the Coming of Dawn;* God is both good and evil: he is a fire issuing out of his own abysmal darkness, devouring and life-giving; God, too, is a stirring towards consciousness from elemental power to "lovely light."

We should keep in mind that all of transcendent speculation, since the time of Plotinus, runs into a grievous paradox: the need to posit as a starting point an unthinkable concept and almost a contradiction in terms. The God to whom thought leads, from whom the world has issued, is as close to Nothing as thought can make him, for he must come before any determination; yet he must have in himself the power to bring forth the world and all it contains in determination: he must be, strictly speaking, all and nothing in one. Some such paradox occurs inevitably whenever speculation ventures deep enough into the foundation of things. We have seen this explicitly formulated by Cusanus. The present-day physical theories about the structure of the void are skirting it in their own way. In traditional Neoplatonism, the manner in which the All proceeds from the initial Nothing is given by the theory of emanation, borrowed largely from the Stoics.

Boehme gives of that theory a new version. We can hardly expect it to be more rational, but it is powerfully dramatic. In fact, its strength lies in having abandoned scholastic rationality altogether. Real religious experience expresses itself only in symbolic language. It is a language which is not of concepts but of significant images: it has a vocabulary and a grammar all of its own. The original Christian experience had found essentially human symbols, such as fatherhood, union, willfulness, atonement, redemption. Boehme's symbology is more naturalistic, and more abstruse too. It finds a natural expression in the alchemical language. Its conceptual frame amounts to this: in the essence of God there must be a plurality of moments, there must be differentiation, initial contrast, or nothing will happen. "Nothing can reveal itself without resistance." God is not only the Yes but also the No which opposes it, or he could not bring forth awareness and joy; there would be no divine will either, for pure unity has nothing in itself that it could will.

Now we can give Boehme's own imagery. It starts from the dark Nothingness, whence the Deity "generates" itself perpetually. What issues from that Dark is a desire, an eternal hunger, a kind of suction of the Abyss (*Urgrund*) which seeks after Being to absorb it but can only twist and fall back upon itself; it brings about as it were a whirl, a wheel of insatiate dark fire. Such is the core of life, a self-consuming fire, such is Nature too in its elemental urge, for the process is mirrored in "becoming." It generates by contrast, centrifugally as it were, the *will* to overcome the inherent destruction and that it is that shines forth as light, clarity, spirit.

Desire, the elemental appeal of the Father, is conceived as harsh attraction and a kind of perpetual pressure and collapse, one image given being the dull crumbling embers which "drive" the clear free flame out of the log. But the other simile of the magic fire-wheel points to more complex ancestral representations of hoary antiquity.

Such is the cosmogonic drama and the birth of Nature as it takes place forever in the eternal Now. "It has to be written bit by bit for the sake of my reader's lack of understanding," but it is strictly outside of time, even as the Son's self-sacrifice which brings light to the spirit.

It takes place in time under the aspect of Nature, and also as our own inner experience of darkness and light. If beings separate themselves from it, they experience only the No, the "wrath of God," elemental and unintentional, which is also the "foundation of Hell," This is the reality of evil in the world, for evil is an intrinsic part of being and growth, "God against God." The harshness and bitterness have to be there in the green fruit, to be matured by the sun's warmth. The fear and pain in the struggle with the self are equally of the essence of the process. The bitter quality is in God also. There is an intrinsically irrational and confusing element in God, in the world, and in man too, and there has to be in thought, but it is a kind of broken, "troubled" development towards rationality and clarity.

The fateful word "development" has entered the philosophical language here for the first time, not in the old sense of "unwinding" but in the new sense implied by our own idea of "evolution." Difference impulse and growth are expressed in the coming to the fore of different qualities. And here is where Boehme the non-humanist beautifully misunderstands the official science of his time. "Quality" in philosophy is a static grammatical attribute of being, it is "whichness" or "howness," but in Boehme's homespun etymology it comes from *quallen, Quelle,* welling forth from a source. "Quality is the mobility or impulse of a thing." Here, as in Bruno, the dynamic element of Renaissance thought has broken loose from the prison of formal systems and is moving towards new possibilities. Two laws have been suggested, if only as psychological experiences: the law of contrast, and the law of development as progressive unfolding of difference. They express a profound change from the past, which is reflected in the different conception of the Godhead. In Plato and Aristotle, the philosophers of "design," God had been forever "actualized" thought, in which the achieved forms existed eternally. Growth was only in matter. The origin of this conception lies in the Greek mathematical ideal, however much of it may have been forced into new functions. The God of Boehme, instead, is himself a potentiality, he is always in the act of "becoming"—and so, consequently, is reality in its essence. Inner contrast and unfolding are unmathematical conceptions from the start; they are an original attempt at presenting a reality unamenable to mathematics.

Boehme's thought, to be sure, remains strictly on the ground of religious speculation, but on one free of all confessional boundaries. The process of the soul takes place wherever man is man, and in this Boehme is no less universal than if he believed in the natural religion of Bodin or Grotius. He is also a Protestant, in that he deals with the individual conscience alone.

On one more point, and it is an essential one, Boehme steers a very sure and revolutionary course: it is on the problem of free will. Pantheism, of which he was wrongly accused, considers the universe as God himself and so cannot admit evil as such. Theism proclaims free will but leaves God somehow responsible for all evil decisions, as the creator of the soul. Newton's God does not escape that responsibility. The third course is that suggested by Boehme: the soul is not a mode of the divine substance or an invention of the Creator, it is absolutely self-existent. Good and evil, God and the devil, heaven and hell, are opposed possibilities within the mystery of consciousness, in relation to which the soul possesses real liberty of choice, as it brings them forth itself as it were. With this, modern philosophy has entered on its course. And we do not mean only idealistic philosophy but any type of thought which has to deal with the issue of freedom.

Modern opinion would probably phrase that issue more or less thus: If there is to be a world of genuine choice, it must permit choices the outcome of which will destroy each other; in other words it cannot be a harmonious world. Disharmony is essential to freedom; when it affects peoples' lives, the experience is evil. This can be said of social disharmonies, of cosmic disharmonies such as the Lisbon earthquake of which Voltaire was to make so much, or of conflict in the human soul.

The crazy-quilt mystical pattern of Boehme's ideas may look as if it were fetched from the darkest medieval lore, but we have said enough to show that a new symbolism was of the essence, and that the intellectual design underlying it is strikingly free and advanced. To realize how much, one should think of the contemporary remnants of medieval rationalism, namely, of the intellectual contraptions worked out by Counter-Reformation theologians about the same time to solve the problems of Grace and Free Will, on which Pascal poured such devastating ridicule in his *Provinciales*. The actual components of the Jesuit construction are the most refined concepts of scholastic theory, yet the quibbling technique with which they are put together reminds one of Rube Goldberg machinery with its steamrollers, calliopes, cogwheels and teakettles connected by strings.

Boehme is a sincere Lutheran, but he too, like the Socinians, is trying to replace as obsolete a feature that a modern Christian thinker, Nikolai Berdiaeff, has recently called the stage-setting of rational theology: an immobile God of benevolent fatherly attributes who arbitrarily invents the universe in order to get some praise that he obviously does not need and hereby sets the stage for a foreseen sequence of mistakes, anger, misery, and atonement. Needless to say, this word of "stage-setting" does less than justice to the profound spiritual experience carried by the Tale. Boehme is suggesting in his own untutored way a scheme different from "natural religion" and more adequate to the actual metaphysical content of that experience, namely, freedom.

Heraclitus the Obscure, the philosopher of Living Fire, had said quite early in the game: "However far you go, you shall not find the boundaries of the soul, so deep it is." It was only to be expected that Boehme's animistic-naturalistic imagery should break down before reaching those boundaries, as all others have done. But in its very simplicity in front of the unconscious depths, in its unexplained visions of apocalyptic strife, it may yet have reached a farther limit than Hegel's ambitious skyscraper of antitheses and syntheses that was to follow, rigged up with the tubular scaffolding of a new rationality.

From *The Confessions:**

*Jacob Boehme, *The Confessions*, ed. W. Scott Palmer, Introduction by Evelyn Underhill. New York: Harper & Brothers; London: Methuen & Co. Ltd., 1954.

[I never desired to know anything of the Divine Mystery, much less understood I the way to seek and find it. I knew nothing of it, which is the condition of poor laymen in their simplicity. I sought only after the heart of Jesus Christ, that I might hide myself therein from the wrathful anger of God . . .

In this way my earnest and Christian seeking and desire (wherein I suffered many a shrewd repulse, but at last resolved rather to put myself in hazard than leave off), the Gate was opened to me, that in one quarter of an hour I saw and knew more than if I had been many years together at an University, at which I exceedingly admired and thereupon turned my praise to God for it.

So that I did not only greatly wonder at it, but did also exceedingly rejoice; and presently it came powerfully into my mind to set the same down in writing, for a memorial for myself, though I could very hardly apprehend the same in my external man and express it with the pen. Yet, however, I must begin to labour in this great mystery as a child that goes to school.

I saw it as in a great deep in the internal; for I had a thorough view of the Universe, as a complex moving fulness wherein all things are couched and wrapped up; but it was impossible for me to explain the same.

Yet it opened itself in me, from time to time, as in a young plant. It was with me for the space of twelve years, and was as it were breeding. I found a powerful instigation within me before I could bring it forth into external form of writing; but whatever I could apprehend with the external principle of my mind, that I wrote down.

Afterwards, however, the Sun shone upon me a good while, but not constantly, for sometimes the Sun hid itself, and then I knew not nor well understood my own labour. Man must confess that his knowledge is not his own but from God, who manifests the Ideas of Wisdom to the soul, in what measure he pleases.

It is not to be understood that my reason is greater or higher than that of all other men living; but I am the Lord's twig or branch, and a very mean and little spark of his light; he may set me where he pleases, I cannot hinder him in that.

Neither is this my natural will, that I can do it by my own small ability; for if the Spirit were withdrawn from me, then I could neither know nor understand my own writings. . . .

Men have always been of the opinion that heaven is many hundred, nay, many thousand, miles distant from the face of the earth, and that God dwells only in that heaven, and rules by the power of the Holy Spirit in this world.

Some have undertaken to measure this height and distance, and have produced many strange and monstrous devices. . . .

But when God had given me many a hard blow and repulse, doubtless from the Spirit, which had a great longing yearning towards me, at last I fell into a very deep melancholy and heavy sadness, when I beheld and contemplated the great Deep of this World, also the sun and stars, the clouds, rain and snow, and considered in my spirit the whole creation of the world.

Wherein then I found, in all things, evil and good, love and anger; in the inanimate creatures, in wood, stones, earth and the elements, as also in men and beasts.

Moreover I considered the little spark of light, man, what he should be esteemed for with God, in comparison of this great work and fabric of heaven and earth.

And finding that in all things there was evil and good, as well in the elements as in the creatures, and that it went as well in this world with the wicked as with the virtuous, honest and godly . . . I was thereupon very melancholy, perplexed and exceedingly troubled, no Scripture could comfort or satisfy me though I was very well acquainted with it and versed therein; at which time the Devil would by no means stand idle, but was often beating into me many heathenish thoughts which I will here be silent in.

Yet when in this affliction and trouble I elevated my spirit (which then I understood very little or nothing at all what it was), I earnestly raised it up into God, as with a great storm or onset, wrapping up my whole heart and mind, as also all my thoughts and whole will and resolution, incessantly to wrestle with the Love and Mercy of God, and not to give over unless he blessed me, that is, unless he enlightened me with his Holy Spirit, whereby I might understand his will and be rid of my sadness. And then the Spirit did break through.

The greatness of the triumphing that was in my spirit I cannot express either in speaking or writing; neither can it be compared to any thing but that wherein life is generated in the midst of death. It is like the resurrection from the dead.

In this light my spirit suddenly saw through all, and in and by all, the creatures; even in herbs and grass it knew God, who he is and how he is and what his will is. And suddenly in that light my will was set on by a mighty impulse to describe the Being of God.

But because I could not presently apprehend the deepest movings of God and comprehend them in my reason, there passed almost twelve years before the exact understanding thereof was given me.

And it was with me as with a young tree, which is planted in the ground and at first is young and tender, and flourishing to the eye, especially if it comes on lustily in its growing; but does not bear fruit presently, and though it has blossoms they fall off: also frost and snow and many a cold wind beat upon it before it comes to any growth and bearing of fruit.]

[From *Signatura Rerum* (The Signature of All Things).*

CHAPTER I.

1. All whatever is taught of God, without the knowledge of the signature is dumb and void of understanding; for it proceeds only from an historical conjecture, from the mouth of another, wherein the spirit without knowledge is dumb; but if the spirit opens to him the *signature,* then he

*The Works of Jacob Behmen, vol. 4, trans. William Law. London: G. Robinson, 1781.

understands the speech of another; and further, he understands how the spirit has manifested and revealed itself (out of the essence through the principle) in the sound with the voice. For though I see one to speak, teach, preach, and write of God, and though I hear and read the same, yet this is not sufficient for me to understand him; but if his sound and spirit out of his signature and similitude enter into my own similitude and imprint his similitude into mine, then I may understand him really and fundamentally, be it either spoken or written, if he has the hammer that can strike my bell. . . .

4. And then secondly we understand, that the signature or form is no spirit, but the receptacle, container, or cabinet of the spirit, wherein it lies; for the signature stands in the essence, and is as a lute that lies still, and is indeed a dumb thing that is neither heard or understood; but if it be played upon, then its form is understood, in what form and tune it stands, and according to what note it is set. Thus likewise the signature of nature in its form is a dumb essence; it is as a prepared instrument of music, upon which the will's spirit plays; what strings he touches, they sound according to their property. . . .

6. Man has indeed all the forms of all the three worlds lying in him; for he is a complete image of God, or of the Being of all beings; only the order is placed in him at his incarnation; for there are three work-masters in him which prepare his form [or signature], viz. the threefold fiat, according to the three worlds; and they are in contest about the form, and the form is figured according to the contest; which of the masters holds the predominant rule, and obtains it in the essence, according to that his instrument is tuned, and the others lie hid, and come behind with their sound, as it plainly shews itself. . . .

9. And thus also it happens to the good man, that when the wicked man strikes his hidden instrument with the spirit of his wrath, that then the form of anger is stirred up also in the good man, and the one is set against the other, that so one might be the cure and healer of the other. For as the vital signature, that is, as the form of life is figured in the time of the fiat at the conception, even so

is its natural spirit; for it takes its rise out of the essence of all the three principles, and such a will it acts and manifests out of its property.

10. But now the will may be broken; for when a stronger comes, and raises his inward signature with his introduced sound and will's spirit, then its upper dominion loses the power, right, and authority; which we see in the powerful influence of the sun, how that by its strength it qualifies a bitter and sour fruit, turning it into a sweetness and pleasantness; in like manner how a good man corrupts among evil company, and also how that a good herb cannot sufficiently shew its real genuine virtue in a bad soil; for in the good man the hidden evil instrument is awakened, and in the herb a contrary essence is received from the earth; so that often the good is changed into an evil, and the evil into a good. . . .

15. Everything has its mouth to manifestation; and this is the language of nature, whence everything speaks out of its property, and continually manifests, declares, and sets forth itself for what it is good or profitable; for each thing manifests its mother, which thus gives the essence and the will to the form.

Chapter II

1. Seeing then there are so many and divers forms, that the one always produces and affords out of its property a will different in one from another, we herein understand the contrariety and combat in the Being of all beings, how that one does oppose, poison, and kill another, that is, overcome its essence, and the spirit of the essence, and introduces it into another form, whence sickness and pains arise, when one essence destroys another.

2. And then we understand herein the cure, how the one heals another, and brings it to health; and if this were not, there were no nature, but an eternal stillness, and no will; for the contrary will makes the motion, and the original of the seeking, that the opposite sound seeks the rest, and yet in the seeking it only elevates and more enkindles itself. . . .

3. . . . For each thing desires a will of its likeness, and by the contrary will it is discomfited; but if it obtains a will of its likeness, it rejoices in the assimulate, and therein falls into rest, and the enmity is turned into joy.

4. For the external nature has produced nothing in its desire, except a likeness out of itself; and if there were not an everlasting mixing, there would be an eternal peace in nature, but so nature would not be revealed and made manifest; so that each thing elevates itself, and would get out of the combat into the still rest, and so it runs to and fro, and thereby only awakens and stirs up the combat.

5. And we find clearly in the light of nature, that there is no better help and remedy for this opposition, and that it has no higher cure than the liberty, that is, the light of nature, which is the desire of the spirit.

7. Seeing now that man's life consists in three principles, viz. in a threefold essence, and has also a threefold spirit out of the property of each essence, viz. first, according to the eternal nature, according to the fire's property; and secondly, according to the property of the eternal light and divine essentiality; and thirdly, according to the property of the outward world: Thereupon we are to consider the property of this threefold spirit, and also of this threefold essence and will; how each spirit with its essence introduces itself into strife and sickness, and what its cure and remedy is.

8. We understand that without nature there is an eternal stillness and rest, viz. the Nothing; and then we understand that an eternal will arises in the nothing, to introduce the nothing into something, that the will might find, feel, and behold itself.

9. For in the nothing the will would not be manifest to itself, wherefore we know that the will seeks itself, and finds itself in itself, and its seeking is a desire, and its finding is the essence of the desire, wherein the will finds itself.

10. It finds nothing except only the property of the hunger, which is itself, which it draws into itself, that is, draws itself into itself, and finds itself in itself; and its attraction into itself makes an overshadowing or darkness in it, which is not in the liberty, viz. in the nothing; for the will of the liberty overshadows itself with the essence of

the desire, for the desire makes essence and not the will.

11. Now that the will must be in darkness is its contrariety, and it conceives in itself another will to go out from the darkness again into the liberty, viz. into the nothing, and yet it cannot reach the liberty from without itself, for the desire goes outwards, and causes source and darkness; therefore the will (understand the reconceived will) must enter inwards, and yet there is no separation.

12. For in itself before the desire is the liberty, viz. the nothing, and the will may not be a nothing, for it desires to manifest in the nothing; and yet no manifestation can be effected, except only through the essence of the desire; and the more the reconceived will desires manifestation, the more strongly and eagerly the desire draws into itself, and makes in itself three forms, viz. the desire, which is astringent, and makes hardness, for it is an enclosing, when coldness arises, and the attraction causes dread, and stirring in the hardness, an enmity against the attracted hardness; the attraction is the second form, and a cause of motion and life, and stirs itself in the astringency and hardness, which the hardness, viz. the enclosing, cannot endure, and therefore it attracts more eagerly to hold the dread, and yet the sting is thereby only the stronger.

13. Thus the compunction willeth upwards, and whirls crossways, and yet cannot effect it, for the hardness, viz. the desire, stays and detains it, and therefore it stands like a triangle, and transverted orb, which (seeing it cannot remove from the place) becomes wheeling, whence arises the mixture in the desire, viz. the essence, or multiplicity of the desire; for the turning makes a continual confusion and contrition, whence the anguish, viz. the pain, the third form (or sting of sense) arises.

14. But seeing the desire, viz. the astringency, becomes only the more strong thereby (for from the stirring arises the wrath and nature, viz. the motion), the first will to the desire is made wholly harsh and a hunger, for it is in a hard compunctive dry essence, and also cannot get rid and quit of it, for itself makes the essence, and likewise possesses it, for thus it finds itself now out of nothing in the

something, and the something is yet its contrary will, for it is an unquietness, and the free-will is a stillness.

15. This is now the original of enmity, that nature opposes the free-will, and a thing is at enmity in itself; and here we understand the centre of nature with three forms, in the original, viz. in the first principle, it is Spirit; in the second it is Love, and in the third principle Essence; and these three forms are called in the third principle Sulphur, Mercury, and Sal. . . .

28. The desire of the liberty is meek, easy, and pleasant, and it is called good; and the desire to nature makes itself in itself dark, dry, hungry, and wrathful, which is called God's anger, and the dark world, viz. the first principle; and the light world is the second principle.

29. And we are to understand, that it is no divided essence, but one holds the other hidden or closed up in it, and the one is the beginning and cause of the other, also its healing and cure; that which is awaked and stirred up, that gets dominion, and manifests itself externally with its character, and makes a form and signature according to its will in the external after itself. A similitude whereof we see in an enraged man or beast. . . .

30. The third form is the anxiousness which arises in nature from the first and second form, and is the upholder or preserver of the first and second; it is in itself the sharp fiat; and the second form has the Verbum, viz. the property to the word, and it consists in three properties, and makes out of herself with the three the fourth, viz. the fire; in the external birth, viz. in the third principle, it is called Sal, or salt, according to its matter; but in its spirit it has many forms; for it is the fire-root, the great anguish, it arises betwixt and out of the astringency and bitterness in the harsh attraction; it is the essentiality of that which is attracted, viz. the corporality, or comprehensibility; from Sulphur it is of a brimstone nature and from Mercury a blaze or flash; it is in itself painful, viz. a sharpness of dying, and that from the sharp attraction of the astringency: It has a twofold fire, one cold, another hot; the cold arises from the astringency, from

the sharp attraction, and is a dark black fire; and the hot arises from the driving forth the sting of grief in the anguish in the desire after the liberty, and the liberty is its enkindler, and the raging sting is the cold's fire's awakener.

31. These three forms are in one another as one, and yet they are but one, but they sever themselves through the original into many forms, and yet they have but one mother, viz. the desiring will to manifestation, which is called the father of nature, and of the Being of all beings.

32. Now we are to consider the hunger of the anxiety, or the salt-spirit, and then also its satiating or fulfilling: The anguish has in it two wills, from the original of the first will out of the liberty to the manifestation of itself; viz. the first will is to nature, and the other reconceived will is the son of the first, which goes out of the manifestation again into itself into the liberty; for it is become an eternal life in nature, and yet possesses not nature essentially, but dwells in itself, and penetrates nature as a transparent shining, and the first will flees outwards, for it is the desire of manifestation; it seeks itself out of itself, and yet amasses the desire in itself; it desires to educe the internal out of itself.

33. Thus it has two properties; with the seeking in itself it makes the centre of nature: For it is like a poison, a will of dreadful aspiring, like a lightning and thunder-clap; for this desire desires only anguish, and to be horrible, to find itself in itself, out of the nothing in the something; and the second form proceeds forth as a flagrat [after-flash], or produces sound out of itself, for it is not the desire of the first will to continue in the horrible death, but only thus to educe itself out of the nothing, and to find itself.

34. And we understand by the centre in itself, with the aspiring wrathfulness, with the wrathful will to nature, the dark world, and with the egress out of itself to manifestation, the outward world; and with the second will out of the first, which enters again into the liberty, we understand the light world, or the kingdom of joy, or the true Deity.

The desire of the dark world is after the manifestation, viz. after the outward world, to attract and draw the same essentiality into it, and thereby to satisfy its wrathful hunger; and the desire of the outward world is after the essence or life, which arises from the pain and anguish.

Its desire in itself is the wonder of eternity, a mystery, or mirror, or what is comprehended of the first will to nature. . . .

. . . A similitude whereof we may apprehend in the thunderstorm; the flash, or lightning, or ethereal blaze, goes always before, for it is the enkindled salniter; thereupon follows the stroke in the flagrat of the coldness; as you see, as soon as the stroke is given the stringent chamber is opened, and a cool wind follows, and oftentimes whirling and wheeling; for the forms of nature are awakened, and are as a turning wheel, and so they carry their spirit the wind.]

CHAPTER XI

Galileo

MOST OF RENAISSANCE THOUGHT TENDS TO SHOW AN almost visionary intensification of the idea of Life as the primal truth. "Biological" is not quite the same for it; life tends to be translated in terms of soul, and what we have is a higher form of animism: monistic panpsychism. This is indeed a general characteristic; it is the way in which the epoch tries to reabsorb the abstract cathedrals of medieval thought and to project the formative power into new shapes. We have seen how even the Pythagorean tradition as embodied in Kepler does not escape this pupating process, as it were; although the power of Number and Design embodied in it keeps it moving away from simple animism, while it strives to penetrate the mystery of creation by way of mathematical Necessity.

A singular example for this is Galileo himself. Galileo Galilei (1564-1642), as a modern scientific intellect, and as the creator of the new physico-mathematical structure of nature, belongs by right, to the next century and the next volume. However, there has been too much emphasis in history on his technical thought. There is more to him than the theory of dynamics and the distinction between primary and secondary qualities of matter. Born in the year of Michelangelo's death, dead in the year of Newton's birth, he is a prodigiously complex and at times contradictory transition between the Renaissance and modern times. All the themes of the past are present in his thought, but harmonized in a new manner.

As an Archimedean, Galileo creates a science of motion: he achieves it by showing that motion is not simply a general word for designating change as Aristotle had used it, but that within the *changes in motion* mathematical laws will reveal themselves. Thus he discovers the law of falling bodies. This is and remains a heresy for scholastics: motion was supposed to be the way in which a being achieves its own good, and mathematics is not supposed to deal with the good. But under the invocation of Plato, the protector of mathematics, Galileo insists that a comprehensive mathematical order is a higher good in itself. He is so convinced of the need for harmony and geometrical order in the universe that no motion can be natural to his mind that is not circular and uniform.

The actual development of his thought shows that he, too, moves from the cosmological frame of mind of the philosophers. That is why he insists that he is philosopher first, and then only mathematician. He has concentrated on the problem of motion as providing an essential clue to the mystery of nature, and the decision between Aristotle and Copernicus. If the projected stone can be shown to move by the same law which controls the motion of the moon, namely, inertia, then the moon, and the Earth itself in its rotation, are no different in nature from the earthly missile, the Earth loses its privileged unique condition and is found to be "in heaven too." When the telescope showed that the moon *was* made of ordinary rock, the circle of proof was concluded in his mind. Copernicus had been right, geometry with its circles is more basic than qualities. To those wondrous circles he was going to hang on even beyond reason.

Against the scholastics who protest in the name of empirical evidence that there is such a thing, and on earth only, as straight motion up and down, against his own discovery of constant acceleration in fall, Galileo stands by the Pythagorean circles: he is even willing to forgo the proper formulation of the inertial law of which he himself is the author, since straight inertial paths would disarrange the beautiful order of things. Not content with the necessary truths as they come one by one out of his own "resolutive method," he is in tireless search of the architecture into which they must fit. The metaphysical assumption is stated flatly: the universe must be conceived as a most perfect work of art, or there would be no sense in trying to understand it. Hence we must look for a groundwork of the

highest possible rationality, and only mathematics can reveal that groundwork, since its truth is pure necessity itself.

Galileo, the so-called empiricist, is in fact an unyielding scientific rationalist. His mind is far from being
"washed clear of opinions" as Bacon prescribes. It is only
fair to insist on this. If there is any dealing with physical
nature by trial and error in the Renaissance, it is rather on
the side of the magic-mystic materialists and alchemists,
whom we have described as of the Stoic descendance. It
is they who tirelessly concoct, distill, extract, combine and
separate, operate with fire, with acids, with solvents and
coagulants—always in the effort to move qualities around
experimentally, to derive one thing by way of another.
Galileo, in the proper mathematical spirit, operates with rational abstractions, he tends to explain "what is" by way
of "what is not." His unscientific predecessors, insofar as
they dealt not with material operations, had insistently
gazed at nature, but they asked it to speak to them through
its many names or its "signatures," or searched for words
to speak to it in a language to which it could respond,
which is indeed what not only mystic metaphysicians but
poets are apt to hope for and expect. Galileo believes
instead that "the book of Nature is written in mathematical
characters," which means, if we follow his thought where it
leads us, that out of "indubitable" premises arising from
points where nature shows measure, weight, and number,
we can set the deductive course of our reasoning as
geometers do, and come back to nature only to check the
conclusion. This is what Galileo means by the experimental
approach. The word "experiment," widely used by all,
meant at the time nothing else but sensible experience:
that is why Galileo has to create a new term, "the ordeal
of experience." Nature is faced with what lawyers call
the adversary method, she cannot tell her own story but is
cross-examined with questions to which the answer can
only be "yes" or "no"; and instead of verbal questions, we
use the rack of experiment. The world, which had been in
Greek thought a closed "republic," as it were, of men, gods,
and things in harmonious coexistence, is beginning to take
on the modern aspect of an open field for the permanent

warfare of man against nature, a campaign of unending breakthroughs.

Thus Galileo the scientist is creating a situation incompatible with the vision of Galileo the philosopher, and he is far from unaware of the powerful dialectical conflict in this thought; but wherever the force of his "necessary conclusions" reaches out is a point of no return.

In one way, Galileo can find philosophical reassurance if he needs it: it is by showing that the architecture of natural philosophy that precedes him is "incongruous and puerile," of essentially poor design and unworthy of the majesty of the Cosmos. He can show that much of the hallowed medieval cosmology degenerates under inspection into shabby literary commonplace. The following criticism of the Aristotelian heavens is taken from his *Dialogue on the Great World Systems*,* which earned him the famous trial and sentence of 1633, on "vehement suspicion of heresy":

[I cannot without great wonder, nay more, disbelief, hear it being attributed to natural bodies as a great honour and perfection that they are impassible, immutable, inalterable, etc.: as, conversely, I hear it esteemed a great imperfection to be alterable, generable, and mutable. It is my opinion that the Earth is very noble and admirable by reason of the many and different alterations, mutations, and generations which incessantly occur in it. And if, without being subject to any alteration, it had been all one vast heap of sand, or a mass of jade, or if, since the time of the deluge, the waters freezing which covered it, it had continued an immense globe of crystal, wherein nothing had ever grown, altered, or changed, I should have esteemed it a wretched lump of no benefit to the Universe, a mass of idleness, and in a word superfluous, exactly as if it had never been in Nature. The difference for me would be the same as between a living and a dead creature. I say the same concerning the Moon, Jupiter, and all the other globes of the Universe. The more I delve into the consideration of the

*Edited and annotated from the Salusbury translation by Giorgio de Santillana. Chicago: University of Chicago Press, 1953. © The University of Chicago, 1953.

vanity of popular discourses, the more empty and simple
I find them. What greater folly can be imagined than to
call gems, silver and gold noble, and earth and dirt base?
For do not these persons consider that, if there were as
great a scarcity of earth as there is of jewels and precious
metals, there would be no king who would not gladly give
a heap of diamonds and rubies and many ingots of gold to
purchase only so much earth as would suffice to plant a
jessamine in a little pot or to set a tangerine in it, that he
might see it sprout, grow up, and bring forth such goodly
leaves, fragrant flowers, and delicate fruit?

It is scarcity and plenty that makes things esteemed and
despised by the vulgar, who will say that here is a most
beautiful diamond, for it resembles a clear water, and yet
would not part with it for ten tons of water. These men
who so extol incorruptibility, inalterability, and so on,
speak thus, I believe, out of the great desire they have to
live long and for fear of death, not considering that, if
men had been immortal, they would not have had to come
into the world. These people deserve to meet with a
Medusa's head that would transform them into statues of
diamond and jade, that so they might become more perfect
than they are.]

HERE WE SEE A PROFOUNDLY NEW IDEA OF THE UNIVERSE
taking shape, ancient and powerful in its roots, incalculable
in its expansion, and as different from the Aristotelian
caricature taught in the schools as it is from the scant and
angular mechanistic dogmatism that Descartes was to introduce a few years later and Newton was reluctantly to adopt
as a basis for his theories. Not quite biological, for Galileo
is essentially a physicist; not mechanical, surely, for the underlying reality is imagined to be a flow of transforming
and vivifying energy which ought to be in essence, as will
be revealed eventually, light itself. It is what Galileo does
not shy from calling by its proper name, the "Pythagorean
philosophy."

The mystical and contemplative overtones which had
been transmitted as part of that philosophy are originally
reinterpreted in a way not very different from what ancient
Philolaus himself would have meant, and we see Galileo

finding expressive symbols of the unifying power of reason in the creative force of life:

[It seems to me that, if the celestial bodies concur to the generation and alteration of the Earth, they themselves are also of necessity alterable; for otherwise I cannot understand how the application of the Sun and Moon to the Earth to effect production should be any other than to lay a marble statue in the chamber of the bride and from that conjunction to expect children.]

THE SAME SEARCHING CRITICISM IS BROUGHT TO BEAR ON the assumed dimensions of the universe:

[SALVIATI: I could wish, Simplicius, that, suspending for a time the affection that you bear to the followers of your opinion, you would sincerely tell me whether you think that they do in their minds comprehend that magnitude which they reject afterwards as impossible for its immensity to be ascribed to the Universe. For I, as to my own part, think that they do not. But I believe that, as, in the apprehension of numbers, when once a man begins to pass those millions of millions, the imagination is confounded and can no longer form a concept of them, so it happens also in trying to comprehend immense magnitudes and distances; so that there intervenes to the comprehension an effect like to that which befalls the sense. For when in a serene night I look towards the stars, I judge, according to sense, that their distance is but a few miles and that the fixed stars are not a jot more remote than Jupiter or Saturn or than the Moon. . . . In a word, I ask of you, oh foolish men, does your imagination comprehend that vast magnitude of the Universe, which you afterwards judge to be too immense? If you comprehend it, will you hold that your apprehension extends itself further than the Divine Power? Will you say that you can imagine greater things than those which God can bring to pass? But if you apprehend it not, why will you pass verdict upon things beyond your comprehension?

SIMPLICIUS: All this is very well, nor can it be denied but that Heaven may in greatness surpass our imagination, as also that God might have created it thousands of times vaster than now it is; but we ought not to grant anything to have been made in vain and to be idle in the Universe. Now, since we see this admirable order of the planets, disposed about the Earth in distances proportionate for producing their effects for our advantage, to what purpose is it to interpose afterwards between the highest sphere of Saturn and the starry sphere a vast vacancy, without any star, that is superfluous and to no purpose? To what end? For whose profit and advantage?

SALVIATI: I think we arrogate too much to ourselves, Simplicius, when we take it for granted that only the care of us is the adequate reason and limit, beyond which Divine Wisdom and Power does or disposes nothing. I will not consent that we should so much shorten its hand, but desire that we may content ourselves with an assurance that God and Nature are so employed in the governing of human affairs that they could not apply themselves more thereto if they truly had no other care than only that of mankind. And this, I think, I am able to make out by a most pertinent and most noble example, taken from the operation of the Sun's light, which, while it attracts these vapours, or heats that planet, attracts and heats them as if it had no more to do; yea, in ripening that bunch of grapes, nay, that one single grape, it does apply itself so that it could not be more intense, if the sum of all its business had been the maturation of that one grape. Now if this grape receives all that it is possible for it to receive from the Sun, not suffering the least injury by the Sun's production of a thousand other effects at the same time, well might we accuse that grape of envy or folly if it should think or wish that the Sun would appropriate all of its rays to its advantage. I am confident that nothing is omitted by the Divine Providence of what concerns the government of human affairs; but that there may not be other things in the Universe that depend upon the same infinite wisdom, I cannot, of myself, by what my reason holds forth to me, bring myself to believe. Surely, I should not forbear to believe any reasons to the contrary laid before me by some higher intellect. But, as I stand, if one should tell me that an immense space, deprived of stars and idle, would be vain and useless, as likewise that so great an immensity for receipt of the fixed stars as exceeds our utmost comprehension would be superfluous, I would reply that it is rashness to go about to make our shallow reason judge of the works of God, and to call vain and superfluous whatever thing in the Universe is not of use to us.]

THIS IS NO DOUBT DEEPLY MEANT; BUT WE CAN SEE A NEW tension building up nonetheless. Whatever the care of Providence, this is not going to be a world that is "meant for man." The essentially divine is in nature, it is outside of us, and we look at it as would admiring guests, with a love that is purely of the intellect, *amor intellectualis*. When Galileo reminded the Church authorities that it would be ruinous for the souls to construe the Word of God so that it comes to be in contradiction with the works of God, and that Scripture concerns itself only with supernatural truth, he was in a strictly orthodox position, but he was implying that the personality of man and his fate might well be found to be less than centrally relevant to the pattern of the universe; hence we may understand the resistance of traditionalists.

A prelude to this position is to be found in Pico della Mirandola. The universe, says Pico, was achieved and complete in all its order when God put man in it: "no archetype available from which to create a new progeny, no heritage to receive, no seat in the universe to settle in." A wonderful image of naturalistic thought which projects a closed and consistent conception of reality with no place for itself. Hence his original attempt to bring thought back, on the scene with the idea of man as the unrelated being outside that order, the Protean free entity that is no single thing because it is potentially all things. The matured understanding of Galileo brings now Pico's magic vision into focus: man's abstract intellect, and that alone, is able by way of mathematics to identify itself with the logic underlying all reality. This is Galileo's metaphysical—and daring— theory of knowledge, concluding with a hymn to the greatness of man in the true Renaissance spirit.

[SALVIATI: We should have recourse to a philosophical distinction and say that the understanding is to be taken

two ways, that is *intensively* or *extensively*. *Extensively,*
that is, as to the multitude of intelligibles, which are infinite, the understanding of man is as nothing, though he
should understand a thousand propositions; for a thousand
in respect of infinity is but as zero. But as for the understanding *intensively,* inasmuch as that term imports perfectly some propositions, I say that human wisdom understands some propositions as perfectly and is as absolutely
certain thereof, as Nature herself; and such are the pure
mathematical sciences, to wit, Geometry and Arithmetic.
In these Divine Wisdom knows infinitely more propositions, because it knows them all; but I believe that the
knowledge of those few comprehended by human understanding equals the Divine, as to objective certainty, for it
arrives to comprehend the necessity of it, than which there
can be no greater certainty.

SIMPLICIUS: This seems to me a very bold and rash
expression.

SALVIATI: These are common notions far from all um-
brage of temerity, or boldness, and detract not in the least
from the majesty of Divine Wisdom; as it in no ways di-
minishes its omnipotence to say that God cannot make
what once happened not to have happened. I believe, Simplicius, that your scruple arises from your having possibly
misunderstood my words somewhat; therefore, the better
to express myself, I say that as concerns the truth, of which
mathematical demonstrations give us the knowledge, it is
the same as that which the Divine Wisdom knows. But this
I must grant you, that the manner whereby God knows the
infinite propositions of which we understand some few is
much more excellent than ours, which proceeds by ratiocination and passes from conclusion to conclusion, whereas
His is done at one single thought or intuition. For example,
we, to attain the knowledge of some property of the circle,
which has infinitely many, begin from one of the most
simple and, taking that for its definition, do proceed with
argumentation to another, and from that to a third, and
then to a fourth, and so on. The Divine Wisdom by the
simple apprehension of its essence comprehends, without
temporal ratiocination, all these infinite properties which

are also, in effect, virtually comprised in the definitions of
all things; and, to conclude, being infinite, are perhaps but
one alone in their nature and in the Divine Mind. Neither
is this wholly unknown to human understanding, but only
beclouded with deep and dense mists which in part come
to be dissipated and clarified when we are made masters of
any conclusions firmly demonstrated and made so perfectly
ours that we can speedily run through them.]

And here, finally, is an epoch-making decision in the
central problem of philosophy—the quest for essences:

[To speculate on the intrinsic essence of things I hold as
hopeless an undertaking and as vain an endeavor in substances close to us as is those far away in the heavens, for
I know as little truly about the substance of the Earth as
of the Moon, about clouds as about sunspots. . . . I may
feel I "know" clouds when I am told that they are water,
and water we are familiar with, we can feel and handle; but
such knowledge is only closer, it is not more intrinsic than
that I had of the clouds; it is a collection of particulars all
equally unknown in themselves, through which I go wandering and discoursing with little or no gain as to the real
thing. Thus, too, I understand nothing more of the essence
of earth or fire, as of that of the Sun or the Moon; for that
is the kind of knowledge which awaits us when we have
moved beyond this world onto the state of beatitude, and
not before. But if we keep to the properties of that essence,
then we may reasonably hope to attain knowledge of a
number of them, and indeed to attain it no less securely
in bodies extremely remote from us than in those around
us: at times, perchance, more exactly in those far away
than in those nearby.]

CHAPTER XII

Hakluyt

THE NAME OF RICHARD HAKLUYT (1552?-1616) IS TIED
to the greatest and most successful adventure of the Renaissance—the discovery of our planet. Froude called his
book the prose epic of the modern English nation. Much
of Renaissance thinking cannot be understood except within the frame of such achievements. While literary humanism is looking obstinately backwards, a new breed of men
are opening up the world. Still, they are men of Renaissance culture, and the great motifs of that thought are
working in their imagination. Columbus himself had not
been looking for new continents, but for a new route to
the land of silk and spices that the ancient geographers had
set as a goal; on landing in the Windward Islands, he does
not describe what his eyes see, but what his passionate
ancestral memory suggests: here are truly the Islands of
the Blessed in the region of the Setting Sun where reigns
perpetual spring, and where the nightingale sings from the
boughs. The nightingale that Columbus heard in the Carib-
bean springs surely from his fancy, Olschki remarks; he
was only evoking the descriptions of the Garden of Eden
which had been in his mind since childhood. No less than
Dante at the top of the seven-storied Mountain of Purgatory, he knew what he was going to find. The new reality
was too different from the known one for the mind to
discern it: it blended with familiar dreams.

Some such attitude persists in the sixteenth century, even
in the attentive Pigafetta, in the prodigiously informed
Hakluyt. The new American continent is by now a massive
reality extending from Arctic to Antarctic, but is still only a
hindrance to their vision, and a "lump of idleness," as

Galileo would say. They are not looking at it, they are looking "around" it. Since the Iberians seem to have monopolized the southern route around, Hakluyt's gaze, like Gilbert's and Frobisher's, is obstinately set on the discovery of the North-West Passage. But the new colonizing and imperial mind is at work already; the first step, he suggests, would be to stake out the North American shores and establish stations along that route. In other words, it would be a good idea to invent some kind of New England. This is the plan that he submits to his sponsors, Sir Philip Sidney and Secretary Walsingham, and this, in fact, is what Raleigh undertakes to do immediately after, with the Virginia settlements. It has been said that to Hakluyt England was indebted for her American colonies more than to any other man of that age.

While Spain goes on taking possession only with *encomiendas,* Hakluyt has the vision of the new era of European expansion. Like the ancient philosophers and legislators of the seafaring Ionian republics, he sees populations swarming overseas to colonize new continents. But since he has to be practical, he suggests using the territories as an immediate outlet for convicts. It is arresting to see Hakluyt, a man of very different temper from Sir Thomas More, disturbed by the same blind ferocity of penal law which went on hanging poor people "twenty at a clap out of one gaol" for insignificant offenses. (This hanging by twenties, which also drew More's compassion, seems to have appealed to the primitive sense of rhythm of authorities.) Sir Thomas had been pleading for reason and mercy, and he got neither. Hakluyt is able to suggest a practical solution, and it will eventually result in the Australian settlements, with the moderate delay of a century and a half, which is a fair minimum for authorities of sound practical judgment to get an idea.

We can see, in the introduction to *Divers Voyages Touching the Discovery of America* (1582), Hakluyt's thought moving through the epic phase of the philosophy of discovery into the intellectual phase, and laying down the requirements for scientific theory and equipment. When he dwells on the creation on the part of Spain of the new

academic dignity of master pilots, he is, in fact, boldly and
romantically announcing the values that English civilization, from Francis Bacon onward, will put into technological achievement; Harriot, a mathematician, was
to go with Sir Walter Raleigh on the first Virginia
voyage. Hakluyt is still only suggesting a puny £40 lec-
tureship in the new subject of navigational science, but a
century later, in 1714, the prize set by the British government for the first working chronometer fit for longitude
measurements was to be £20,000. John Harrison, a self-
taught Yorkshire carpenter, won the prize, and brought
into being, out of nothing as it were, the new technology
of clockmaking, from which were to come James Watt
and the first steam engineers. Thus the course set by
Hakluyt's navigators, as they emerge from the mist of
heroic legend, leads far into the future.

[PREFACE TO "DIVERS VOYAGES TOUCHING THE DISCOVERY
   OF AMERICA" (1582)*

A Very Late and Great Probability of a Passage by the
Northwest Part of America in 58 Degrees of Northerly
Latitude

An excellent learned man of Portingale, of singular
gravity, authority, and experience, told me very lately that
one Anus Cortereal, captain of the Ile of Tercera, about
the year 1574 (which is not above eight years past) sent
a ship to discover the Northwest Passage of America, and
that the same ship, arriving on the coast of the said America in fifty-eight degrees of latitude, found a great entrance
exceeding deep and broad, without all impediment of ice,
into which they passed above twenty leagues and found it
always to trend toward the south, the land lying low and
plain on either side; and that they persuaded themselves
verily that there was a way open into the South Sea. But
their victails failing them, and being but one ship, they
returned back again with joy. This place seemeth to lie
in equal degrees of latitude with the first entrance of the
Sound of Denmark between Norway and the headland
*London: The Hakluyt Society, 1850.

called in Latin *Cimbrorum promontorium,* and therefore like to be open and navigable a great part of the year. And this report may be well annexed unto the other eight reasons mentioned in my epistle dedicatory for proof of the likelihood of this passage by the northwest.

To The Right Worshipful and Most Virtuous Gentleman, Master Philip Sidney, Esquire

I marvel not a little, right worshipful, that since the first discovery of America (which is now full four-score and ten years), after so great conquests and plantings of the Spaniards and Portingales there, that we of England could never have the grace to set fast footing in such fertile and temperate places as are left as yet unpossessed of them. But again, when I consider that there is a time for all men, and see the Portingales' time to be out of date and that the nakedness of the Spaniards and their long-hidden secrets are now at length espied, whereby they went about to delude the world, I conceive great hope that the time approacheth and now is that we of England may share and part stakes (if we will ourselves) both with the Spaniard and the Portingale in part of America and other regions as yet undiscovered. And surely if there were in us that desire to advance the honour of our country which ought to be in every good man, we would not all this while have foreslown the possessing of those lands which of equity and right appertain unto us, as by the discourses that follow shall appear most plainly. Yea, if we would behold with the eye of pity how all our prisons are pestered and filled with able men to serve their country, which for small robberies are daily hanged up in great numbers, even twenty at a clap out of one jail (as was seen at the last assizes at Rochester), we would hasten and further every man to his power the deducting of some colonies of our superfluous people into those temperate and fertile parts of America, which, being within six weeks' sailing of England, are yet unpossessed by any Christians, and seem to offer themselves unto us, stretching nearer unto her Majesty's dominions then to any other part of Europe. We read that the bees, when they grow to be too many in their own hives at home, are wont to be led out by their captains to swarm abroad, and seek themselves a new dwelling-place. If the examples of the Grecians and Carthaginians of old time and the practise of our age may not move us, yet let us learn wisdom of these small, weak, and unreasonable creatures. It chanced very lately that upon occasion I had great conference in matters of cosmography with an excellent learned man of Portingale, most privy to all the discoveries of his nation, who wondered that those blessed countries from the point of Florida northward were all this while unplanted by Christians, protesting with great affection and zeal that if he were now as young as I (for at this present he is three-score years of age) he would sell all he had, being a man of no small wealth and honor, to furnish a convenient number of ships to sea for the inhabiting of those countries and reducing those gentile people to Christianity. Moreover, he added that John Barros, their chief cosmographer, being moved with the like desire, was the cause that Bresilia was first inhabited by the Portingales, where they have nine baronies or lordships and thirty engines or sugar mills, two or three hundred slaves belonging to each mill, with a judge and other offices and a church, so that every mill is, as it were, a little commonwealth; and that the country was first planted by such men as for small offenses were saved from the rope. This he spake not only unto me and in my hearing, but also in the presence of a friend of mine, a man of great skill in the mathematics. If this man's desire might be executed, we might not only for the present time take possession of that good land, but also in short space by God's grace find out that short and easy passage by the northwest which we have hetherto so long desired and whereof we have many good and more then probable conjectures, a few whereof I think it not amiss here to set down, although your Worship know them as well as myself. First, therefore, it is not to be foregotten that Sebastian Cabot wrote to Master Baptista Ramusius* that he verily believed that all the north part of America is di-

* G. B. Ramusio (1485-1557) is the Italian Hakluyt. Master John Verarzanus is Giovanni da Verrazzano, the discoverer of Manhattan Island.

vided into ilands. Secondly that Master John Verarzanus, which had been thrice on that coast, in an old, excellent map which he gave to King Henry the Eight and is yet in the custody of Master [Michael] Locke doth so lay it out as it is to be seen in the map annexed to the end of this book, being made according to Verarzanus' plat. Thirdly, the story of Gil Gonsalva recorded by Franciscus Lopes de Gomara, which is said to have sought a passage by the northwest, seemeth to argue and prove the same. . . . Seventhly, the experience of Captain Frobisher on the hither side and Sir Francis Drake on the back side of America, with the testimony of Nicolaus and Anthonius Zeni, that Estotilanda is an iland, doth yield no small hope thereof. Lastly, the judgment of the excellent geographer Gerardus Mercator, which his son Rumold Mercator, my friend, shewed me in his letters and drew out for me in writing, is not of wise men lightly to be regarded. . . . "You write," saith he to his son, "great matters, though very briefly of the new discovery of Frobisher, which I wonder was never these many years heretofore attempted. For there is no doubt but that there is a straight and short way open into the west, even unto Cathay, into which kingdom if they take their course aright, they shall gather the most noble merchandise of all the world and shall make the name of Christ to be known unto many idolatrous and heathen people." And here to conclude and shut up this matter, I have heard myself of merchants of credit that have lived long in Spain that King Philip [II] hath made a law of late that none of his subjects shall discover to the north-wards of five and forty degrees of America, which may be thought to proceed chiefly of two causes: the one, least passing farther to the north they should discover the open passage from the South Sea to our North Sea; the other, because they have not people enough to possess and keep that passage, but rather thereby should open a gap for other nations to pass that way. Certes if hetherto in our own dis-coveries we had not been led with a preposterous desire of seeking rather gain then God's glory, I assure myself that our labors had taken far better effect. But we forgot that godliness is great riches and that if we first seek the kingdom of God all other things will be given unto us,

and that as the light accompanieth the sun and the heat
the fire, so lasting riches do wait upon them that are
zealous for the advancement of the kingdom of Christ and
the enlargement of his glorious Gospel; as it is said, "I
will honor them that honor me." I trust that now, being
taught by their manifold losses, our men will take a more
godly course and use some part of their goods to his
glory; if not, he will turn even their covetousness to serve
him as he hath done the pride and avarice of the Spaniards and Portingales, who, pretending in glorious words
that they made their discoveries chiefly to convert infidels
to our most holy faith (as they say), in deed and truth
sought not them, but their goods and riches. Which thing
that our nation may more speedily and happily perform,
there is no better mean in my simple judgment then the
increase of knowledge in the art of navigation and breeding of skilfulness in the seamen: which Charles [V] the
emperor and the king of Spain that now is, wisely considering, have in their contractation-house in Sivill appointed
a learned reader of the said art of navigation and joined
with him certain examiners, and have distinguished the
orders among the seamen, as the groomet (which is the
basest degree), the mariner (which is the second), the
master (the third), and the pilot (the fourth), unto the
which two last degrees none is admitted without he have
heard the reader for a certain space (which is commonly
an excellent methematician, of which number were Pedro
di Medina, which writ learnedly of the art of navigation,
and Alonso di Chavez and Hieronimus di Chavez, whose
works likewise I have seen), and being found fit by him
and his assistants, which are to examine matters touching
experience, they are admitted with a great solemnity and
giving of presents to the ancient masters and pilots and
the reader and examiners as the great doctors in the universities, or our great sergeants at the law when they proceed, and so are admitted to take charge for the Indies.
And that your Worship may know that this is true, Master
Steven Borrows, now one of the four masters of the queen's
navy, told me that newly after his return from the discovery of Moscovy by the north, in Queen Marie's days,
the Spaniards, having intelligence that he was master in

that discovery, took him into their contractation-house at their making and admitting of masters and pilots, giving him great honor, and presented him with a pair of perfumed gloves worth five or six ducats. I speak all this to this end, that the like order of erecting such a lecture here in London or about Ratcliffe in some convenient place were a matter of great consequence and importance for the saving of many men's lives and goods, which now, through gross ignorance, are daily in great hazard. . . .

For which cause I have dealt with right worshipful Sir Francis Drake, that seeing God hath blessed him so wonderfully he would do this honour to himself and benefit to his country, to be at the cost to erect such a lecture; whereunto in most bountiful manner at the very first he answered that he liked so well of the motion that he would give twenty pounds by the year standing and twenty pounds more beforehand to a learned man, to furnish him with instruments and maps, that would take this thing upon him; yea, so ready he was that he earnestly requested me to help him to the notice of a fit man for that purpose, which I, for the zeal I bear to this good action, did presently, and brought him one who came onto him and conferred with him thereupon, but in fine he would not undertake the lecture unless he might have forty pound a year standing, and so the matter ceased for that time; howbeit, the worthy and good knight remaineth still constant, and will be, as he told me very lately, as good as his word. Now if God should put into the head of any noble man to contribute other twenty pound to make this lecture a competent living for a learned man, the whole realm no doubt might reap no small benefit thereby.

CHAPTER XIII

Giordano Bruno

HISTORY HAS NOT YET REGISTERED A STABLE APPRAISAL for Giordano Bruno (1548-1600). He has reappeared in contemporary consciousness (and he would have appreciated the irony of it) largely through *Finnegan's Wake*, across which he flits as "Mr. Brown," "Bruno Nolan," "the firm of Brown and Nolan," and many other travesties, for he is a central figure in the thought of James Joyce. He is not one of those minds which shed a pure and equable light to reveal a new landscape of ideas; with the fire of his temperament there went a good deal of smoke. But his power of living thought no less than the greatness of his death make him full worthy to stand as a terminal symbol of Renaissance audacity.

"Academician of no academy"—thus he introduces himself sarcastically—"called the insufferant" (*il fastidito*). He does not issue from the great centers of learning. He is a lonely figure from the start. Insufferance flung him, at the age of twenty-eight, from his home town in Nola near Naples, where he had been made to lead from adolescence the life of a Dominican monk. For the next sixteen years, he was to be an itinerant scholar, a displaced person without status—"the man from Nola" as he refers to himself in his dialogues; a tormented figure, "gay in sorrow, sorrowful in gaiety," difficult to his friends, insufferant and insufferable by turns. The object of his search had been far from clear to him at the start. Intense early reading led him, like so many others, to the vaster mystical horizons of Neoplatonism, and from thence to the Learned Ignorance of Nicholas of Cusa. He searched for the sources of doctrine in antiquity, in the natural philosophy of the early Greeks, in Zeno's subtle paradoxes concerning the One and the Many, in the "wisdom of Solomon and Pythagoras." The discovery of Copernicanism, the revived "Pythagorean theory" as it was currently called, seems to have been the spark that ignited the mixture. From then on, he became the prophet of a new knowledge and the denizen of cosmic Infinity.

Moving out of Catholic territory, he tried to settle in Geneva but was repelled by the Calvinists; he moved on to France where he found some peace, and the favor of the king. But wherever he taught for a time, he had to cope "with the three-headed hellhound of Aristotle, Ptolemy and dogma." In the retinue of the French ambassador, he crossed over to England, where he was to spend the three most productive years of his life.

Elizabethan England had become, at that time (1583), a focal point of European culture. One might speak of a certain phase of the Renaissance as the "circle of Sir Philip Sidney." Its political minds were Leicester, Walsingham, Fulke Greville, while other friends, Raleigh, Hakluyt, Frobisher and Drake, were opening up new worlds to adventure; on the side of the arts were Spenser and the Areopagus Society. The engaging figure of young Sidney himself, roving ambassador, soldier, courtier, and himself a poet of distinction, held together its many strands in a subtle intellectual "Architectonicke" such as he liked to conceive in the realm of the arts. Giordano Bruno, although he spoke no English, found himself completely at ease in this cosmopolitan circle, where everyone knew one of the "polite languages" in addition to Latin; the Italian intellectual coming from the cradle of humanism was subtly molded in his turn. In Marlowe, whom he probably met, he found an intellect as reckless as his own. If Sidney had revived the Petrarchan sequence of sonnets in *Astrophel and Stella,* why, he would write sonnet sequences too, and more intricate in conceit; in the heroic atmosphere of imperial adventure, he was inspired to write his masterpiece of poetic thought, the *Heroic Exaltations.* His dedications to Sidney and Walsingham are no empty formalities.

This happy phase could not last: he came into conflict with the Oxford authorities over Copernicus and by 1585 he was again on the move.

"If you want to know why," he wrote, "I dislike unanimity and I hate commonality. I am suspicious of majorities. It is the One which wins my love; the One that gives me freedom in my bondage, peace in my torment, wealth in my poverty, life in my death. . . . Thus it comes to pass that when a steep ascent rises before me I withdraw not my footsteps in weariness from the stony path. . . ."

Germany was his next goal, that, too, far from peaceful. The Lutheran university of Wittenberg received him well, and he thanked them in handsome style, but he could not be reconciled to their doctrine, as he had not been to Calvanist predestinationism. He felt, like Erasmus, that to deny the free will of man was "a corruption of laws and religion." As he scornfully remarked: "Trying to look wise, they have damaged many peoples, making them into worse barbarians than they were, contemptors of good actions, and reckless in every vice and ribaldry, because of the conclusions that they draw from such premises." Luther's "pecca fortiter" seemed a temperamental absurdity to Bruno's essentially humanist judgment.

A yearning for his homeland drew him south, and a half-formulated desire to come to terms with Rome. He hoped to be divested of his religious obligations by his Church and to be allowed to live at peace with it as a layman. He deemed Venetian territory safe enough for such soundings; but a false protector betrayed him into the hands of the Inquisition. He was then forty-four years of age. He was to spend the next eight years in the Roman prison of Castel Sant'Angelo, while his case was being investigated at interminable length. Another great philosophical temperament, Tommaso Campanella (see p. 22), no less adventurous and unruly, like him a Dominican, and promised to dreadful vicissitudes in years to come, was doing a "stretch" too in the Castle, at that time. A poem of his refers to their common plight:

> As to the centre all things that have weight
>> Sink from the surface: as the silly mouse
>> Runs at a venture, rash though timorous,
>> Into the monster's jaws to meet her fate:
> Thus all who love high Science, from the strait
>> Dead sea of Sophistry sailing like us
>> Into Truth's ocean, bold and amorous,
>> Must in our haven anchor soon or late. . . .
> Knowledge, grace, mercy, are an idle dream
>> In this dread place. Nought but fear dwells in it,
>> Of stealthy Tyranny the sacred seat. *

Throughout those years, Bruno fought for his life. He pitted his resourcefulness and his vast learning against the Inquisitional mind, to prove that he had never deviated from the essential orthodoxy; it took on the other side the learning and resourcefulness of Bellarmine, the great Jesuit consultant of the Inquisition, to pin him down at last on eight propositions that he was challenged to accept or deny, without further comment. Bruno appealed against them to the pope himself, and was turned down, his appeal unread. He refused to submit, and was sentenced to death as a confirmed heretic. "You are more afraid of this than I am" he told the judges who read him the sentence. He ignored repeated entreaties for a last-minute repentance, and was solemnly burned at the stake on Campo di Fiori on February 19, 1600. A wedge had been stuffed in his mouth, as was done in those cases, to prevent him from blaspheming. He turned his face away from the proffered crucifix and died in silence.

In after times, Giordano Bruno has been glorified as a martyr for free thought, secularism, and even democracy. This is fairly absurd, for Bruno was highly diffident of the untutored multitude, and hardly a secularist. From the other side, much ado has been made of his trimming and shifting throughout his long ordeal, to prove that he was an irresponsible, vainglorious and unbalanced individual.

In reality, Bruno was quite consistent to a line of his own, but it has not been largely understood:

*Translated by J. A. Symonds.

〔 True propositions are never offered by us to the vulgar,
but only to the wise, who can reach an understanding of our
point of view. This is why truly religious and learned
theologians have never challenged the freedom of philosophers; while the true, civilized and well-organized
philosophers have always favored religions. Both sides are
aware that religion is needed for restraining rude populations, which have to be ruled, whereas rational demonstration is for such, of a contemplative nature, as know how
to rule themselves and others. 〕

THIS IS NOT INTELLECTUAL SNOBBERY, NO MORE THAN HAD
been Copernicus's shyness and reserve. In Bruno's fondness
for symbolistic allegory, in his recognition of the learned
class as something superior and apart, we find anew the traditional concept of a sacred science as belonging not to all
but only to such as would make safe use of knowledge.
Nor does it involve contempt for the simple, who always
had in them the spark of truth, but only for their exploiters.
"There is no nation," says Bruno, "which ever actually
worshipped cocks, crocodiles, onions or turnips, but the
light of the divine principle shining through them, which
in different times and places will shine from other equally
mortal objects."

Clearly, Bruno was no more of a Christian when he
wrote this than a modern Unitarian would be, but he had
a profound religious feeling and could tell his judges truly
that he had gone along with Calvinists, Anglicans and
Lutherans in turn only as a matter of philosophical
savoir-vivre; he had certainly been always closer to
humanistic Catholicism than to any of the sects, "those
sticklers for niceties who are nowadays infesting Europe."

In modern terms, Bruno would be against the separation
of the Church from the state, but he considers the true
philosopher to be above both, and in this he remains
close to Plato. Having discovered, as he thinks, the mission of the true philosopher, which is to understand how
the freedom of God is all one with rational necessity, it
appears to him clear that only the sage, as he imagines
him, in his aristocratic detachment, is capable of living

at this intellectual level. A similar philosophic realization, taking place in the mind of Spinoza, will lead to far more modern and drastic political conclusions, but this is a matter for the next century.

It cannot be denied that, in his very personality and style, Bruno embodies the uncertainties and contradictions of the Renaissance. Lofty and penetrating speculations are often drowned in a stream of embellishments flowing from the too-well stocked memory of the rhetorician, or interrupted by irrepressible Neopolitan clowning and outrageous satirical slapstick. There is in him an overflowing vitality which violates the bounds of form, an overweening certainty which shoves persistently at the reader half-baked notions and preposterous paramathematics as means to the ultimate conclusions, and then complains of not being understood. But such extravagances in no way obscure Bruno's overwhelming philosophical vision; they indicate, rather, aspects of it for which he had no adequate means of expression.

The vision has its source, as we said, in the Copernican idea—whose logical implications Bruno spoke out boldly where Copernicus had still been hesitant. Copernicus had reasons for his restraint. He did not dare ascribe infinity to his universe because in Christian doctrine infinity belongs only to the Creator, not to his creation. A universe which shared with God the attribute of infinity would lose, so to speak, its creatureliness and become, in one sense at least, equal to its maker.

The Church had even taken away from Aristotle the one "extensive" infinity that he granted the universe, that in time. Bruno knows only too well who it was that had insisted on infinity, both spatial and temporal, in the past; it was that Godless atomist, Lucretius. But he takes it up unafraid, as he states his doctrine thus in the first questioning by the Inquisition:

I hold the universe to be infinite, as being the effect of infinite divine power and goodness, of which any finite world would have been unworthy. Hence I have declared infinite worlds to exist beside this our Earth; I hold with

Pythagoras that the Earth is a star like all the others which are infinite, and that all these numberless worlds are a whole in infinite space, which is the true universe. Thus there is a double sort of infinity, in size of the universe and in number of worlds; this it is which has been understood to disagree indirectly with the truth according to faith. However, I place in this universe a universal providence whereby each thing grows and moves according to its nature; and I understand it two ways, one the way in which the soul is present in the body, all in all and in each part, and this I call nature, and shadow and vestige of the Deity; the other way is the ineffable one in which God is present in all, not as a soul, but in a way which cannot be explained.]

WITH THIS AMPLE STATEMENT OF HIS DOCTRINE, BRUNO was suggesting that it should be compatible philosophically with Christianity. But the plurality of worlds was hardly compatible with Christ's Incarnation as a unique event in time; moreover, it was clear that the Platonic and Christian idea of a deity *transcendent* to the Universe and to Being itself was replaced here by the new idealist conception of a God *immanent* in the Universe. However much he might insist that it was meant "strictly on the philosophical plane," this was indeed Bruno's idea: the Universe as an autonomous living being, operating by internal forces and necessity, with God as its soul, hardly to be distinguished from Nature itself. One cannot but respect the scrupulousness of the Inquisition, which took eight years to make up its mind that the doctrine, however acceptable its religious content, could not be reconciled with dogma.

Bruno had no scientific education, but he had grasped to the full the Principle of Sufficient Reason, which is a foundation of scientific rationalism. He expresses it metaphysically, e.g., "It would not be worthy of God to manifest himself in less than an infinite universe," and no doubt this is the aspect of it which was most clearly present to his mind. In the same double aspect, logical and metaphysical, the principle is still the base of Leibniz's thinking, but the logical aspect predominates.

The same scientific instinct leads Bruno to seek the invariance of the universe in its physical, quantitative substance, in those atoms which move into the focus of his thought in the last period; but he tries to identify them with the Pythagorean monads and the "minima" of Cusanus: it is a new kind of pantheistic monism which is born, and will find its rational achievement in Spinoza.

But then, is Bruno's ideal purely rational? Hardly. He is representative of a deep change whereby in the later Renaissance, Humanism tends to become Naturalism while preserving its original inspiration. It is not the modern setting up of a nature alien to man, as appears already incipient in Galileo. It is a shifting of the initial humanistic concept of *virtù*, an enlarging of it to embrace both nature and man. The Nature of Bruno is not mechanical as it will be for the materialist, or darkly inimical as it will be for later pessimists. It is conceived as containing our highest values "according to its own principles." It is as if in the group of southern Italian philosophers, Telesio, Bruno and Campanella, the pre-Socratic vision lived again, not as a simple certainty, but rather as a tormenting nostalgia. Pythagoras and Zeno are invoked as tutelary deities. In the "minima" of Nature, in Zeno's analysis of the material point refracted through Cusanus, Bruno sees the implicit richness of the universe, and such truths cannot be explored by investigating phenomena, but by going deeper into oneself. At the other end, the Copernican infinity provides a model for the unitary nature of the cosmos, where the divine reality becomes clear, where minimum and maximum coincide at last.

The creative aspect of Bruno's thought would seem to lie in his wholehearted commitment to the concept of infinity, which is going to prove so fertile in the seventeenth century, both mathematically and metaphysically. He does not merely contemplate the illimitable ocean of Being; one might say that he "goes overboard" in it. In the fullness of this Being he finds a new freedom. The center of gravity, as it were, has tilted for the whole of thought. The relationship of man to God is depersonalized, because God, being infinite necessity, can no longer come down to man. It is man who must raise himself up to him by transcending his own limits in an effort which can have no end.

Spinoza can still see philosophy as an "adequation of the intellect to its object," but for Bruno no such adequation is possible, only the flight of the soul in that direction. The objects of knowledge have to be conquered in ever new and inexhaustibly different approaches, and this becomes here the source of passionate ethical emotion; the illimitable vistas of never-ending research become a positive value. It is the way for man to receive the Godhead "in his own will." The old word *humanitas,* that we met at the beginning of this survey, takes on the new meaning of the unchecked openness of man's being in the direction of infinity: for the flight upwards of the spirit brings him always back "to his own terrain," to the depths of his own soul.

Thus, also, what to Spinoza can be detached "intellectual love" has to be for Bruno a "heroic frenzy," for the aim is not merely rational or contemplative, it is a progressive *poiesis,* an inspired "making," as the Greeks understood it: a discovery which takes on aesthetic shape and thus also expression; the goal is the point "where truth, art and music meet," and it is reached only by the "God-intoxicated" mind.

The achievement of Bruno, then, does not lie in organization of knowledge. It lies in a new understanding of a possible relationship of man to the universe. It has much in common with the depths reached by Paracelsus and Boehme, but it meets more directly and resolutely the dramatic experience that we called "the breaking of the circle." Man is reconciled to the new freedom offered to him by science. If we look for systematic thought, there is hardly any: only the hope of it, a keen dialectic, and a great intuition, a passionate acceptance of the Open Universe.

This is the historic reason why Bruno, who had been ready to adjust, compromise and retract in matters of orthodoxy, stiffens into intransigence at the last when

asked to give up his philosophical tenets. He sees the time
has come, as he had prophesied unknowingly in his own
fable of Actaeon, to will the destruction of his own contingent being, so that his *Deus Absconditus,* which could
not but elude the thinker, may be "realized" in himself.

In the act of sacrifice, Giordano Bruno knew he was
fully resolving the mistakes of his life, the conflicts of his
nature, the insufficiency of his intellect, the inadequacy of
his equipment. As a man, he knew he had been a failure;
but the philosopher in death was transcending that sense
of metaphysical failure which dogs the life of the scholarly
philosopher however great, and makes him look for a
substitute bliss in the fond hope of being raised some time
from the purgatory of the footnote to the paradise of the
paragraph. He was surely not facing the flames for a rational proposition—no one does, and it was only sensible
of Galileo, thirty-three years later, to decline the doubtful
honor of martyrdom.

The Platonic inspiration of Bruno's dialogues was also
that of his final decision. He knew that it was only in death
that Socrates had begotten in his disciple's mind ideas
which were to prove henceforth immortal. Like Socrates,
he was offering himself up not for a mature doctrine but
for free thought itself as a "beautiful risk"; not for an
ideology but for an idea. Unlike Socrates, he was not allowed to give words to the inflexible simplicity with which
he met his fate. But we like to imagine that he would not
have disdained—for he too was capable of lightheartedness
—the words of a contemporary of ours, Lauro de Bosis,
written before meeting a similar fate: "There is a message
which has to be delivered; whether I live or die has little
importance. But if I die, there is a chance that it may go
registered and special delivery."

What follows out of the dialogue *Ash Wednesday (La
Cena delle Ceneri)** is not part of the convivial argument
about Copernicus, which takes two thirds of the text, but
a (very condensed) version of Bruno's trip through "Lon-

*Translated by Giorgio de Santillana and Elisabeth Abbott.

don by night" as he was making his way to Fulke Greville's house. This vivid description of the city in the time of Elizabeth is not a mere comic interlude; we are warned in the preface that it might be "a moral geography" and "more allegorical and tropological" than it appears. The philosopher has chosen the light-hearted Falstaffian vein to tell us of his ordeal in life, and what he had had to confront in the way of ignorance, wrong doctrines, prejudice and hatred. The transposition is fanciful, but there is a flash of poignant vision, truer than Bruno could imagine, in his closing mention of Campo di Fiori, where he was to be burned fifteen years later amid the jeers of the same multitude he describes so disdainfully here.

Of the characters in the dialogue, the Nolan, is, of course, the author himself, who never appears in the first person as was the custom, but uses "Theophilus" as a spokesman. John Florio is well-known as the author of the classic translation of Montaigne. He was the son of a Siennese Protestant emigré.

[THEOPHILUS. . . . We had been invited for the night of Ash Wednesday, the Nolan and I, to the house of the most honorable Signor Folco Grivello [Fulke Greville] who had gathered a company to hear the reasons which favor of the motion of the Earth according to Copernicus. . . . We set out, after dark, with Messer John Florio and Master Matthew Gwinne, and we thought it prudent to shorten our way through London by turning towards the Embankment and taking a boat.

We reached the river near Lord Buckhurst's [Thomas Sackville's] palace and there spent as much time crying out "oars" (for so they call for a gondola in that country) as would have been more than enough to reach our host's dwelling on foot.

Two ancient boatmen answered at last, and came in as slowly as if it had been their way to the gallows. After many questions and answers concerning whence, where, why, how, and how much, they agreed to tie up. As we descended into the creaking thing, said the Nolan: "I daresay this is older than the *lux perpetua,* and might rival Noah's ark in antiquity. Maybe it is a leftover from the Deluge. Listen to the sounds it makes. They say the walls of Thebes resounded, but never like this." We laughed, but as Hannibal is said to have done before his last battle.

PRUDENTIUS: *Risus sardonicus*.

THEOPHILUS: Anyway we did our best to respond to that sweet harmony as love does to disdain, and we sang to its accompaniment. John Florio, as if in memory of past loves, sang "Dove, senza di me, dolce mia vita," and the Nolan took up from him with "Il Saracin dolente." And so we whiled away the time, while our two Charons were rowing us along with strokes that would be dwarfed by the waving of a lady's fan. But a little beyond the Temple, not even a third of the way, the boatmen put us ashore. All our expostulations were in vain. That was where they lived, they said, and they were going no further.

PRUDENTIUS: It is the nature of villeins and louts, that they do nothing from duty, and barely something from fear of punishment.

THEOPHILUS—So off we were again through the dark city, and here let the dirtier Muses out of Merlin Coccaio sustain my song. We had only moved a few steps, when we found ourselves floundering in a lake of mud without outlet, held in by two walls, which is what down there they call a street. Said the Nolan, who has more schooling than we, and has traveled widely: "Methinks I discern a swinish passage. Just follow me." He had not done saying when he found himself sunk in the ooze so deep that he could not pull out his legs. But there was little we could do except push forward holding on to each other. We staggered on thus grimly in the dark, hoping for firmer ground, while at each step we went down knee-deep towards the blackness of Avernus. One whistled with rage, another sighed and stumbled, another snorted, another swore under his breath; we had given up trying to figure our way, all we could do was to push on through that sea of slime which was tardily wending its way toward the wide and winding river.

PRUDENTIUS—Now that's a beautiful clause.

THEOPHILUS—Never mind. Well our tragic resoluteness

256 THE AGE OF ADVENTURE

stood us in good stead. Aristotle says that there is no infinity in act, and indeed we ended up eventually in a gentler kind of marsh, which had some dry ground on the side, and from thence in a sort of rain-trough where one could skip or rather fumble and stumble from stone to stone; and so at last we found ourselves back on the main throughfare, and as we looked around for landmarks, lo and behold we were not more than fifty feet away from the Nolan's rooms whence we had started out.

Despondent and weary, we were tempted to give up. The more so as the prospect was now to find our way through streets inhabited by a populace far from friendly. But with magnanimous and indomitable resolve, we decided to run the gauntlet, come what might.

PRUDENTIUS: These be great words for a middling occasion.

FRULLA:—It is permissible to do as princes are wont to, who prefer to exalt the lowly. What becomes worthy inasmuch as raised by them is that much more notable than when favors are bestowed on the great who have a claim to them through their own greatness. And if ancient poets have written compositions in praise of sauce, of mosquitoes, or flies, or ants or suchlike, and moderns have followed up by taking up as subjects of their song polecats, slippers, roots, draft-dodging, candles, figs, bedpans, and the itch, why should we not honor with ample treatment an ordeal surely more significant? 'Twere better, no doubt, if there were occasion here to raise the flight of our eloquence to speak in fitting terms of that earthly goddess, that singular and incomparable Diana of our times, she who from these frigid regions so close to the Arctic parallel sheds light and glory over the whole terrestrial globe; I mean Elizabeth, who yields to no king on earth in counsel, wisdom, authority or splendor, nor surely to anyone among the learned in her knowledge of the arts and sciences, and in her acquaintance with all civilized languages; who, amid the raging storms of a sea of adversities, has shown the greatness of her heroic soul in holding the ship of state on an unswerving and victorious course these five-and-twenty years past, and, indeed, were Fortune to do her justice, it should grant this great Amphitrite to spread the mantle of her empire over no less than the whole globe.*

But it is not of her that I have occasion to speak, nor yet of the great lords and famous gentlemen and scholars of her council, worthy of all honor and distinction. The substance of my tale concerns, alas, the meanest of her subjects: for England can boast of a lower populace which in disrespect, incivility, coarseness, boorishness and sheer savagery of nature yields to none in the world. They are a kind of people who, when they see a foreigner, become so many wolves and bears, by God, and put on the malevolent look of a disgruntled pig when you take away his trough. This most ignoble kind is divided into two categories——

PRUDENTIUS: *Omnis divisio debet esse bimembris, vel reducibilis ad bimembrem.*

THEOPHILUS:——One of which is composed of workingmen and shopkeepers who, recognizing somehow that you come from abroad, turn up their noses at you, jeer, snigger, give you the bird and call you in their own language dog, traitor and foreigner, which last is the vilest epithet they can bestow and implies that you are fair game for the worst treatment conceivable; it matters not whether you be young or old, a noble or a gentleman, wearing a robe or bearing arms. Now should you by misfortune have occasion to repel one of those who crowd in on you, or put your hand to the sword-hilt, you shall straightway see them come swarming out of their shops as far as the street is long, and you will find yourself surrounded by a mob of rowdies who have sprung up more quickly than did the warriors, fabled by the poets, when Jason sowed the dragon's teeth. It would seem as if the earth disgorged them; but in fact they issue from the shops, taverns and stables and present an impressive and delightful array of longstaves, maces, halberds, partizans and rusty pitchforks which, for whatever worthy purpose the Sovereign may have granted them, are always in readiness for this and similar opportunities. Thus armed they will fall upon you

---

*This praise of a sovereign who was a "perverse heretic" was held against Bruno at the Inquisition trial.

with outlandish fury, not reflecting on whom, why, wherefore or how; there is no concerted action; each is intent
on venting his natural contempt for the stranger; and if
he be not impeded by the very press of folk, all bent on
the same purpose, you shall have the measure of your
doublet taken by fist or rod, and, if you be not wary, you
shall have your hat staved in. All that even if you be accompanied by some person of means or quality—let him
be count or duke, it shall be to his damage and not to
your profit for, in a herd, these folk are no respecters
of rank, and, however he may disapprove, he must stand
aside, look on and await the finish. Then, in conclusion,
when you think you may be allowed to repair to your bar-
ber and rest your weary and much abused body, you will
find these same people turn police and constables to claim
that you have touched someone, somehow. And no matter
how sore your back and legs may be, they will beat and
kick you till you run as if you had the wings of Mercury
or were mounted on the horse Pegasus or astride Perseus's
steed or riding Astolfo's hippogriff or leading Madian's
dromedary or trotting on one of the giraffes of the Three
Wise Men; they will urge you on with such mighty fists it
were far better for you were they the kicks of an ox, an
ass or a mule. Nor will they leave off till they have flung
you into prison; and here, *me tibi comendo.*

PRUDENTIUS: *A fulgure et tempestate, ab ira et indigna-
tione, malitia, tentatione et furia rusticorum . . .*

FRULLA: . . . *Libera nos, domine.*

THEOPHILUS: And then there be those carrying water or
beer or ale, who are big enough to knock down a house
with their load; and going on their way will jostle you
as if inadvertently, and crack your head open with the
corner of their barrel—but of them one should not complain, as they are not of the rational genus, and have more
of the mule than the man in their composition. Whereas I
should less forgive, for being closer to the semblance of
human kind, those that issue at a run from a shop as if
bent on some pressing errand, and go for your ribs with the
charge of a bull—all in good sport, of course, as happened
the other day to poor Messer Alessandro Citolino, who

to the great delight of the assistance got his arm and ribs fractured, and the judge had to tell him there was nothing he could do. Still less would I excuse those who come up close with friendly mien as if to say good evening, and then give you a jolt of a sudden. Of which, from one sort or another, we got a baker's dozen before we were through, and the last was for the Nolan, at the pillar which is in front of the palace amid three streets—a big nice fat shove as might count for ten, and he fetched up against the wall with a thud worthy another ten, for which he said, "Thankee, master," no doubt because the fellow had used his shoulder and not the stave he was carrying.

PRUDENTIUS:—*Aries primum, inde Taurus.*

THEOPHILUS:—And then we come the other kind, the servants. Now I am not speaking of the top ones, they are gentlemen's gentlemen—among those one may find courtesy. Beneath them, however, are such as wear their master's insignia, and then those who wear none, and then comes the last class, the servants of servants.

PRUDENTIUS: *Servus servorum non est malus titulus usquequaque.*

THEOPHILUS: Those in the second class, the ones who wear the livery, are usually bankrupt merchants, artisans or students, who have failed—escaped from shop or school. Those in the third class are cowardly fellows who, to get out of hard work, have left a freer profession; they are either runaway sailors, or landsmen who have tossed away their plows. The last, in the fourth class, are a mixture of desperadoes, vagrants, scullions thrown out by their masters, jackanapes, castaways, unemployables, the useless and the shiftless, those who find no opportunity for stealing, together with fugitives, jailbirds and crooks ready to ply their trade. These hang about the Old Change and the doors of St. Paul's. In Paris you will find their like in front of the courts of Justice; in Naples, on the steps of San Paolo; in Venice on the Rialto; in Rome, at the Campo di Fiori. . . .]

THE LAST REMARK OF PRUDENTIUS IS A POINTER. "SERVANT of Servants is never a bad title anyway." The pompous quacking (*usquequaque*) is but a thin disguise for the pointed reference to the Pope and his cohorts. If we were to write a program to this music, we might say that the sea of mud is ignorance and school philosophy, the bellicose shopkeepers are the vested academic interests, and the lower class of servants the kind of monks that Erasmus (whom Bruno loves to quote), had already caught in his sights. It is they, indeed, who are waiting for their victim in Campo di Fiori.

The following is from the dialogue *de l'Infinito Universo e Mondi* (of the Infinity of the Universe and of the Worlds) in Arthur Livingston's translation, published here for the first time. The character of Fracastoro, who appears here, is historic. Girolamo Fracastoro (1483-1553) was a physician and philosopher, a powerfully original mind who would have deserved a section in this book, if justice could be done to all the significant figures of the period. Bruno, of course, had never known him, since he died in Verona when Bruno was only five years old; he is presented here, with Platonic freedom, in the character of an intelligent listener and a judge of the argument. Philotheus is, as previously Theophilus ("the lover of God"), Bruno himself. Burchio is the usual academic scholar or intelligible ass (see p. 64), and the exchange of amenities occurring towards the end is a reasonably faithful mirror of the controversies which beset Bruno at every turn in his way of sorrows.

[ELPINO: How can the universe be infinite?

PHILOTHEUS: How can the universe be finite?

ELPINO: Do you think that this infinitude can be demonstrated?

PHILOTHEUS: Do you think this finiteness can be demonstrated?

ELPINO: Why this inordinate expansion?

PHILOTHEUS: Why these narrow boundaries?

BURCHIO: Come to some point soon, Philotheus, because I shall be much amused at hearing this fable, this fancy of yours.

FRACASTORO: Softly, Burchio; what will you say if you should happen to be convinced that it is true?

BURCHIO: Whether it's true or not, I'm not going to believe it. This infinite can't find room in my head. However, to tell the truth, I wish it were as Philotheus says, for if by mischance I should tumble off this world, I'd be sure to find a place to go.

ELPINO: Of course, Philotheus, if we intend to make our senses judges, or even give them that importance due to them from the fact that all we know is derived from them, we shall find it perhaps not so easy to come to your conclusion.

PHILOTHEUS: There is no sense capable of seeing the infinite, nor is there any from which this conclusion of mine can properly be demanded. The infinite cannot be the object of sense; and a person who asks to obtain an idea of it through the senses might as well expect to see substance and essence with his eyes. If he wished to deny it for the reason that it is not sensible, visible to the senses, he would be obliged to deny also his own substance and being. We must fix limits to our expectations of evidence from the senses. We admit their testimony only on things perceptible to them; and even then not without appeal, unless their judgment be controlled by reason. Think of how variable they are in determining such a thing as the horizon. When we know from experiment how readily we are deceived by them in matters pertaining to the surface of this globe on which we live, how much more should we suspect them in what they tell us of the limits of the starry dome?

ELPINO: Of what use are the senses then, tell me?

PHILOTHEUS: They serve only to rouse the reasoning faculty, to suggest possibilities, to point the way, to testify in part; not to give final evidence. . . .

ELPINO: Where is truth then?

PHILOTHEUS: In the sensible object as in a mirror; in the reason, through inference and discussion; in the intellect, through premise or conclusion; in the mind, in absolute living form.

ELPINO: Very well then, on with your arguments.

PHILOTHEUS: I will do so. If the world is finite, and beyond the world there is nothing, I ask you, where is the world? Where is the Universe? Aristotle answers: in itself. The convex surface of the sphere of fixed stars is a universal place; and that of the first container is not in any other container. For "place" is only the surface and extremity of a containing body. Therefore a thing that has no containing body has no place. Well, Aristotle, what do you mean by that dictum of yours: "place is in itself"? What definition will you give me for "a thing outside the world"? If you say there is *nothing* there, well, then, heaven, the world, certainly, will be nowhere. . . .

FRACASTORO: Right. The world will be nowhere, and the whole will be inside nothing. The argument is fair. . . . Elpinus, you are not a sophist because I see you admit what cannot be denied.]

THE NEXT STEP IS TO PROVE THAT, SINCE THERE IS SPACE outside our world, this world of ours might be supposed to be anywhere in it, hence where it is not, other worlds "can be, must be and are," in order to make it as full as it is here. In modern terms, if this space is isotropic, it has to be all full because a section of it certainly is. And as this our world is perfect, the fullness will all be of perfection.

[PHILOTHEUS: . . .Thus, from the exact identity of all space, it is ill for all space not to be full. Consequently the universe will be of infinite dimensions and the worlds will be innumerable.

ELPINO: Why should they be so many and not simply one?

PHILOTHEUS: Because, if it is ill that this world should not be, or that this plenitude should not exist, is it equally true of this space or of any other space equal to it?

ELPINO: I say it is ill as regards what is in this space, which might be in any other space equal to it, without distinction.

PHILOTHEUS: If you will carefully consider, you will see that it all amounts to the same thing. For the propriety of this corporeal being which is in this space, or could be in another equal to it, accounts for and concerns only that due propriety and perfection which can be in just such and so much space as this is, or in another equal to it; it does not concern that propriety which may be in innumerable other spaces like it. If it be right for a finite good, a limited perfection, to exist, all the more is it right for an infinite good to exist; for where a finite good exists through propriety and right, the infinite exists through absolute necessity.

ELPINO: The infinite good certainly exists, but it is incorporeal.

PHILOTHEUS: On that point we are agreed, as regards the incorporeal infinite. But how does that affect the utter propriety of there existing the corporeal infinite good, the corporeal infinite being? Or how does that prevent the infinite, implicit in the most simple and individual first principle, from unfolding itself rather into this its infinite and boundless image, with capacity for innumerable worlds, than into such narrow boundaries? Really it is almost blasphemous not to admit that this body which to us seems so great and vast, is only a dot, ay, a nothing, in comparison to the divine presence.

ELPINO: Just as the greatness of God does not consist in any way in corporeal dimensions (I grant you that the world adds nothing to him), so we must not think that the greatness of his image consists in the greater or lesser dimensions of its mass.

PHILOTHEUS: That is a very good answer, but it does not touch the kernel of the problem. I do not demand infinite space, nor does nature have infinite space, for the dignity of corporeal dimension and mass, but for the dignity of corporeal natures and species. For the infinite excellence manifests itself incomparably better in innumerable individuals, than in those which are numerable and finite. Therefore, it is necessary that of an inaccessible divine countenance there be an infinite image, in which innumerable worlds, such as the others above us, exist as infinite members. So in view of the innumerable grades of perfection which must represent the unfolding of the divine incorporeal excellence in a corporeal way, there must be innumerable individuals, and namely these great animate beings, of which the earth is one, the earth, our divine mother who has borne us and nourished us and at last will take us back into her bosom. . . .

FRACASTORO: I believe that there is no one to persevere obstinately in the false denial that as for space it can infinitely contain, and as for the individual and collective excellence of infinite worlds that they can be contained, any less than this world which we know. Each of them has a reason for appropriate existence. For infinite space has infinite aptitude, and that infinite aptitude attains its glory in an infinite act of existence, whereby the infinite efficient is saved from being deficient, and aptitude from being fruitless.

*   *   *   *   *   *   *   *   *

ELPINO: However, I should be glad to hear the rest you have to say about the eternal beginning and efficient cause, whether this infinite effect is required by them; and whether, after all, the effect is really such.

PHILOTHEUS: . . . To begin then, Why should we, how can we, think that the divine power is inactive? Why should we assume that divine goodness, capable of infinite extension to infinite things, should will to be scarce, to restrict itself to nothing, assuming that any finite thing in comparison with the infinite is nothing? Why should you think that that kernel of divinity, which can expand infinitely into an infinite (if I may so speak) sphere, chose, as it were, in envy to remain sterile, rather than to become reproductive, a father, prolific, adorned and beautiful? Chose to impart itself rather in stinted portions and, more exactly, not at all, than with a bounty commensurate with its glorious power and being? Why should its infinite capacity be foiled? The possibility of infinite worlds within reach deluded? Compromised the excellence of the divine image, which ought to be more brilliant when reflected in a mirror, unconfined, vast as its infinite being? Why should we make this assumption, which, when posited, entails so many difficulties, and without promoting law, religion, faith or morality in any way, destroys so many philosophical principles? Why should you think that God, both in potentiality, in operation and effect (which are in him all the same thing), is limited, and as it were the bound of the convexity of a sphere, rather than conceive him, so to say, as the unbounded boundary of an unbounded thing? I say boundary unbounded, because the infinity of God is different from the infinity of the universe; for he is the whole infinite in its totality and complexity, but the universe is all in all (if indeed we can say in a certain sense totality where there is neither part nor end) dependently and not totally; so that God appears as the limit, the universe as the limited, not with the same distinction that prevails between finite and infinite, but in the sense that one is infinite and the other limiting with reference to the total and to his total existence in all that which, although it is all infinite, is not however totally infinite. For this is quite different from dimensional infinity.

ELPINO: That is not quite clear to me. So you would do me a favor by explaining yourself more fully on what you say is all in all totally, and all in all the infinite and the totally infinite.

PHILOTHEUS: I call the universe infinite as a whole because it has neither boundary limit nor surface; I consider it not totally infinite because each part of it we may select is finite, and of the innumerable worlds it contains, each one is finite. I say that God is entirely infinite because no boundary is applicable to him and every one of his attributes is one and infinite. I call God totally infinite, because his whole self is in all the world and in each of its parts, infinitely and totally. . . .

ELPINO: I see. Well, go on with your exposition.

PHILOTHEUS: . . . Why are we required to believe that an agent which has power to work an infinite good works rather a finite good? Or conversely, if he has made it finite, why should we believe he has power to make it infinite, since in him power and action are the same thing? Because he is immutable, he feels no conditioning forces in his operation or in his productive power, but from a certain and definite productive power there must immutably proceed a certain and definite effect. *He cannot be therefore other than he is; he cannot be something that he is not; he can do nothing except what he has power to do; he can will only what he wills; necessarily he can do only what he does, for to have power distinct from the act belongs only to mutable things.*

FRACASTORO: Surely a thing which never was, is not, and will never be cannot have as attributes possibility and potency; and if the first efficient can will only what it actually wills, it can do only what it actually does. Nor do I see how some people justify what they say of infinite active potency without its corresponding infinite passive potency, and their idea that He who create the innumerable in the infinitely immense, creates only the one and the finite; for his action is necessary from the fact that it proceeds from a will which, from being in the highest degree immutable, in fact immutability itself, amounts to actual necessity. *Hence it is that liberty, will, necessity, are identical; and further, action is identical with will-power and being.*

I might add a couple of syllogisms arranged like this: if the first efficient willed to do other than what it wills to do, it could do other than what it does but it cannot will to do other than what it wills to do; therefore it cannot do other than what it does. And so when we posit a finite effect, we must posit finite operations and potency. Again —which amounts to the same thing—the first efficient can do only what it wills to do; it can will to do only what it does; therefore it can do only what it does. Therefore, if we deny the infinite effect, we must deny the infinite potency.

PHILOTHEUS: Your syllogisms are not simple, but they are unanswerable. Nevertheless, I understand the reluctance of some worthy theologians to accept them. With shrewd foresight they realize that uncultivated and ignorant minds with this view of necessity come to lose all notion of individual responsibility and of the dignity and merits of justice. . . .

*   *   *   *   *   *   *   *   *

ELPINO: I will accept your theory as true, if you are able to answer a very important objection, by which Aristotle was induced to deny the infinity of divine power intensively although he admitted it extensively. The reason for his negative was that since in God potency and act are the same thing, with his power for moving infinitely he would move infinitely with infinite power; in which case the heavens would be moved in an instant; for if the stronger the motor, the greater the velocity, the motor of greatest strength would move with the greatest velocity, and that of infinite strength would produce instantaneous motion. The reason for his affirmative was, that God regularly and throughout eternity moves the first mobile heaven according to the regular law by which he moves it. You see then why Aristotle attributes to him extensive infinity [in time], while denying him absolute and also intensive infinity. So I consider that just as his infinite motive potency is restricted in the act of motion to finite velocity, so his similar potency for creating the immense and innumerable has been restricted to the finite and numerable. This is approximately the opinion of some theologians. . . . So, just as we are certain that this motion, notwithstanding its derivation from infinite potency, is finite, so, with equal facility, the number of worlds may be considered limited.

PHILOTHEUS: The argument in truth is of great persuasiveness and likelihood. But you should first observe that since the universe is infinite and motionless, it is idle to look for the one who moves it. Secondly, since the worlds contained in the universe are infinite in number, the masses of earth, of fire and the other varieties of bodies called stars, they all derive their motion from an internal force, which is their own soul, as we have elsewhere shown. It is vain therefore to go looking for any motor extrinsic to them. With the result that the first cause is not a motive force, but, placid and motionless itself, it imparts the power of motion to infinite and innumerable worlds, animate beings great and small placed in the spacious region of the universe, each of which has its mobility, impelling force and other accidents. . . .

BURCHIO: Oh, why not turn the world upside down and have done with it!

FRACASTORO: With a world downside up as it stands, that would not be such a bad idea.

BURCHIO: (*thundering*) You are wantonly bent on nullifying a world of labor and devotion, all the effort represented by Aristotle's book on *Physics,* on *Heaven* and on the World. Yet such books have cost countless hours of application to generations of commentators, men who have paraphrased and glossed, written compendia and summaries, scholia and translations, reducing them to questionnaires and theorems. These are the works that have formed our *doctores profundi, subtiles, aurati, magni, inexpugnabiles, irrefragabiles,* our angelics, our seraphics, our cherubics, our divines!

FRACASTORO: With a goodly dose of nut-crackers, pinch-hitters, tub-thumpers, dummy-chuckers, horn-butters, and kick-swingers; and a pinch of far-sighteds, palladians, olympics, firmamentals, celestial empirics, and loud-thunderers.

BURCHIO: And I suppose if you have your way we'll throw them all in the cesspool. A fine mess the world will be in when we have discarded and brought into contempt the thought of the best philosophers of the world. According to you Plato is an imbecile and Aristotle an ass.

FRACASTORO: My dear coconut, I never claimed that they were donkeys and that you people were their colts, or that they were monkeys and you their peanuts. As I said at the outset, in my eyes they are the heroes of the earth. I refuse, however, to believe everything they say unquestioningly, much less admit theories of theirs which, as you have heard if you have any ears at all, are flatly contradictory to the truth.

BURCHIO: Well, who is going to decide what the truth is?

FRACASTORO: That is the prerogative of every careful and wide-awake intelligence, of everybody who is as judicious and free from obstinacy as he can be and is willing to admit defeat when he is no longer able to defend their view of matters or refute ours.

BURCHIO: Even if I can't defend their case, it is due to my own weakness and not to their defects; just as your victory is due not to the soundness of your doctrine, but to your low sophistries.

FRACASTORO: If I were consciously ignorant of the case

in dispute, I should refrain from passing judgment. If I were as flat-footed in my convictions as you, I should call myself as learned by faith and not by knowledge.

BURCHIO: If you had better manners, you would see yourself as a presumptuous ass, a sophistical assailant of good letters, an assassin of reputations, a disturber of the established order, a perverter of truth and a suspect of heresy.

PHILOTHEUS: Up to this point we could see that this fellow had little information. Now he insists on proving he is a man of little judgment and no manners.

ELPINO: But don't forget to appreciate his lungs. He can argue louder than a Franciscan friar. My dear Burchio, your faith is above reproach and beyond praise. You said at the outset that even if what we said were true, you would refuse to believe it.

BURCHIO: And you would be wiser than Aristotle, if you were not an ass, a pauper, a nameless and homeless beggar without visible means of support, an oat-eater, a hungry-gut, begotten of a tailor, dropped by a washerwoman, with a cobbler for grandfather, offspring of a slandering panderer in a litter of donkey-shoers. And the devil take you, too, for you are no better.

ELPINO: I hope, my dear sir, that hereafter you will not go to the trouble of visiting us but will wait for a call from us.]

FINALLY, HERE IS A CENTRAL MYTH OUT OF BRUNO'S OWN Platonic-style *Symposion,* the *Heroici Furori* (Heroic Exaltations), also in Arthur Livingston's translation.

This group of dialogues is dedicated "to the most illustrous and excellent Knight, Sir Philip Sidney," and in its sequence of sonnets it is a reminder of Sidney's own Petrarchan sequence, *Astrophel and Stella;* but Bruno's aim is transcendent abstraction, and the treatment markedly more Baroque in style. The ideas are presented allegorically in a series of emblems and poems, and then worked out symbol by symbol in philosophical comment. The concluding dialogue is between two women, Laodomia and Giulia (a reminder of Plato's Diotima) who express themselves only in song.

The series of ten dialogues rings all the changes on the theme of Intellectual Love. The technique is strange and contrived, not, however, out of any subservience to convention. In these same dialogues, Bruno expresses new and strikingly modern aesthetic views with respect to the reigning conventions in poetics. Good or bad, Bruno's reasons are his own, and tie up with his own idea of the role of symbol in thought. By formalizing his treatment to the utmost, he gives the impression of writing an early set of *Goldberg Variations*. But one comes to realize that this technique itself is symbolic of the "circling approach" of the mind to the Absolute as he describes it in the section we quote here.

In this section, Bruno finds a deeply significant form in which to express the "understanding" that he is searching for, the point where knowledge and creation meet. It is the ancient fable of Actaeon, the daring hunter who beheld Diana herself bathing in a stream, and was turned by her into a stag so that his own staghounds tore him to pieces. In order to behold the truth, man must accept to be destroyed by it, in his own contingent being.

TANSILLO:* Here we note the constituent aspects of heroic love, in so far as it tends toward its own object, which is the supreme good, and of the heroic intellect, in so far as it strives to attain to its own object, which is primal or absolute truth. In the first consideration we find a general statement of the situation and the trend of the discussion, which will be systematically developed in five other considerations. It says accordingly:

Young Actaeon is running his mastiffs and hounds through
     the woods,
When fate drives his dangerous and imprudent course
Along the trails of the forest beasts.

*Luigi Tansillo, a poet and friend who had died when Bruno was in his twentieth year, and for whom he entertained a lifelong attachment. Cicada is probably Odoardo Cicada, a Neapolitan shipowner.

And lo, in a stream he sees the fairest face and form,
In purpose, gold and alabaster
That eye of god or man e'er saw.
And the great hunter at once becomes the game.

A stag become, into the thickest woods
He turns his fleeter feet;
But the great pack of his own huge dogs devours him.

Upon a lofty prey so I let loose my thoughts,
And they, turning upon me,
Give me a cruel death in their fierce and cruel fangs.

Actaeon represents the human intellect, intent on the pursuit of divine wisdom, on the apprehension of divine
beauty. He *is running his mastiffs and hounds*. Of these
the hounds are fleetest of foot, the mastiffs are most powerful, for the operation of the intellect precedes the operation of the will, but the latter in turn is the more vigorous
and efficacious; since divine goodness and beauty is more
lovable than comprehensible to the human intellect, and
love moreover is what prompts and impels the intellect to
go before it as a lantern in the dark. *Through the wood:*
wild and solitary, visited and explored by very few men,
and therefore with few traces of human footsteps. The
youth has little experience and practice, for his life has
been short and his enthusiasm uncertain. He has little
competence then for the course of searching reason and
passionate impulse, outlined in the character of Pythagoras.
There the path is most rugged, thorny and deserted, making the greatest demands on skill and patience: yet here it
is that he is running his mastiffs and hounds *along the trails
of the forest beasts*. These beasts are the intelligible aspects
of ideal concepts. They are in their fastnesses, hunted by
very few, discovered by fewer still, and very rarely captured. *And lo, in a stream,* that is, in the mirror of symbol,
figuring the subject of the higher waters above the firmament and the lower waters beneath the firmament, *he sees
the fairest face and form*.

CICADA: I suppose the linking of divine with human apprehension, *the eye of god or man,* refers not so much to manner of cognition, where they are vastly different, as to the subject, which is identical in both cases.

TANSILLO: Of course. He says in *purple, gold and alabaster,* because it symbolizes the purple of divine power, the alabaster of divine beauty, the gold of divine wisdom, towards which things Pythagoreans, Chaldeans, Platonists and others strive as best they can to rise. *The great hunter becomes the game:* he was the huntsman, but he became the prey through the operation of the intellect whereby he converts the apprehended things into himself.

CICADA: He shapes the intelligible species in his own way, proportions them to his own capacity, for they are always received in the manner of those who acquire them.

TANSILLO: This hunt takes place through the operation of the will, through the actuality of which he is converted into the object.

CICADA: I see: because love transforms, converts him into the thing he loves.

TANSILLO: You are aware that the intellect apprehends things intelligibly, that is, in its own fashion; and the will pursues things naturally, that is, according to the manner in which they exist in themselves. So Actaeon with those thoughts of his, those dogs, seeking without themselves goodness, wisdom, beauty, in other words, *the forest beasts;* and the moment he came into the true presence, carried away, beside himself, at the spectacle of such great beauty, he saw himself changed into the thing he was hunting; and he discovered that he himself had become the longed-for prey of his own dogs, his thoughts; for, now that he had compressed divinity into himself, there was no longer any occasion to hunt for it elsewhere.

CICADA: Yes, it is well said that the kingdom of God is within us and that divinity dwells within our souls through virtue of the regenerate intellect and will.

TANSILLO: Precisely; Actaeon then has become the prey of his own dogs, he is pursued by his own thoughts; and he *turns his* new stag *feet* (now refashioned for a divine course) to the thickest woods, the regions of incompre-

hensible things. Formerly he was common man of the multitude; he has become outstanding and heroic, he has
high ideas and character and leads a life of unusual excellence. At this point *the great pack of his own huge dogs
destroys him;* his life according to the manner of the
thoughtless, sensuous, blind and fantastic world is over;
he begins to live in intellect, the life of a god, feeding on
ambrosia and becoming drunk with nectar. . . . He is
dead to the world, free from the prison of matter. The
walls are now cast down, with full unobstructed vision
he looks out upon an unbroken horizon. He is beginning
to see the whole as a unit, no longer through differences
and numbers; to behold Amphitrite, the fountain of all
numbers, species, classes; to behold the Monad, the true
essence of the being of them all—the monad which is nature, wherein the divine monad may be contemplated in
reflection as the sun in the moon, by which it gives us
light, when it has passed into the hemisphere of intellectual substances. . . .

Then, under guise of another likeness, he describes the
manner whereby he girds himself for the conquest of his
object and he says:

My solitary sparrow, build thy nest
In that place which clouds and fills all my thought.
There continue thy doings, there expend thy industry and
      thy art.

Be reborn there, there rear thy beauteous chicks
Now that fierce fate completed its course
Against the emprise from which it was wont to keep thee.

Go, a nobler dwelling
I wish thee to enjoy and a god will guide thee
Who is called blind by those who cannot see.

Go, and kindly to thee be
Every divinity of this spacious creation
And come not back to me, since thou art not mine.

The progress represented above by the hunter driving his dogs, is here symbolized by a bird, a winged heart, being sent forth from the cage in which it sat idle and at rest, to build its nest on high for the rearing of its chicks, its thoughts. For the time has come when the thousand exterior obstacles and the native dullness within have ceased offering impediment. He bids it godspeed then on its ascent to a more splendid state, now that the potencies of the soul are more fully fledged. The Platonists likewise represent these potencies by two wings. As a guide he gives him that god who by the blind multitude is called blind and mad, namely Love; and love, under the grace and favor of heaven, is able, as it were, to transform it into that other nature to which it aspires, or into that state from which it has been wandering an exile. That is why he said: *And come not back to me for thou 'rt not mine,* so that I may not inappropriately say with the poet:

"Thou hast left me, heart of mine,
"Light of my eyes, thou art no longer with me."

Next comes the death of the soul, called by the Cabalists the "death of the kiss," and represented in the song of Solomon, when the dear one says: "Let him kiss me with the kisses of his mouth, for I am sick with love." By others it is called sleep, as when the Psalmist says: "I will not give sleep to mine eyes, or slumber to mine eyelids, until I find out a place for the Lord."

The enthusiast, then, feels as if his soul were dead in itself and alive in the object. He would fain recall his heart, but it is rebellious as a hawk gone wild, it has strayed too far ever to return. The soul then grieves, not through real sorrow, but through torment of love, while the heart is flying toward a place it cannot arrive at, striving to a goal it cannot attain, trying to embrace what it cannot comprehend, and withal, even though its departure from the soul is in vain, becoming more and more inflamed with ardor toward the infinite.

CICADA: How come it, Tansillo, that the spirit, in this progress upward, is content with its suffering? What is the source of that urge which spurs it forever onward beyond what it already possesses?

TANSILLO: I was coming to that. When the intellect has arrived at the apprehension of a certain definite intelligible form, and the will at an out-reaching commensurate to that apprehension, the intellect does not stop at that point: for its own light brings it to realize that it contains within itself every genus of the intelligible that is desired, up to the point of its apprehending in its vision the supreme source of ideas, the ocean of all truth and goodness. It results from this that whatever species is presented to the intellect and is comprehended by the will, from the very fact that it has been so presented and comprehended, the intellect concludes that above this species are greater and greater ones, and so it is in a constant state of a certain kind of activity toward new motion and abstraction. . . . From the beautiful that is comprehended and as a result limited, and therefore beautiful only by participation, it makes a perpetual progress toward that beautiful which is truly beautiful without limit or constriction whatsoever.

CICADA: A futile search, it seems to me.

TANSILLO: Not at all. It is contrary to the facts of nature that the infinite should be comprehended, thereby becoming finite. If that were the case, it would no longer be infinite. It is however perfectly in accord with nature that the infinite, from the very fact of its infinitude, should be infinitely pursued, the pursuit of course not partaking of the nature of physical motion in space, but of a cerain metaphysical motion, which progresses not from the imperfect to the perfect, but goes circling through the degrees of perfection till it reaches that infinite center which is neither form nor formed.

CICADA: I would like to know how by going in a circle you can ever reach the center.

TANSILLO: I can't imagine.

CICADA: Then why do you say so?

TANSILLO: Because that is something I can do, leaving you to think it out. . . .]

L'Envoi

(From Bruno's *de l'Infinito Universo e Mondi***)**

Who gives me wings and who removes my fears
Of death and fortune? Who inflames my heart?
Who breaks the chains and makes the portals start
Whence but a rare one, freed at last, appears?

Time's Children and his weapons, ages, years,
Months, days, and hours, all that host whose art
Makes even adamant and iron part
Have now secured me from his fury's spears.

Wherefore I spread my wings upon the air
No crystal spheres I find nor other bar
But flying to the immense I cleave the skies

And while from my small globe I speed elsewhere
And through the ethereal ranges further rise
I leave behind what there is seen from far.

(Translated by W. C. GREENE)

Recommended Further Reading

General Works on Renaissance Thought

Cassirer, Ernst. *The Individual and the Cosmos in Renaissance Philosophy,* translated and with an introduction by Mario Domandi. Philadelphia: University of Pennsylvania Press, 1963.

Debus, Allen G. *Man and Nature in the Renaissance.* Cambridge; New York: Cambridge University Press, 1978.

Kristeller, Paul Oskar. *Renaissance Thought and Its Sources,* edited by Michael Mooney. New York: Columbia University Press, 1982.

Webster, Charles. *From Paracelsus to Newton: Magic and the Making of Modern Science.* Cambridge; New York: Cambridge University Press, 1982.

NICHOLAS OF CUSA

The Idiot, translated by Clyde Lee Miller. New York: Abaris Books, 1979.

Nicholas of Cusa on Learned Ignorance: A Translation and an Appraisal of De Docta Ignorantia, by Jasper Hopkins. Minneapolis: Arthur J. Banning Press, 1981.

Hopkins, Jasper. *A Concise Introduction to the Philosophy of Nicholas of Cusa.* Minneapolis: University of Minnesota Press, 1978.

Jaspers, Karl. *Anselm and Nicholas of Cusa,* translated by Ralph Mannheim and edited by Hannah Arendt. New York: Harcourt Brace Jovanovich, 1966.

Sigmund, Paul E. *Nicholas of Cusa and Medieval Political Thought.* Cambridge: Harvard University Press, 1964.

LEONARDO DA VINCI

Treatise on Painting, translated by A. Philip McMahon, with an introduction by Ludwig Heydenreich. Princeton: Princeton University Press, 1956.

The Literary Works of Leonardo da Vinci, edited by Jean P. Richter. Berkeley: University of California Press, 1977.

Calder, Ritchie. *Leonardo and the Age of the Eye*. New York: Simon & Schuster, 1970.

Philipson, Morris (ed.). *Leonardo da Vinci: Aspects of the Renaissance Genius*. New York: G. Braziller, 1966.

SIR THOMAS MORE

The Complete Works of St. Thomas More. New Haven: Yale University Press, 1963-.

Utopia: A New Translation, Backgrounds, Criticism, translated and edited by Robert M. Adams. New York: Norton, 1975.

Logan, George M. *The Meaning of More's Utopia*. Princeton: Princeton University Press, 1983.

Reynolds, E. E. *The Field is Won: The Life and Death of Saint Thomas More*. Milwaukee: Bruce, 1968. (reissued as *The Life and Death of St. Thomas More*. New York: Barnes & Noble Books, 1978.)

Sullivan, E. D. S. (ed.). *The Utopia Vision: Seven Essays on the Quincentennial of Sir Thomas More*. San Diego: San Diego State University Press, 1983.

MACHIAVELLI

The Portable Machiavelli, translated and edited by Peter Bondanella and Mark Musa. Hammondsworth, England: New York: Penguin Books, 1979.

The Prince; A New Translation, Backgrounds, Interpretations, Peripherica, translated and directed by Robert M. Adams. New York: Norton, 1977.

Anglo, Sydney. *Machiavelli: A Dissection*. New York: Harcourt, Brace & World, 1970.

Prezzolini, Giuseppe. *Machiavelli*, translated by Gioconda Savini. New York: Farrar, Straus & Giroux, 1967.

ERASMUS

The Praise of Folly, translated with an introduction and commentary by Clarence H. Miller. New Haven: Yale University Press, 1979.

Bainton, Roland H. *Erasmus of Christendom*. New York: Scribner, 1969.

Tracy, James D. *Erasmus: The Growth of a Mind*. Geneva: Droz, 1972.

LUTHER

Martin Luther, Selections from His Writings, edited with an introduction by John Dillenberger. Garden City, New York: Doubleday, 1961.

The Table Talk of Martin Luther, translated by William Hazlitt and edited with an introduction by Thomas S. Kepler. New York: World Publishing, 1952.

Atkinson, James. *Martin Luther and the Birth of Protestantism*. Hammondsworth, England; Baltimore: Penguin, 1968.

Erikson, Erik H. *Young Man Luther: A Study in Psychoanalysis and History*. New York: Norton, 1958.

DÜRER

Writings, translated and edited by William Martin Conway, with an introduction by Alfred Werner. New York: Philosophical Library, 1958.

Anzelewsky, Fejda. *Dürer: His Art and Life*, translated by Heide Grieve. New York: Alpine Fine Arts Collection Ltd., 1981.

Bongard, Willi and Matthias Mende. *Dürer Today*, translated by Patricia Crampton. Bonn: Inter Nationes, 1971.

COPERNICUS

On the Revolutions of the Heavenly Spheres, translated by A. M. Duncan. New York: Barnes & Noble Books, 1976.

Kuhn, Thomas S. *The Copernican Revolution: Panetary Astronomy in the Development of Western Thought*. Cambridge: Harvard University Press, 1957.

MONTAIGNE

The Complete Works of Montaigne, translated by Donald M. Frame. Stanford: Stanford University Press, 1957.

Essays, translated with an introduction by J. M. Cohen. Hammondsworth, England: Penguin, 1958.

Frame, Donald M. *Montaigne: A Biography*. New York: Harcourt, Brace & World, 1965.

PARACELSUS

Debus, Allen G. *The English Paracelsians*. New York: F. Watts, 1966.

Pagel, Walter. *Paracelsus: An Introduction to Philosophical Medicine in the Era of the Renaissance* (2nd rev. ed.). Basel; New York: Karger, 1982.

KEPLER

Caspar, Max. *Kepler*, translated and edited by C. Doris Hellman. New York: Abelard-Schuman, 1959.

Knight, David C. *Johannes Kepler and Planetary Motion.* New York: F. Watts, 1962.

Koestler, Arthur. *The Watershed: A Biography of Johannes Kepler.* Garden City, New York: Anchor Books, 1960.

BOEHME

Bailey. Margaret Lewis. *Milton and Jakob Boehme: A Study of German Mysticism in Seventeenth-Century England.* New York: Haskell House, 1964.

Walsh, David. *The Mysticism of Innerworldly Fulfillment: A Study of Jacob Boehme.* Gainsville: University Presses of Florida, 1983.

GALILEO

Drake, Stillman. *Galileo at Work: His Scientific Biography.* Chicago: University of Chicago Press, 1978.

Geymonat, Ludovico. *Galileo Galilei: A Biography and Inquiry into His Philosophy of Science*, translated by Stillman Drake, with a foreword by George de Santillana. New York: McGraw-Hill, 1968.

Golino. Carlo L. (ed.). *Galileo Reappraised.* Berkeley: University of California Press, 1966.

HAKLUYT

Hakluyt's Voyages: The Principal Navigations, Voyages Trafiques and Discoveries of the English Nation. edited by Irwin R. Blacker. New York: Viking Press, 1965.

The Hakluyt Handbook, edited by David Beers Quinn. London: The Hakluyt Society, 1974.

GIORDANO BRUNO

Nelson, John Charles. *Renaissance Theory of Love: The Context of Giordano Bruno's Eroici Furori.* New York: Columbia University Press, 1958.

Paterson, Antoniette Mann. *The Infinite Worlds of Giordano Bruno*. Springfield, Illinois: Charles C. Thomas Publisher, 1970.

Yates, Frances A. *Giordano Bruno and the Hermetic Tradition*. Chicago: University of Chicago Press, 1964.

Index

Meridian (0452)

LIVES IN HISTORY

☐ **CRAZY HORSE AND CUSTER by Stephen E. Ambrose.** Crazy Horse, leader of the Oglala Sioux, and General George Armstrong Custer. Both were men of aggression and supreme courage, and became leaders in their societies at very early ages. Their parallel lives would pave the way, in a manner unknown to either, for an inevitable clash between two nations—one red, one white—fighting for possession of the open prairie. "Movingly told and well written."—*Library Journal*
(008026—$8.95)

☐ **F.D.R. AN INTIMATE HISTORY by Nathan Miller.** A fair and unflinching portrait that captures all sides of America's only four-term president: the brilliance, charm, and remarkable talents of both the political and the private personality. This fascinating and comprehensive biography brings F.D.R. to life for Americans who remember the Roosevelt years as well as those who never knew him.
(006767—$10.95)

☐ **THE LIFE AND DEATH OF MARY WOLLSTONECRAFT by Claire Tomalin.** This penetrating biography does full justice to this liberated woman of the eighteenth century who brilliantly exposed the inequities of society's treatment of women, but whose life had a soap-opera plot of passionate affairs, an illegitimate child, daring involvements during the French Revolution, suicide attempts, and tragic premature death.
(006562—$7.95)

☐ **CHRISTOPHER COLUMBUS, MARINER by Samuel Eliot Morison.** This saga of Columbus, told by a modern scholar who was himself an accomplished sailor, recreates the terror and excitement of the first Atlantic voyage, the discovery of land, the loss of the Santa Maria, and the tragedy of the subsequent voyages with all the intensity of a firsthand account.
(007674—$5.95)

Prices slightly higher in Canada.

Buy them at your local bookstore or use this convenient
coupon for ordering.

NEW AMERICAN LIBRARY
P.O. Box 999, Bergenfield, New Jersey 07621

Please send me the books I have checked above. I am enclosing $_____
(please add $1.50 to this order to cover postage and handling). Send check or money order—no cash or C.O.D.'s. Prices and numbers are subject to change without notice.

Name _____

Address _____

City _____ State _____ Zip Code _____

Allow 4-6 weeks for delivery.
This offer subject to withdrawal without notice.

Plume

 Meridian

READINGS IN ART HISTORY

(0452)

☐ **THE NOTEBOOKS OF LEONARDO DA VINCI selected and edited by Pamela Taylor.** A cloud of mystery still hovers about the person of Leonardo da Vinci, the mind that could both conceive and execute the perfection of a *Last Supper*, and design a flying apparatus. Now the greatest mind of the Renaissance is revealed in this brilliant selection from his own notebooks. With 16 pages of drawings by Leonardo himself. (258464—$8.95)

☐ **A FIELD GUIDE TO AMERICAN ARCHITECTURE by Carole Rifkind.** From the simple wood houses of the seventeenth century to the steel and glass towers of our own day, this invaluable handbook traces the fascinating development of architectural styles in the United States. Here are the periods, the styles, the form and function of historical buildings from colonial times to today—with more than 450 illustrations for easy identification. (257735—$11.95)

☐ **AESTHETICS TODAY readings selected, edited, and introduced by Morris Philipson and Paul J. Gudel.** Revised and updated with sixteen new essays from the past twenty years, this classic collection brings together the writings of Edward Said, Frederic Jameson, Meyer Schapiro, E.H. Gombrich, Michael Fried, J. Hillis Miller, Stanley Cavell, and many others. This new edition includes a wide range of commentary and criticism on post-modern art. (006643—$9.95)

☐ **GOTHIC ARCHITECTURE AND SCHOLASTICISM by Erwin Panofsky.** In this inquiry into the analogy of the arts, philosophy, and religion in the Middle Ages, Panofsky succeeds in showing how architectural style and structure provided visible and tangible equivalents to the scholastic definitions of the order and form of thought. This volume is not only an important contribution to the history of art, but to the history of ideas as well. (008344—$7.95)

Prices slightly higher in Canada.

To order use coupon on next page.

Meridian

(0452)

THE MAKING OF AMERICAN HISTORY

☐ **LOOKING FAR WEST: The Search for the American West in History, Myth, and Literature. Edited by Frank Bergon and Zeese Papanikolas.** Here is an extraordinary collection of writings about the American West as both a historical reality and a realm of the imagination. Here in song and story, myth and firsthand report is an anthology that gives full expression to the West in all its complex meanings. (007585—$5.95)

☐ **LEE AND GRANT by Gene Smith.** One was the great personification of the Southern beau ideal; the other was a graceless, small-town Midwesterner. Both reached their summits of glory in a war that filled them with horror and each had to build a new life in the war's aftermath. In this book—as in life—they illumine and define each other's greatness, and give human meaning to the conflict that the struggle between them decided. (007739—$10.95)

☐ **FACING WEST: The Metaphysics of Indian-Hating and Empire-Building by Richard Drinnon.** Following the course of American expansion westward historian Richard Drinnon examines the eerie similarities of attitude and action on the part of three centuries of representative Americans. The vision of the American past that emerges is as disturbing as it is meticulously portrayed. (006325—$10.95)

☐ **ABRAHAM LINCOLN: The Man Behind the Myths by Stephen B. Oates.** He has been called the Great Emancipator and a white racist, a devotee of democracy and an incipient tyrant. His life has been cloaked in the mists of time and distorted by both the devotion and the enmity that he inspired. With his pioneering research Oates offers us a picture of Lincoln as he really was. (007348—$6.95)

Prices slightly higher in Canada.

Buy them at your local bookstore or use this convenient
coupon for ordering.

NEW AMERICAN LIBRARY
P.O. Box 999, Bergenfield, New Jersey 07621

Please send me the books I have checked above. I am enclosing $_____
(please add $1.50 to this order to cover postage and handling). Send check
or money order—no cash or C.O.D.'s. Prices and numbers are subject to
change without notice.

Name _____

Address _____

City _____ State _____ Zip Code _____

Allow 4-6 weeks for delivery.
This offer subject to withdrawal without notice.